PERFORMING ANIMALS

 **ANIMALIBUS** VOL. 11
OF ANIMALS AND CULTURES

Nigel Rothfels, General Editor

ADVISORY BOARD:
Steve Baker (University of Central Lancashire)
Susan McHugh (University of New England)
Garry Marvin (Roehampton University)
Kari Weil (Wesleyan University)

Books in the Animalibus series share a fascination with the status and the role of animals in human life. Crossing the humanities and the social sciences to include work in history, anthropology, social and cultural geography, environmental studies, and literary and art criticism, these books ask what thinking about nonhuman animals can teach us about human cultures, about what it means to be human, and about how that meaning might shift across times and places.

Other titles in the series:

PERFORMING

ANIMALS

HISTORY, AGENCY, THEATER

EDITED BY **KAREN RABER** AND **MONICA MATTFELD**

THE PENNSYLVANIA STATE UNIVERSITY PRESS | UNIVERSITY PARK, PENNSYLVANIA

An earlier version of chapter 9, "Miss Mazeppa and
the Horse with No Name," by Kari Weil, appeared as
"Purebreds and Amazones: Saying Things with Horses
in Nineteenth-Century France," *differences* 11, no. 1
(1999): 1–37.

Library of Congress Cataloging-in-Publication Data

Names: Raber, Karen, 1961– , editor. | Mattfeld,
    Monica, 1982– , editor.
Title: Performing animals : history, agency, theater /
    edited by Karen Raber and Monica Mattfeld.
Other titles: Animalibus.
Description: University Park, Pennsylvania : The
    Pennsylvania State University Press, [2017] | Series:
    Animalibus: of animals and cultures | Includes
    bibliographical references and index.
Summary: "A collection of essays that explore the role
    of performing animals in literature, theater, art,
    and other media prior to the twentieth century,
    and discuss recent theoretical work in animal
    studies, materialism, and post humanism"—
    Provided by publisher.
Identifiers: LCCN 2017009262 | ISBN 9780271078342
    (cloth : alk. paper)
Subjects: LCSH: Animals in the performing art—
    History. | Human-animal relationships in the
    performing arts—History. | Animals as rep-
    resented on the stage—History. | Equestrian
    drama—History.
Classification: LCC PN1590.A54 P474 2017 | DDC
    791.8—dc23
LC record available at https://lccn.loc.gov/201700926

Published by The Pennsylvania State University Press,
University Park, PA 16802-1003

The Pennsylvania State University Press is a member
of the Association of American University Presses.

It is the policy of The Pennsylvania State University
Press to use acid-free paper. Publications on uncoated
stock satisfy the minimum requirements of American
National Standard for Information Sciences—
Permanence of Paper for Printed Library Material,
ANSI Z39.48–1992.

This book is printed on paper that contains 30%
post-consider waste.

CONTENTS

ILLUSTRATIONS

INTRODUCTION

KAREN RABER AND MONICA MATTFELD

What does it mean to say that an animal performs? Is it even possible to make such a claim? These questions continue to perplex everyone, from philosophers, to critics of popular culture, to individual animal owners. The assertion that animals perform might merely involve observing that animals play roles in a broad variety of ritual, theatrical, and other types of events where they display the results of training, something that has probably been the case since humans and animals first took up cohabitation. But to suggest that animals are *capable* of acting, of doing more than simply obeying cues or past training, raises a host of subtle expectations and assumptions both about how we define animals, either in distinction to or in relation to humans, and about what "performance" entails. Can an animal, for example, be said to act or perform as a self-conscious creature aware of the effects of calculated acts of deception? And must "performance" always involve an element of entertainment? What if the word is used in different registers to indicate either a demonstration of achievement (in the sense that a creature achieves a high level of skill at some kind of sport or art), or the linguistic and structural sense of execution, bringing into existence: does eliding the issue of self-consciousness solve the conundrum?

How these questions are answered has varied dramatically depending on how animals are situated categorically by philosophy, theory, or cultural practice. Whether we believe that an animal has self-consciousness, reason, a sense of the fictive, the desire to satisfy a crowd of spectators, the desire to rise to some abstract standard of achievement, or the depth of emotion required of a great stage actor often depends on how "human" we imagine an animal to be, and on whether we consider the divide that separates one from the other to be porous, movable, or simply absent. Many scholars working on animals have accepted a historical narrative in which the Enlightenment—particularly Cartesian skepticism—ushered in a period that demoted animals to machinelike status, leading to the erasure of animals as potential subjects, actors, and agents. Human exceptionalism, such a history proposes, was a more vexed problem for pre-Cartesian thinkers, but once Descartes banished animals from human company on the basis of their lack of demonstrated rational capacity, philosophy, science, and the humanities engaged in a far-reaching and triumphal anthropocentrism.[1] Such a narrative, it's worth pointing out, requires that we ignore the day-to-day experiences of many people who either did not agree or simply did not enter into the historical philosophical debate about animals, and did not necessarily ponder its consequences. In other words, even after Descartes, people saw animals engaged in marvelous actions, and believed what they saw. That is not to say that the public's encounters with performing animals upset the anthropocentric tea cart, but rather that whether pre- or post-Descartes, there has always been tension over what status animals hold among different groups of humans; the resulting disputes over how their actions can be interpreted may involve issues of gender, social class, religious belief, and ethnic or national identity. Public acceptance and embrace of the idea that animals who provide spectacles or performances are genuine "actors," feeling and projecting emotion, aware of an audience and appealing to it, might be branded naive sentimentalism by a "scientific" elite—but that has not eliminated or reduced the cultural influence of such positions. Certainly, *human* emotional engagement with animals on display often occurs without reference to any philosophical debate about animal status. Yet even the audience most empathetic to animals on display or in diverse kinds of spectacles is implicated in the construction of relations of social, political, economic, and moral power, made complicit in the drawing or erasure of boundaries between species, between observer and observed (with all the issues of control and agency those terms connote).

Recent work in both the sciences and the humanities has provided new tools for scholars to investigate the problem of animal performance from all angles, and among a broad array of constituencies. This volume capitalizes on the recent "animal turn" in theory and scholarship to assess what new perspectives it makes possible regarding the place of "the animal" as a performer, and what new accounts of performing animals can be constructed as a result. The essays collected here address the question of performance from a number of different angles, using diverse methodologies across historical periods—but all involve pre-twentieth-century examples of animals being asked in some fashion to act (in all the possible senses of that word) for an audience. The volume's historical orientation is meant to accomplish a number of things. First, it avoids the complications presented to the topic by the necessarily presentist bent of film studies, while providing a kind of prehistory to the excellent work being done in that field. Second, it moves among pre- and post-Enlightenment examples in order to suggest both historical patterns and differences that put the idea of a Cartesian divide in question. And third, it seeks to expand the ways in which we think about what "performing" means in the first place.

Animals have been part of human-engineered spectacle for as long as humans have been capable of recording their lives—from ritual slaughter, to cockfighting, to the pageantry of the hunt, animal death in particular has been an organizing focus of human representation, but delight in animal antics has made nonhuman creatures equally important as entertainers. Medieval cycle plays included animals as part of their spectacles, and, as Lisa Kiser observes, "virtually every common European

animal . . . took some part, large or small, in games, spectacles, menageries, performances, tournaments and displays during the period, even if the documentary
evidence of their presence is limited."[2] The Renaissance capitalized on the ubiquity of
performing animals: Louis B. Wright observed in his 1927 work on the topic that the
early modern theater frequently used animals in stage plays because there was such
a large pool of well-trained creatures to draw on, given their presence in interludes,
masques, bearbaiting arenas, and other, less formal environments.[3] Eight decades later,
Erica Fudge returned to the question of animal performances in tracing the ideological uses of "the animal" in philosophy, natural history, and other domains in early
modern England. Her treatment of the Bear Garden, where bears were tormented or
"baited" by dogs, turns away from the drama being played out between animals and
instead examines that being experienced by onlookers. Bearbaiting locked human
and animal in a troubling mirror relation that "revealed a struggle over the nature of
being human itself."[4]

In the eighteenth and nineteenth centuries, visiting displays of exotic plants and
creatures became a widespread pastime, an occasion for marveling at nature's prolific
variety. Meanwhile, the use of animals as entertainers expanded to generate entirely
new forms of spectacle: out of the traditions of the horse ballet, manège riding, and
fairground tricks, for example, Philip Astley invented the first, wildly popular, version of the circus. Foxhunting became the preferred country pastime and spectator
sport for both men and women, while horse racing gained new prominence as an
increasingly professional sport, in part through Charles II's enthusiasm for it, which
resulted directly or indirectly in the founding of Newmarket and the development
of the Thoroughbred breed. Throughout the period, the use of animals in stage plays
and events continued with the development of, and subsequent mania for, large hippodramatic spectacles in London's theaters, where nonhuman actors literally took
center stage, while the growth of the British Empire saw the import and display of
ever more exotic animals in private menageries, circuses, and public zoos.[5]

Animal performances are now most widely experienced in connection with
sports, in zoos, and on film. The presence of animals in these genres has been scruti-
nized by critics who take up diverse, sometimes opposing positions: most famously,
John Berger's explanation for why we look at animals, particularly those in zoos,
emphasizes their disappearance from people's everyday and increasingly mechanized
life, and their consequent burden of the one-directional human gaze, where they
become objects of human knowledge, always thereby only increasing the distance that
divides "us" from "them."[6] Steve Baker's 1993 *Picturing the Beast* gives an account of
how animals are deployed to construct human identity in a variety of visual media;
his discussion of the "disnification" of the animal through its reduction to a simplistic, cartoonish device, often generating discomfort or conflict with creatures, fleshes
out this negative dimension of representation.[7] Akira Lippit also turns to animals'

filmic appearances to extend Berger's argument: if, for Berger, the loss of mutuality in animal-human relations is a past fact, for Lippit, animals are spectral reminders of loss, perpetually reanimated, perpetually under erasure.[8] Jonathan Burt and Anat Pick both resist this retrospective narrative of privation, attempting to recover the positive effect of animals' inclusion in film. For Burt, film is more complex and diverse in its attempts to render either animals or a politics of the gaze; attempting to "cast a positive slant on the loss that previous theories have reinforced," Burt finds affective power and a degree of agency in film animals' effect on human audiences.[9] Pick's analysis of both literature and film relies on the insights of Simone Weil into the aesthetics of vulnerability, particularly embodied vulnerability, the shared creatureliness of both human and animal.[10]

All of these interpretive stances regarding animals in film belong to specific historical contexts. Berger, writing in the late 1970s and early 1980s, broke ground simply by asking what ideological ends were achieved by art and other visual genres, while Baker's poststructuralist readings introduced theories of power, identity, and representation to animals. But Lippit, Burt, and Pick come to their subjects informed by twenty-first-century critical animal studies, whatever the degree to which they directly acknowledge this or not. The very recent focus on animals in theory, philosophy, and criticism has occasioned a reevaluation of the Western metaphysical tradition and a newly expanded concern about how we apprehend—or ignore—animals in nearly every discipline. Matthew Calarco summarizes the field's aspiration to do more than reevaluate content, and to generate "an alternative ontology of animal life, an ontology in which the human-animal distinction is called radically into question."[11] In this project, too, performance and the capacity to act produce a useful friction. In *The Animal That Therefore I Am*, for example, Derrida investigates Lacan's claim in the *Écrits* that an animal cannot "pretend to pretend." Lacan attempts to make a precise distinction between reaction and response, between a deception made possible in the symbolic order and the kind of pretense that "is found in physical combat or sexual display":

> An animal does not give its word, and one does not give one's word to the animal, except by means of a projection or anthropomorphic transference. One can't lie to an animal, either, especially by pretending to hide from it something that one shows it. . . . But an animal does not pretend to pretend. He does not make tracks whose deception lies in the fact that they will be taken as false, while being in fact true ones, ones, that is, that indicate his true trail. Nor does an animal cover up its tracks, which would be tantamount to making itself the subject of the signifier.[12]

Derrida calls Lacan out on the kinds of logic that ground his claims here, including Lacan's Cartesian depiction of "the animal" as machinelike, and his recourse to the "old (Adamic and Promethean) theme of the animal's profound innocence." Even if we could determine the boundary between pretense and the pretense of a pretense, Derrida remarks, we would still need to know "in the name of what knowledge or what testimony . . . one could calmly declare that the *animal in general* is incapable of pretending pretense."[13]

Lacan is, of course, treading a well-worn path in discussing human distinction not only in terms of access to a certain dimension of symbolic representation, but also in setting up the human-animal boundary through an argument about human defect—from Genesis, to Freud's castration complex, to the pretending-to-pretend human deceit that goes beyond the requirements of nature, the animal's assumed sufficiency establishes it as the Other the human requires, and inscribes the animal as that which only ever is, but does not have, an Other. Paradoxically, human defect and animal perfection end up justifying Heidegger's observation that the animal is "poor in world," or shut away from relationality. Undoing Lacan, Derrida calls attention to the specularity of these formulations, beginning with his famous example of the cat who returns his gaze and ending with the dizzying problem of the theater of philosophy, its circularity and the vertigo it creates.[14]

Where Derrida challenges Lacan on the grounds of philosophy, others in both the sciences and the humanities are changing forever the way we evaluate his claims about pretense and deception in animal communication. Theories of zoosemiotics, for instance, question the validity of the boundaries that supposedly distinguish animal from human language systems: the example of animal signaling, the evolutionarily beneficial behaviors of begging, display, warning, and other forms of communication, is instructive, since no sooner did signaling emerge as a focus for evolutionary biologists than disputes arose over the amount and nature of *deceptive* signaling.[15] In theory, signaling is nearly always reliable, both because over time false signaling won't work, leading the group to suffer the loss of a valuable survival tool, and because there is a high cost to whatever behavior is involved (so, for instance, unusual size or coloring might be an advantage in mating but carry a cost in terms of food and energy consumption). Yet a propensity to deceptive signals does occur in some animal populations. Deception in signaling might not be conscious, scientists are often quick to assert—displaying a kind of determined anthropocentrism in their aversion to what might sound like anthropomorphic projection in the idea that nonhuman creatures are capable of deliberate, conscious trickery. Yet at its foundation, zoosemiotics insists that we acknowledge that humans and animals developed communication systems through a common evolutionary process. Indeed, taking Derrida's skepticism to heart, zoosemiotics edges into the world of zoopoetics, the recognition that "animals dwell imaginatively, rhetorically and culturally on the earth."[16]

Brian Massumi mounts a full frontal assault on the idea that because animals are judged to be creatures only of instinct, they cannot be self-aware, creative, or conscious in the way that humans are assumed to be. Massumi focuses on supposedly instinctual animal play, which, he asserts, "creates the conditions for language," since its "metacommunicative action builds the evolutionary foundation for the metalinguistic functions that will be the hallmark of human language." For Massumi, play consists of dramatic action, gestures performed in the ludic mode, "with a mischievous air, with an impish exaggeration or misdirection"; play may be part of an animal's education in fighting, but it is only the "improvisational process" of play that lets the animal succeed in a real fight. Thus, even if play is instinctual for animals, the idea that instinct forecloses any creative, plastic, aesthetic, or self-reflexive dimension gets things exactly backward: an animal whose fighting was entirely rote and predictable, which is what a purely instrumental concept of instinct would have it do, would be quickly killed. Rather, as Massumi points out, instinct is "sensitive" to environment, to particular situations, to relations among participants, and thus to the singularity of lived experiences.[17]

Lacan and Derrida are heirs, however skeptical or unwilling, to Cartesianism, the terms of their arguments to some degree determined by its prior delimiting of the grounds of philosophy. Although many theorists and philosophers are, like Massumi, intervening in this legacy, science and the humanities generally continue to contend with it. But plenty of laymen and -women in many historical periods have framed the whole debate quite differently—perhaps because "instinct" and "reason" both suggested that the Cartesian framework failed to explain their own lived experiences. From Aristotle to Aquinas, philosophers agreed that animals lacked reason, but this certainty was almost as often challenged by those who actually knew and worked with animals. James I, for example, famously disputed the conclusion of a debate at Cambridge regarding whether hunting dogs were able to construct syllogisms, by suggesting that the antagonist in that debate should "thinke better of his dogs or not so highly of himself."[18] Similarly, Descartes's patron William Cavendish, Duke of Newcastle, argued uncontroversially that his horses were reasoning creatures capable of thought entirely comparable to that of humans.[19] Michel de Montaigne might count as a philosopher, but it was playing with his cat that gave him a memorable lesson in skepticism: "When I am playing with my Cat, who knowes whether she have more sporte in dallying with me, then I have in gaming with her? We entertaine one another with mutuall apish trickes. If I have my houre to begin or to refuse, so hath she hirs."[20] Direct engagement with animals before and after the Cartesian divide resulted in alternative ways of knowing that are vastly different from the objective philosophical vantage point, resulting in an epistemological binary that scholars are only now beginning to challenge.

That said, it is as unclear to many now as it was when Lacan and Derrida debated the issue, or when Descartes and Montaigne pondered the status of animals, whether reason or language is strictly necessary to the pretense involved in theatrical performance, or even to the enactment of deceit in more limited cases. Edward

Topsell's *Historie of Foure-Footed Beastes* (1607), a translation of Conrad Gessner's sixteenth-century natural history *Historia animalum*, is replete with instances of animals signaling quite competently, even to their language-enabled human brethren, and entertaining one another with clever antics. Later in the eighteenth century and well into the nineteenth, an entire genre of literature was dedicated to the exploration of the success and failure of nonhuman language systems within a human world. It-narratives, such as Francis Coventry's *Memoirs of Pompey the Little* (1752), the anonymous *Memoirs of Dick the Little Poney* (1800), and Alfred Elwes's *The Life and Adventures of a Cat and a Fine Cat Too!* (1857), are narrated by nonhumans who are anthropomorphically afforded an ability to falsify, rationalize, and signal both to other members of their species and to their human counterparts.

While we might dismiss these episodes and texts as the quaint traces of a more credulous world, we can't shake the sense that many kinds of animals are quite capable of something beyond mechanical obedience to evolutionary or other biological imperatives. We often sense that animals might indeed perform not just at our command but in ways that go far beyond. Science has begun to amass evidence that our "sense" is quite right. When Nobel Prize winner Karl von Frisch first examined the "waggle dance" of bees in the 1920s and asserted its role as language, he met resistance among fellow scientists; years later, his theories were proved correct, and the concept of animal access to forms of language is increasingly evident.[21] The idea that animals might dance (or posture, or vocalize) not just to inform but to entertain or produce an aesthetic experience is no longer automatically greeted with mockery. Zoosemiotician Thomas Sebeok's work suggests that although animals might not produce verbal forms of art, they respond to and create signals on the basis of aesthetic principles by other means.[22] And when nonhuman animals are placed before a human audience, trainers and handlers attest that they display a desire to prolong their appearance, indicating that they have a sense of the difference between rehearsal and live performance.[23] Indeed, humans' rejection of such claims as projection or anthropomorphism should be regarded with skepticism for its own anthropocentric assumptions; if we insist, in the face of a growing body of evidence, that what looks like animal language, art, culture, or pleasure in performance simply cannot exist, we risk asserting human privilege, and we invite scrutiny of the motivation behind such denial.[24]

Even if we don't believe in animals' ability to perform self-consciously for performance's sake, we certainly feel moved by animal acts in ways that defy the easy relegation of animals to a Cartesian prison. Is it they who generate our emotion, or is it just our projection? And what does either option mean for our understanding of ourselves and the creatures around us? The recent essay collection *Performing Animality*, edited by Lourdes Orozco and Jennifer Parker-Starbuck, begins to answer some of these questions by exploring animals in theatrical traditions. With primary emphasis on modern theater productions such as *War Horse*, the essays in their collection connect the often disparate fields of animal studies and performance studies by investigating what animals in theater can tell us about dramatic performances. In a related volume, *Animal Acts: Performing Species Today*, Una Chaudhuri and Holly Hughes ask us to contemplate the ethical, political, and social ramifications of using animals for entertainment. "The first article of faith of interspecies performance," Chaudhuri writes, "is that we are *trying hard* to talk about actual animals now, even when . . . we cannot help but also see them as symbols for our ideas and metaphors for human dramas." The contemporary performances assembled in *Animal Acts* register the "epistemological crisis" involved in confronting animals through the mediation of "slews of misinformation, prejudice, and ignorance." The volume establishes that this epistemological crisis has deep roots, as do human patterns of recognition and resistance. Chaudhuri and Hughes emphasize that traditional forms of performance featuring actual animals raise questions about the "ethics of training, captivity, and the commercial use of animals."[25] Our own group of essays covers vivisection, horse racing, and meat eating, along with other apparently fully exploitive relationships to animals. Yet many of the essays assembled here challenge the idea that all such relationships must always be, and always are, one-directional, involving the human imposition of conditions and limits on animals; instead, *Performing Animals* remains open to the idea that power and agency travel along tangled paths of connection and disconnection whenever an animal inhabits a role in a human-structured environment.

Even what we mean by *acting* or *performing* is often open to question. The term *performance* has recently been put to a rather different purpose in the work of materialist thinkers. We refer here to a collection of theoretical approaches variously described as the new materialism, new vitalism, Actor Network Theory (ANT), or object-oriented ontology (OOO).[26] The root of the idea of "performativity" lies in the issue of action, and in what kinds or degrees of agency can be discerned when objects, as well as creatures of all kinds, "act" on others or within themselves. Bruno Latour describes objects, animals, humans, and other components of an environment as "actants" that operate in a social network. Because relations are not permanent and do not exist outside actants' continual generation of them, they must constantly be "performed"; since human and nonhuman actants are constructed only through this performance, no definitional distinctions exist to distinguish between them. Clearly, such theory materially decenters the human, much as Derrida does in a philosophical-linguistic register. Karen Barad takes materialist theory a step further, using quantum physics to demonstrate that even component objects do not preexist the moment of their atomic constitution, through what she terms "performativity." Rather than (social or other) interactions between objects determining relationships, Barad argues that the "intra-actions" of objects—that is, the conditions by which they come into being in the first place, before they can interact with other objects—generate the "cuts" that result in putatively or discernably discrete things.[27]

It might seem that these materialist theories have very little to do with traditional ideas of animal performance. But in the course of performing a task, a character, or a role, whether onstage or off, traditional forms of animal entertainment often also engender material categories like "life," "death," "flesh," "tool," or "body," among many others. Take, for instance, the moment in Shakespeare's *Two Gentlemen of Verona* when Lance accuses his dog Crab of a sour nature for failing to weep at Lance's departure from his family, unlike his mother, father, sister, maid, and even "our cat wringing her hands." Lance sets up a miniature play, with his shoes standing in for his mother and father, his staff for his sister, his hat for the maid, and either himself as the dog or the dog as himself.[28] The interchangeability of objects and humans, humans and animals (not to mention servants and masters, or selves and others), bodies and their accoutrements, like hats and shoes, resonates uncannily with current theoretical resistance to privileging one of these over another, or even establishing fixed social, linguistic, or agential categories for all.

The essays in this collection explore both the more traditional and the new materialist approaches to animal performance over a broad historical arc; not only do they interrogate the Cartesian divide, but they also take direct aim at the paucity of understandings of performance that rely on intentionality and bodily awareness as key components of agency. The small and large, living and dead, common and liminal critters discussed in this collection were alive in some form; they were beings who had a direct influence on the lived reality of the human and nonhuman animals who shared their worlds. Their agential selves, whether potentially theatrical, intentional, and knowing or unintentional and entirely material, intra-acted and caused agential cuts through their performances. These essays explore potential answers to a host of questions: did animals communicate, and what did they say? How influential was Cartesian belief among those who shared a bodily world with animals? How does our traditional, iterative, and often theatrical understanding of performance change when animals, in all of their diverse shapes and sizes, are added to the mix?

The question of life and death in performance starts the collection, with Karen Raber's analysis of Renaissance eating practices. Looking to the theatricalities of the animal body as flesh and meat, and at the crossroad between the two states of matter, Raber uses new materialist theories to probe the "rich and complex set of processes and intra-actions" between meat and human producers and consumers. Early modern feasting habits placed the (sometimes dead) animal body at the center of the evening's entertainment, and such positioning was designed in part to highlight human superiority over animal being. However, the theatricality of early modern recipes also points to animal agency in the material item produced for consumption in a way that opens up new possibilities for definitions of agency that cross animal/human and alive/dead binaries.

Examining extant sources rich in evidence for details on animal-human intra-actions and alternative conceptions of agency, Pia Cuneo provides a new take on the equestrian portrait. Focusing primarily on the bronze equestrian statue of Heinrich Julius by Adriaen de Vries of circa 1605, Cuneo argues that we must move beyond traditional art-historical approaches to such works and instead come to see and experience the animal subject as a once living, breathing being. Working within Barad's materialist and performative theories, Cuneo argues for a new scholarly methodology that not only makes visible the previously invisible animal subject but also explores ways in which the viewer or consumer of the artistic product also intra-acts, or generates the object through acts of observing. For Cuneo, a work of art is not "a static object that passively reflects a single true meaning." Instead, it is "the instigator of dynamic processes of interpretation in which physical experiences, not just intellectual strategies, play fundamental roles in the intra-action between the artwork and its viewers." The act of viewing horse and human in a mutually informing relationship as illustrated in art leads in turn to relations between subjects, artist, and viewers that have "personal, social/professional, and political meanings."

Richard Nash plumbs the materiality of scholarly records for new ways of approaching questions of animal agency and the production of the equine animal body through sporting performance. Looking to eighteenth-century manuscript trial books for horse racing, Nash argues that "these records document (in ways that human agents were at some pains to conceal and keep private) specific observations of equine athletic performance. In doing so, they also reveal different models of ownership and jockey behavior, including significant patterns of human collaboration in terms of racing 'confederacies.'" When examined alongside more traditional historical records, such as art and studbooks, the trial books illustrate complex patterns of interaction across species lines that indicate how animal athletic performance influenced understandings of breed identity.

The next chapter delves into the "equestrian sublime" and audience response to animal performance. Monica Mattfeld questions romantic period understandings of animal acting and agency in Matthew Lewis's hippodrama *Timour the Tartar* (1811), as they relate to contemporary constructions of "ideal horseness." Asking whether horses were understood as rational beings, or as beings capable of fictionalizing a performed identity, Mattfeld interrogates what a "horse" became onstage. The constructions of "horse" from outside the theater environs, Mattfeld argues, were a fundamental component of equine performed identity onstage, and of audience interpretations of hippodramatic spectacles. Relying heavily on an equestrian and sympathetic sublime, Lewis invited his audiences to align themselves with the nonhuman performers onstage in an inter- and cross-species lesson in patriotism that points to new understandings of equine agency, thespian ability, and human-animal relations from the stage to the pit.

Rob Wakeman also investigates audience responses to animal performance with an exploration of late medieval English nativity plays. Taking issue with current scholarship that argues that animal participations in early plays "only served as spectacles of violence," Wakeman argues that animal performers served more as vehicles through which, and upon which, human communities of faith were built. In addition, Wakeman questions the often idealized notion of "the animal" as the harbinger of truth, and argues for a late medieval understanding of nonhumans that in turn destabilizes prevalent conventions of anthropocentric social and world hierarchies.

Sarah Parker picks up theater's inherent "spectacles of violence" in her chapter on the use of animals in scientific experiments during the early modern period. Pointing directly at some of the ethical questions inherent in performing and performative animals, Parker asks whether performance necessarily involves movement, action, or the fictive dimension we've been discussing so far. Working with Galen's accounts of animal experimentation, Parker argues that vivisection as scientific theater allows an animal "a kind of voice" that reaffirms human exceptionalism, but also a voice that provides new insights into how early moderns understood suffering and pain. Long before Jeremy Bentham wrote, "The question is not, Can they *reason*? nor, Can they *talk*? but, Can they *suffer*?," vivisected creatures raised the same questions, not only about animal suffering but also about the signs by which suffering could be made known, and how the animal's "linguistic assemblages" might be understood by those who witnessed them.[29]

Moving from the literary world to the scientific, Jessica Wolfe examines early modern entomology, with a particular emphasis on flea circuses. Focusing specifically on Mark Scaliot's *circus minimus*, Wolfe argues that insects in general and circus fleas in particular were unsettling beings. Early moderns considered insects particularly "theatrical" in their malleability between and transgression of established natural categories. Often considered liminally situated between life and death, or animal and machine, insects just didn't fit. Wolfe interrogates what it means for animals, and the scientific experiments that study them, to be theatrical, and sheds new light on some of the most contested questions in animal studies: what is alive? What is not? How do we know?

Todd Borlik continues the discussion of insects with a direct exploration of the question "who, or rather what, counts as an actor" in the world of Shakespearean England. Looking to the emerging field of entomology for clues, Borlik argues that Shakespeare based his famous fairy folk on period understandings and theatrical treatments of insects. Shakespeare's fairies do not fit with traditional conceptualizations of the wee folk popular throughout England, a point consistently puzzling to literary scholars but one that Borlik sees as the direct result of Shakespeare's interest in natural history. Shakespeare's "arthropomorphic humans" were the result of "bio-mimicry," and they point to interesting reconceptions of theatrical agency and early modern notions of human versus animal attributes onstage.

How horses and humans acted on and offstage, and the many social and personal ramifications of performance, is the subject of the two concluding chapters. Gender transgressions, so prevalent within hippodrama as a genre, are the topic of Kari Weil's chapter. Weil follows the career of one of the greatest female equestrians to grace the stage: Adah Menken and her horse "performed and transgressed categories, not only of gender and race but also of species" in the nineteenth-century smash hit *Mazeppa*. Tracing Menken's career as represented in the Parisian press, Weil argues that Menken's sensationalized interaction with her horse, within an environment already famous for social and political playfulness, was sublime, but sublime in a way that "materialized into an alluring but potentially dangerous spectacle of interspecies corporeality—an image with which male riders were only beginning to be saddled."

The final chapter, by Kim Marra, examines the 1889 play *Shenandoah*, set during the American Civil War. In this popular hippodramatic spectacle, the physical presence of horses resulted in the destabilization of theatrical representation and reenactment, but the "horses also crossed other conventional boundaries, queering cultural norms of gender and sexuality and interlocking categories of species, race, class, region, and, ultimately, life and death." The presence of equine actors upset normative masculine gender performance through their large, unpredictable, and physical presence, and opened up a space in which women could increasingly enact femininities that pushed against social norms. Conversely, the equine body also created opportunities for the reinscription of gendered and racialized conventions in a contradictory and queer performance of self.

These essays weave back and forth between historical periods, and between the small and the large nonhuman creatures who inhabited these periods. They interrogate assumptions not merely about what might distinguish animals from humans, or their respective performance abilities, but about what we think is going on when we see animals "perform." We hope in this way to expand the dimensions of debates that concern both animals and humans in order to engage more consciously in the creaturely pleasures that entangle us so profoundly with our fellow actors, human and nonhuman alike.

NOTES

1. Fudge's *Brutal Reasoning* gives a thorough summary of Descartes's position (147–62), as does Shannon's *Accommodated Animal,* esp. 183–98. Both also account for resistance to Descartes's arguments from various constituencies: as Fudge points out, "the debates about reason outlined by philosophers and divines were at some distance from the lived realities of early modern men and women" (164).

2. Kiser, "Animals in Medieval Sports," 103.

3. Wright, "Animal Actors on the English Stage."

4. Fudge, *Perceiving Animals,* 1; her chapter "Screaming Monkeys: The Creatures in the Bear Garden" (11–33) describes how bears, apes, dogs— and people who succumbed to the temptations of cruelty, pleasure, and vice—all came to occupy, for some witnesses, the same rank of creation. See also Bliss, "Property or Performers," which notes that animals could be used as actors or as property on

Renaissance stages, requiring a constant redrawing of the boundary between animal and actor.

5. For more on how menageries and zoos stage animals, see Rothfels, *Savages and Beasts;* Berger, *About Looking;* and Burt, *Animals in Film.* An unusual angle on display and the idea of the "zoo" informs Poliquin's *Breathless Zoo.*

6. Berger, *About Looking,* 3–28.

7. Baker, *Picturing the Beast,* 165–86.

8. See Lippit, *Electric Animal.*

9. Burt, *Animals in Film,* 197.

10. Pick, *Creaturely Poetics.*

11. Calarco, *Zoographies,* 141.

12. Lacan, *Écrits,* quoted in Derrida, *Animal That Therefore I Am,* 129.

13. Ibid., 130, 135.

14. Ibid., 151, 155.

15. See Sebeok, *Perspectives in Zoosemiotics.*

16. Moe, "Zoopetics," 30; see also Moe, *Zoopoetics.*

17. Massumi, *What Animals Teach Us,* 8, 9, 13.

18. Mayor, "King James I," 93.

19. Cavendish gives a practical lesson on "reason" and how horses demonstrate its use in his *General System of Horsemanship,* where he makes this rebuke to Descartes: "If he [the horse] does not think (as the famous philosopher Des Cartes affirms of all beasts) it would be impossible to teach him what he should do" (12).

20. Montaigne, *Apology of Raymond Sebond,* 260. Laurie Shannon calls Montaigne a better skeptic than Descartes in *Accommodated Animal,* 192.

21. Frisch's *Aus dem Leben der Bienen* was first published in 1927, translated into English as *The Dancing Bees.*

22. See Sebeok, "Prefigurations of Art."

23. Tait, *Wild and Dangerous Performances,* 195.

24. See Ingold, "Introduction," in *What Is an Animal,* 1–16. Ingold uses Mary Midgely's description of "species solipsism" in questioning the way claims of anthropocentrism reject actual evidence that animals are capable of the same things humans are.

25. Una Chaudhuri, "Animal Acts for Changing Times 2.0: A Field Guide to Interspecies Performance," in Chaudhuri and Hughes, *Animal Acts,* 4–5, 8, 6.

26. On Actor Network Theory, see Latour, *Reassembling the Social;* on object-oriented ontology, see Bogost, *What Is Object-Oriented Ontology?*

27. Barad, "Posthumanist Performativity." In her work, Barad joins everyone from Foucault to Haraway and Latour to Butler in embracing the body, and in resisting what she calls representationalism (the primacy of language in constructing realities), but she addresses what she sees as a gap in these theorists' work, the specific process by which discourse and bodies interact. Barad argues for the body's, and all matter's, agential realism (an account of human and nonhuman ontology that takes seriously the idea of matter's agency, so that rather than "words" and "things," the world consists of relationalities that are material in nature). Her neologism "intra-action" insists that there are no preexisting entities before relationship, that only through intra-action do the boundaries of phenomena come to exist.

28. Shakespeare, *The Two Gentlemen of Verona,* 2.3.4–22.

29. Bentham, *Principles of Morals and Legislation,* 311n122.

1

ANIMALS AT THE TABLE

Performing Meat in Early Modern
England and Europe

KAREN RABER

John Wecker's *Secrets of Art and Nature* (Latin, 1582; English translation by R. Read, 1660) offers a recipe for roasting a goose alive. Advising the application of a ring of fire to some "lively Creature," the recipe includes pots of water to slake the dying goose's thirst, while it "fl[ies] here and there" within the fire ring. The cook should baste the goose's head and heart so that "her inward parts" will roast before she dies: "when you see her giddy with running, and begin to stumble, her heart wants moisture: she is Rosted, take her up, and set her upon the Table to your Guests, and as you cut her up she will cry continually, that she will be almost all eaten before she be dead."[1] Thus far, recipes like this one have attracted limited scholarly analysis. Wecker's recipe appears, for instance, in the introduction to Patricia Fumerton and Simon Hunt's collection *Renaissance Culture and the Everyday*, where it serves as a reminder of the casual cruelty of Renaissance practices, which in turn estrange everyday early modern culture for a generation of historicist critics.[2] In her account of the abattoir that was the early modern kitchen, Wendy Wall describes scenes of far more bloody violence accompanying the preparation of meals, drawing from them consequences for the gendering of household labor.[3] Culinary historians might situate the recipe as an example of the new interest in food's aesthetic complexity during the Renaissance. To animal lovers and vegetarians, the recipe would speak for itself, highlighting the intolerable suffering of living creatures rendered as mere meat for the table: recent work by posthumanist scholars like Simon Estok and Erica Fudge have discussed early modern resistance to, and rare embrace of, vegetarianism based on the dehumanizing influence of meat eating exemplified by extreme cases of torture like Wecker's recipe.[4]

Wecker's goose is no lonely outlier. Fumerton mentions such other examples of kitchen barbarity as a pig whipped to death and a capon "pulled" and gutted while alive as evidence that the goose's fate was a common one in early modern cookery. Eels, apparently, were regularly eaten while alive, their motion part of the experience of consumption. A recipe in *The Vivendier*, a mid-fifteenth-century French cookbook, offers a comic take on the goose's lyric performance:

> Get a chicken or any other bird you want, and pluck it alive cleanly in hot water. Then get the yolks of 2 or 3 eggs; they should be beaten with powdered saffron and wheat flour, and distempered with fat broth or with the grease that drips under a roast into the dripping pan. By means of a feather glaze and paint your pullet carefully with this mixture so that its colour looks like roast meat. With this done, and when it is about to be served to the table, put the chicken's head under its wing, and turn it in your hands, rotating it until it is fast asleep. Then set it down on your platter with the other roast meat. When it is about to be carved it will wake up and make off down the table upsetting jugs, goblets and whatnot.[5]

What happens to the naked chicken after it amuses the guests is not reported.

Like many elaborate banquet dishes, Wecker's goose and the *Vivendier*'s chicken accomplish a number of things at once. They collapse the distinction between living and dead, between animal and meat; they also conflate the meal's function as sustenance with its function as entertainment. The latter is not surprising, since the basic job of a banquet or feast for guests was precisely to affirm or create social ties through a ritualized communal event that often featured grandiose dishes, meant more to impress the diner with the host's wealth or status than to satisfy the palate. Feasts were often interspersed with theatrical, musical, or other forms of diversion also nicely calculated to demonstrate the host's authority, good taste, education, and other virtues. Both recipes belong to a long tradition of theatricalized, artistically complex meats served at banquet tables, a tradition that extends back at least to the classical literary example of Trimalchio's feast from Petronius's *Satyricon*. That tradition arguably reached its height during the late Renaissance, which often consciously imitated the excesses of classical feasting.

What the goose and chicken recipes do, then, is ensure that the host will be remembered for providing a most entertaining dish, one that results in a miraculous performance by the entrée itself. But in early modern Europe, changing habits with regard to meat eating required that the animal at the center of this performance take on new roles, new functions. In our own historical moment, meat rules the table, unquestioned monarch of the meal, surrounded by fawning courtiers (vegetables and other side dishes), often enthroned and crowned (resting on beds of starches, or doused with sauces). Recent adventures in pink slime and petri-dish meats have brought home how hard it is to decenter "real" meat from this sovereign position: petri-dish meat in particular offends through its very status as simulacrum.[6]

But it hasn't always been this way. Only at a fairly late date in its etymology, at just the moment when Wecker's goose and the *Vivendier*'s comical chicken took the stage, did the term "meat" begin to signify specifically the flesh of a dead animal meant for human consumption in a meal. Prior to the fifteenth century, meat was almost uniformly used as a generic term for all food. The alternative to the current association of "meat" with cooked animal is the more obsolete use of the word "flesh," but in the Middle Ages this word referred as often to human beings as to animal bodies, and so did not restrictively designate a component of a meal.[7] The etymologies of "meat" and "flesh" thus suggest that something was happening culturally during this period that required the role of dead animals at the table to be recoded, to be divided off from other categories of food and bodies.

There are a number of practical reasons why such a transition might have occurred: on the one hand, the Middle Ages' huge appetite for meat was displaced during a subsequent period of agricultural change that saw food animals reduced in number, thus making meat consumption the prerogative of the wealthy, associated with class and affluence.[8] In their survey of French cookery books, Philip and Mary Hyman observe that the very popular *Le thresor de santé* devotes fully half of its pages to recipes for meat.[9] When the advent of more successful and productive agriculture allowed more people access to meat at meals, meat thus gained a tremendous cultural cachet. A growing role for the culinary arts in ever broader segments of society throughout the sixteenth and seventeenth centuries also focused the attention of many (even those who still couldn't afford much) on feats of cookery applied to meat; meanwhile, widening popular concern over the medical role of meat in dietary regimes encouraged people to think carefully about distinctions among meats and between meat and other foods. Whatever the economic, medical, or other practical reasons for meat's changing role, it was also transformed into a cultural focal point through its various representations as an object, one engaged in complex interactions with human bodies, with other meats, with other "players" at the banquet table. But that new status for meat only makes more potent the problem of establishing what it is that "makes meat." Is the living animal already incipient meat?[10] At what point in its metamorphosis does an animal become meat: when slaughtered, when divided by the butcher, when cooked, when eaten? "In the eating encounter," writes Jane Bennett, "all bodies are shown to be but temporary congealments of a materiality that is a process of becoming, is hustle and flow punctuated by sedimentation and substance."[11] Before being consumed, meat acts on human senses and imagination: odor, texture, taste all simultaneously generate responses in human anatomy, and in the human brain, most not fully under the conscious control of an individual. After consumption, flesh melts into flesh, becomes categorically indivisible, yet can generate discomfort, illness in the short term, or obesity and debility in the long term. The simplistic observation "you are what you eat" hides a rich and complex set of processes and intra-actions that this chapter will probe.[12]

As I noted above, most discussions of early modern meat are found in works of culinary history, animal studies, or activist anti-meat criticism. While welcome and a clear inspiration to this project, the various agendas of such recent work have tended to ignore or erase the nuanced process by which cultural dominance is accorded meat as a main part of meals, and the consequent cultural negotiations of meat's inherent complexity as a performer at the table. In this chapter, I focus narrowly on meat's position as an actor in the theater of the meal. In the interests of understanding how (usually mostly) dead matter can be said to perform, I mobilize the work of the "new materialists," particularly Jane Bennett, who offer a way to talk about the metaphors mobilized by and through meats, about meat's role as actant, and about what Bennett calls its "vagabond" quality, and its vitality-in-death.[13] In what follows, I take up the question of what is at stake in the appearance of two groups of performing meats in early modern feasts and banquets: first, zombie meats, in the vein of Wecker's goose and the *Vivendier*'s chicken; second, the related creation of early modern "transgenic" or "masquerading" meats through the technique of engastration (the stuffing of one meat with another, or several others) and engastration's close analogues, "re-dressed" meats—meats made up to look like living versions of themselves, or like other creatures or objects. What these "performing meats" have in common is the multidimensionality of their required signification. They do not simply entertain, although certainly that is part of their purpose. Rather, I argue that their performances at the dinner table illuminate early modern ideas and desires about the living animals that provided a newly meaningful dietary mainstay. I will not argue that early moderns in any way were appalled or revolted by the collapse of theatrical performance and the rendering of animals as meat—that is, I do not suggest that Wecker's or any other such recipe aroused ethical concerns about animals themselves. Rather, I argue that early modern banquets created performed and performing meats that violated species and other categories, and that while this theater of meat announced and celebrated human exceptionalism and human control over nature by testifying to the creative and transformative power of the human cook (and host), it also revealed the limits of that power by conceding or granting to animal flesh a type of agency—what Judith Butler might call the "performativity" of meat—in the process of making it act out a part in a meal.[14] Ultimately, I argue that what meat "performed" was itself—all the distortions, complications, and ideological dimensions of its production *as meat*.

Zombie Meats

Whether Wecker's recipe for cooking a goose alive is meant to be a real recipe is debatable. For one thing, it is included in a book called *The Secrets of Art and Nature*, suggesting that it belongs to the genre of alchemical or occult literature; the volume shares some aspects with natural philosophies, including, for example, remedies for various diseases, and offering a compendious and inclusive treatment of the various creatures it discusses, alongside recipes and other kitchen lore. Wecker's may not be the only recipe of its kind in early modern cookbooks, but no corresponding descriptions of a "live" animal consumed at table during an actual banquet seem to survive (apart from those involving eels)—not to mention the fact that it isn't clear whether the recipe could even work reliably. Yet if it does not represent a material practice regarding meat in the past, it certainly represents a *fantasy* about what cooking and eating can achieve. The question I address in this section is: what is that fantasy, and what are its implications? What is the appeal of Wecker's zombie goose? What role, exactly, did it perform for his readers, and to what ends?

The theatricality of early modern banqueting has been amply charted by historians and literary-cultural scholars. Ken Albala remarks about the theater of cooking and eating that "any meal . . . contains a script. It might be said that every participant in the eating event is equally an actor."[15] Roy Strong describes the elaboration of food items in late medieval and early modern banquets, noting that "eating [had] become an element in a vast theatrical production." At one feast given by Gaston IV at Tours in 1457, a series of entremets divided numerous courses; "mobile scenery, costumed actors, singers, musicians and dancers" enlivened the scene, along with a culinary "finale" involving a "heraldic menagerie sculpted in sugar: lions, stags, monkeys, and various other birds and beasts, each holding in paw or beak the arms of the Hungarian king" who was being honored. As medieval appetites for both food and spectacle evolved, cookery books and famous cooks ushered in a new era of cuisine, influenced by many factors, including the use of spices, hints of Arab cuisine, new culinary techniques, and so on. One consequence of this expanding importance and investment in food was a new standard for aspects like "form and color"—Strong remarks that "the physical side of eating is being displaced by the aesthetic pleasure of looking." Not displaced, perhaps, but certainly melded with the idea of food as visually consumable as well as gustatorily so. In 1598, *Epulario, or The Italian Banquet*, translated from Italian for English cooks, gives a description of a type of dish now familiar to us only because of its appearance in a nursery rhyme: "To make Pies that the Birds may be alive in them, and flie out when it is cut up" (B4r). Inside a larger "coffin," or shell, the recipe calls for the insertion of a smaller, genuinely edible pie that is surrounded with "small live birds" who will fly out when the larger shell is opened, "to the delight and pleasure shew to the company." The emphasis on "shewing" is recognized a moment later, when the recipe advises that the smaller pie is there for actual eating, "that they [the guests] shall not bee altogether mocked." To be entertained by the performance of the birds evokes pleasure; to make the visual spectacle all would be to mock the diners' appetites for consumption of another kind. Gaze and palate must both be satisfied. Strong describes castles created out of meats, sugars, flour, and other ingredients populated by creatures, among them a full-grown stag, boar, rabbits (the latter clearly "meant to be eaten"), a boar's head breathing fire, fountains of wine, enormous confections large enough to contain human musicians.[16] The crying of Wecker's goose is a much-redacted variant of such a grandiose display, blending gustatory and auditory pleasure when the presumably faint sounds of the goose's voice accompany consumption of her tasty flesh.[17] From the fourteenth through the seventeenth century, food functions as propaganda, display, art, sculpture, and even full-bore theater.[18]

I would isolate two aspects of the recipe to consider more closely: the theatrical performance of the goose's actual death, and its performance for the diner once served. Wecker presumably describes an act of cookery that happens in a kitchen, well away from the guests who will partake of the dish, yet he does so in excruciating detail, constructing a scene that resembles nothing so much as a miniature drama. Surrounded by kitchen staff, including the cook, who must bank the fires that roast her, the goose has an audience to her immediate suffering, mirrored in the reading audience of the cookbook once the recipe is printed. She is active, flying around looking for escape, periodically basted with water to encourage her further struggles. A death scene more lingering and pathetic could hardly be found on the early modern stage, suggesting that what matters in this recipe is not only the eventual dish that results but the pleasure (whatever that consists of) in vicariously witnessing this transition from living, "lively" animation to zombielike living death. That pleasure is so great, so compelling, that readers who might never experience it directly are being invited, through the printing of the recipe, to mentally reenact it. What do Wecker's readers gain from this possibly spurious description? A moment of insight into how life can be preserved in the face of even the most deadly treatment—insight, that is, into the very moment that is obscured to the most educated early modern reader, even to medical experts, in a world where the fact of death was everywhere, but knowledge of what precisely it *was*, nowhere? Or do they enjoy the pleasure of witnessing an act of torture that results, because of its repressed and controlled violence, in a moment of beauty (the "song" as she is eaten)? If this is the consequence, the scene then evokes a tradition of torture and martyrdom that makes the goose a Christ figure, sacrificed in a parody (or is it?) of the Passion and the Eucharist.[19] Is this latter possibility the reason why the goose's consumption and its textual reproduction are different—one involves partaking of the flesh, the other, an imaginative investment in the scene of death itself? If so, what does that make the recipe book? It's hard not to think here of the current craze for food porn, which turns images or representations of recipes into a substitute for sexual pleasure. But in this case, the "sexual" is something else, something closer to a transformative embodied experience that conjures sensory experiences usually absent from ordinary meals.

Wecker's goose had, of course, already been the target of human transformation on a global scale. Geese were both wild and domesticated creatures in early modern Europe. However, because Wecker's recipe comes amid a long section on domesticated fowl of all kinds, including ducks, chickens, and pigeons, we can be reasonably sure that this is the domestic variety. Wecker also advises that the goose is only the preferred fowl for this dish, but also names ducks or "some lively creature" as options. Geese were domesticated as early as three thousand years B.C., and are ubiquitous rather than limited to certain regions. In addition to providing eggs and flesh for the table, geese are good watch-fowl, especially in groups, since they are both extremely loud and potentially aggressive toward other animals or unfamiliar humans. For these reasons, the goose should be considered a touchstone for the entire concept and process of domestication. And domestication is human improvement in its most concrete and generalized form. Before arriving at the dinner table, then, a goose is already a "redressed" creature, one whose physiology and behavior have been meddled with (as the term redress implies, "remedied" to become a domestic creature, but also, as we'll see below, re-dressed in its theatrical garb) by human agency, turned into a mirror for human power over nature. Albala observes that the predominance of domesticated over wild meats grew exponentially in the late sixteenth and early seventeenth centuries, and that the preference for meats generated from human control over nature, instead of those derived directly from nature itself, had moral and cultural connotations, so that wild meats came to be associated with unrefined, or "wild," characteristics in those who ate them. Instead of noble hunters, early modern foodies were beginning to think of themselves equally as scholars and collectors who appreciated the finer, lighter meats.[20]

This goose, then, is being mobilized as a performer in something more complex than the mere display of wealth and privilege: her "speech," her faint movements, even the knowledge of the means of her preparation enhance the aesthetic dimension of the meal itself, while the knowledge of, or report of, the method of her preparation might fashion a new kind of textual experience once translated into print. But it is worth thinking about what is different when a living animal is thus made an actor in the drama of eating. In addition to the animal's being made compliant through a prior process of domestication, the bird's dying here is produced as the sauce to her own demise. While we might think this a horrific thing, early moderns more likely would have appreciated the ideological content of the moment—an animal serenading a diner whose consumption endorses the act of eating as an aestheticized assertion of human control over creation, and therefore also over death. At the same time, however, the "cut" that should mark the goose's flesh as object, as dead and therefore edible meat, instead disrupts any neat distinction:[21] the diner carves into an animal that announces by voice and gesture that she is still animate, conscious, a participant in the drama of the table. The bloody drama usually assumed to end in the kitchen arrives at the table; instead of passive audience, guests become actors on stage, themselves completing the act of killing Wecker's goose, and so fixing it as meat. If the difference between the raw and the cooked is culture, then this goose arrives only rawly cooked. As to the cook and guest who rely on a meal of meat as a demonstration of exclusively human agency, their goose is cooked indeed when they enlist this goose in the performance of her death.

Make Your Own (Dead) Animal

Everywhere in the early modern kitchen, an observer could find examples of transmutation, things being turned into other things, often involving various forms of meat. "Turn your meat," writes Lady Elinor Fettiplace in one recipe, "to pure blood."[22] Wendy Wall notes that cookbooks "underscore the importance of flesh mutating into flesh . . . everywhere hearkening toward dinner's vitality and the precariousness of embodiment."[23] Food was used to create almost anything, from small objects to entire environments: Strong describes fake gardens made of sugar, vessels and instruments, statues and sculptures, even entire buildings made of food.[24] The feast was a "game of deceit," with edible trenchers, cups, and so on—but also featuring meats layered or fused within, around, and on top of other meats, disguised as other creatures or as their own living selves.[25]

Part of the reason for meat's "vagabond" nature in the early modern world is the degree to which it was not yet cultivated to enhance its more consumable qualities— that is, flesh was hard to eat because generally it was quite tough (and early modern teeth were probably not always reliably strong enough to tear and chew it fully). Thus the vast majority of recipes in the period involving meat require its dis-integration through extreme cooking techniques. Nearly every meat is stewed, seethed, or minced, and then mixed, stuffed, or sauced with other ingredients; many meat dishes end with the resulting "paste" reconstituted through baking or incorporation into puddings, hashes, or other blended dishes. Roasted meats are actually fairly rare (usually appearing at larger banquets in the late Middle Ages) and often limited to more tender animals like fowl. What this means is that early modern meat dishes obscure their origins: one could not necessarily perceive in the resulting food the shape or other physical attributes of the living animal. Even the sheer act of butchering transformed food into something vastly different from its first incarnation, while even the simplest styles of cooking were by definition processes of transformation. The preface to John Day's *Travels of the Three English Brothers* (1607) compares playwriting to cooking by noting the additions, subtractions, and obfuscations of both: "Who gives a fowle to his cook to dress / Likewise expects to have a fowle againe, / Though in the Cookes laborious workmanship / Much may be deminisht, som-what added / The losse of feathers and the gaine of sauce."[26] While a diner might expect her cook to send a "fowl" back from the kitchen, she accepted that it might arrive in new, saucy attire following the mysterious process of re-creation applied to it.

At the simplest level, by creating re-formed and re-dressed dishes, cooks were merely restoring visual cues to the animal's identity and a less ambiguous connection between the transformed meat and its prior condition as a live animal. *Epulario*, for instance, includes a recipe for how "to dresse a Peacocke with all his feathers" that produces a dish that "seems to be alive." The cook removes the bird's feathers and skin, cooks its meat, then re-stuffs it with its own flesh and re-feathers it. While this is the most frequent process cited in recipes, it turns out that the disintegration of meat through cooking opened the door to much more inventive results. Rendering meat edible also provided an opportunity to quite literally make meats "cross-dress," like one of Shakespeare's boy actors done up in women's garb. Early modern meat thus becomes the material of experiments with nature, transforming and translating what *was* into what *might be*. If "dressing" (meaning to form, order, arrange, straighten, or manage) referred to meat's preparation either for cooking or for serving, then we might say that meats were also "re-dressed" in other attire for their appearance at the dinner or banquet table: that is, they were re-clothed and amended or remedied in the process.

Consider the turducken, a turkey stuffed with a duck, which is in turn stuffed with a chicken, a dish now primarily served at Thanksgiving feasts in the United States. Although its name is new (dating, according to the *OED*, only to the 1980s), its origins lie in the period we are discussing, in the fascination with engastration that informs many early recipe books and banquet tables. England calls three-bird roasts "royal roasts," and they derive from the very old process of boning and then stuffing a portion of meat for added flavor and texture. The Tudor Christmas pie, which dates back to the tables of Henry VIII if not before, placed an engastrated turkey inside a "coffin" of pastry (probably to allow it to cook well without burning). Turkeys were, Bruce Boehrer notes, objects of "high-end gastronomic desire," owing to their exotic origins and their association with the peacock, a traditional bird at the most splendid feasts.[27] Of course, they were also large enough birds to allow the enclosure of various other game and domesticated fowl within, a not insignificant part of their appeal. It is tempting to link their hidden yet populous interiors with their obscurity in early modern natural histories, since turkeys also presented a challenge to European lineages of species: whether the bird was entirely new, or a true relative of peacocks, was a question with both religious and scientific implications. At the very least, it is possible to observe that the turkey's indefinite origins, in a fortuitous accident of gastronomy, align nicely with its indefinite identity as a highly engastratable bird.

Perhaps the grandeur of the turkey has led us to overlook the smaller animals inside, but from the perspective of the chicken in a turducken, the subsequent layers are a form of cloaking device, concealing its "nature" until the moment when the turkey is carved and reveals itself to be not a singular dead animal but one inhabited by other creatures. It is thus a variation on the many surprise theatrical food-based revelations included in famous banquets. Jeffrey Hudson, court dwarf to Henrietta Maria, was first presented to her leaping out of a piecrust. Pope Gregory XIII offered a miniature model of the Castel Sant'Angelo out of which came rabbits, partridges, and other small creatures.[28] The *Vivendier*'s dormant chicken is one version of these surprises, which incorporated—literally, made part of the corpse—living animals, violating the expectation of dead meat, as well as elements of theater wedded to gastronomic techniques. The chicken at the heart of the turducken continues the experience of novelty and wonder among diners in all these episodes, aided by the turkey's and duck's savory flavors, but also by their function as disguise.

The turducken is really quite a tame critter: the most extreme example of animal experimentation comes in attempts to create entirely new creatures from dead flesh. For his banquet in honor of the French king Francis I at the Field of the Cloth of Gold in 1520, Henry VIII's cooks whipped up a "cockentrice" by sewing together the head of a pig and the rear end of a chicken. While such an object might look like a bizarre violation of nature, it was not so rare a dish, having already graced the table of John Stafford, bishop of Bath, in 1425, and probably many more banquets besides.[29] If Wecker's goose and the *Vivendier*'s chicken are proto-zombies, then perhaps these "re-dressed" meats count as early experiments in transgenesis—the manipulation of animal DNA to produce new species, to recode dead flesh and give it new naturalized-unnatural forms. What cannot be found in nature is produced by human ingenuity and intervention, which amends and improves—that is, redresses—simple meats, giving them new identities.

What do engastric or cross-dressed meats in early modern cookery tell us, either about meat or about what it represents? While the engastration of meats can be assimilated to other forms of transformation at the banquet table (like *Schauessen* or *trionfi*, confections in all sorts of shapes and forms made out of a variety of materials), making meat into a simulacrum of itself or of other meats suggests that "meat" functions as figurative and symbolic *matter*—it is in itself metaphor, or perhaps an example of what Ian Bogost calls "metaphorphosis" in the sense that "meat" as a descriptor of dead flesh detaches from any "natural" or confirmed "thing" in the world and instead becomes a thing in itself.[30] Each of these masquerading dishes is an ontologically confused and confusing thing, its existence made possible precisely because of the mobile (in every sense of this word) thingness of a thing (dead flesh) that was once a living object (the animal). The boundary crossings of these masquerading meats can be assimilated to the same narrative as our performing meats above. However, I think the process of creating re-dressed meats carries a particular cost: by provoking cooks and diners to reconsider meat's inert, passive status and the reliability of meat's self-identity, they raise questions about meat's dangerous potential influence on the identity and status first of the animal who is transformed into meat, and next of the eater who consumes it.

Early modern dietaries and medical texts posited a humoral human body, porous and thus vulnerable to external influences, constantly struggling to achieve equilibrium. Geography, class status, gender, and other factors could influence an individual's basic humoral complexion, while everything from air to food could disturb the precarious balance of that body's internal machinery.[31] Whole categories of meats were understood to define the bodies that ate them: pork, for instance, was a lower-class dish, suitable for crude palates and crude bodies, while tender fowl was for more refined diets. Albala notes that Charles Estienne's *De Nutrimentis* (1550) "excised many foods completely in consideration of health," including onions and garlic because they were only "appropriate for barbers and journeymen."[32] Luigi Cardano found no room for apples in any healthy diet. Food was never simply fuel: it was physic for a range of ailments, with effects on everything from individual morality to national identity. "All acts of ingestion and excretion," Michael Schoenfeldt argues, were "very literal acts of self-fashioning."[33] Gluttony was a frequent target of criticism in dietaries, followed by drunkenness, but excessive consumption of meat also repeatedly drew opprobrium from dietary authors. William Bullein recommended only certain meats for creating "good blood," including many fowl and roasted veal or boiled mutton, while Andrew Boorde praised pheasant as a bird that "doth comfort the brayne and stomach," along with other small birds whose flesh is nourishing but does not "ingender melancholy."[34] Like many English dietaries, Boorde's applauded beef as a dish for Englishmen, as long as it was neither too old nor from a female animal, either of which would cause "leprous humours."[35] Pork was an especially vexed subject, even when it was not remade as an early modern proto-cyborg: Fudge recounts the various positions for and against it, but most agreed that it was risky because of the pig's association with uncleanliness and cannibalism.

If one can't tell the identity of the meat that one consumes, however, then obviously any prescription regarding appropriate consumption of the stuff is rendered ineffectual. Moreover, if meats can be recoded, not merely as different meats (as in the case of layered and blended meats) but as completely new creatures (as in the case of the cockentrice), then the entire edifice that rests on the Galenic system falls apart. Instead of policing social, political, national, and other boundaries, meat violates the whole notion of decipherable categories. Again, Bennett's use of the term "vagabond" describes meat's inherent variability, its itinerant nature, resistant to the kind of fixity required by dietary regimes of the period. In an accident of history and language, we might recall here that early modern stage performers, actors in the public theater, were regarded as vagabonds and "masterless men" by authorities. Like human performers, banquet meats promised a theater of order and discrimination, but in their mobility they might deliver the opposite.

If transgenic meats expose meat's susceptibility to transformation, and re-dressed or masquerading meats suggest the difficulty that diners might have in even recognizing the meat on their plates, then not only does meat not enable the policing of social, moral, political, and other categories, as it is supposed to, but, as a "vagabond," it might lead to the complete collapse of all categories, full stop. The anxiety embodied in meat revolves around its mobility—it is always in the process of becoming something else: animal becoming flesh, flesh becoming "meat," meat being cooked, cooked meats being consumed, consumed meats becoming (human) flesh again, and so on. At each stage, what meat is and isn't is uncertain; in the last stages, when animal flesh is transmuted into human flesh, meat enacts a mingling of bodies that confronts the diner with the porousness of her body and its essential material instability. Matter is never itself; it is always becoming other. Engastric concoctions like the turducken and cross-species confabulations like the cockentrice, I believe, deliberately reproduce this indistinction as a circumscribed by-product of human intervention in the making of meat, rather than in its most global and threatening form as definitional of all flesh, in order to confront and defang the anxieties aroused by the act of eating a dead animal. In light of this possibility, it is useful to consider for a moment the practice of redressing meats as the animals to whom the flesh originally belonged. A peacock dressed up in its feathers is dead meat masquerading as living animal—or, in another formulation, an animal masquerading "as itself," just in a more culinarily compliant form. Such redressing attempts to introduce stability and a different kind of vitality to the dead, confused, and confusing object being presented to diners. But what does it mean to say that the bird is dressed as "itself"? What "self" does the bird—dead, dismembered, mixed with other ingredients, reassembled, shaped, and re-feathered—have? The act of culinary re-dressing imports a fantasy of self-identity, of a prior subjectivity invested in the living animal. While not precisely a process that recognizes some individuality of a bird, re-dressing her at least implies respect for species identity as a partial substitute. One would not want a guest to cut into an object that didn't proclaim itself a specific type of animal.

Early modern meat had to be made, first by the cultivation of living animals as domesticated breeds suitable for consumption, then as flayed and dismembered carcasses, then as transformed culinary objects. What makes meat, however, is also its performance of itself throughout the penultimate stage of transformation, the meat, of itself (of a "self") *as meat*. Only then can a guest recognize the various codes that render meat edible, and take it on its final journey, to mingle with human flesh from within. Wecker's goose is not meat until after her body is cut into by the diner, extending the "making" process from kitchen to table. Cross-dressed meats masquerade as living creatures, as themselves in lively form, until they are dismembered a second time by the diner who restores the certainty of death and renewed life as human, not animal, flesh. At the banquet table, "performance," in its more common sense of theatrical action, bleeds—literally—into "performativity," the construction of matter *as matter*. In its tales of zombie geese and chickens, its transgenic and cross-dressed pheasants, turkeys, and ducks, early modern culinary practice stages the dangerous cultural drama of becoming meat.

NOTES

1. Wecker, *Secrets of Art and Nature*, 148. Wecker's is not precisely a cookbook, but rather a grab bag of "secrets" in various fields, accompanied by recipes for both foods and medicines.

2. Patricia Fumerton, "Introduction: A New New Historicism," in Fumerton and Hunt, *Renaissance Culture and the Everyday*, 2.

3. The afterlife of Wecker's recipe includes its appearance in M. F. K. Fisher's postwar *How to Cook a Wolf*—in a chapter called "How to Make a Pigeon Cry," the title of which actually refers to a quotation from Jonathan Swift—as part of her encouragement to cooks faced with rationing, assuring them that their talents could conquer and transform the most bizarre kinds of meats.

4. See Fudge, "Saying Nothing"; and Estok, "Theory from the Fringes." Fudge is concerned with the justifications of early modern resistance to, versus acceptance of, vegetarianism, while Estok argues that Shakespeare's plays sanction vegetarianism in many of their representations of meat eating.

5. Scully, *Vivendier*, 81.

6. In August 2013, Mark Post, a vascular biologist, offered his lab-grown meat in a publicity stunt for which it was cooked as a hamburger by a famous chef and tasted by two food critics (see Jha, "First Hamburger," and Palmer, "Lab-Grown Burger," for examples of online articles covering the event). Public reaction ran the gamut, but one constant was the momentary wince at the mere thought of consuming meat that did not have its origins in an authentic cow. Safety and cost concerns aside, if meat grown in a petri dish fails, it will be this reaction that kills it.

7. The *OED* gives initial instances from 1325 and 1475 for this more narrow usage; until that moment, meat was anything that could be eaten, from vegetables to sweets. The *Middle English Dictionary* gives numerous definitions of "meat" that refer to all forms of solid food (as opposed to drink); only in one subcategory is "meat" defined as derived from animals, and then it is indistinguishable from the "meat" of fish or any other form of flesh. A review of the Middle

English corpus reveals numerous uses of "meat" for virtually any food, from individual items like onions to concoctions like possets or desserts. Noëllie Vialles, in *Animal to Edible*, 4, notes that the same shift happened to the French *viande*. Meanwhile, "flesh" functioned as a reference to the human body (as in "all flesh is weak") in medieval literature, as well as to communion bread, or to the muscle and other tissues of a living mammal (thus excluding fish or fowl).

8. See Albala, *Banquet*; and Strong, *Feast*. In his introduction to early modern food, Jean-Louis Flandrin points out that over a long stretch of time, from the late Middle Ages through the eighteenth century, archaeological evidence suggests that "diet ceased to be determined by the hazards of production and began to be shaped instead by consumer preference." This was especially true for the social elites, although Flandrin cites the example of a French monastery. Flandrin, "Dietary Choices and Culinary Technique, 1500–1800," in Flandrin and Montanari, *Food: A Culinary History*, 405.

9. Hyman and Hyman, "Printing the Kitchen," 396. Albala observes that because domesticated meats represented the bending of nature to human will, they may have been of increasing value for their symbolic function at the same time. *Banquet*, 33.

10. Vialles points out that requirements for bloodletting as the means of an animal's death in butchering (and proscriptions on using animals that die by disease or accident) and the animal's status as a "permitted species" guarantee that only certain animals, and only living ones, make it to the dinner table. *Animal to Edible*, 5.

11. Bennett, *Vibrant Matter*, 49.

12. The term "intra-action" belongs to Karen Barad, as does a version of the concept of "performativity." I intend both terms to resonate throughout this chapter. What is useful about Barad is that she doesn't stop with the connotations of "performative" as, for example, Butler uses the term, but strenuously resists the tendency to assimilate "performance" back to divided

ontologies of being and representation, problematizing implicit causality in the way we think about these things. See "Posthumanist Performativity."

13. By "vagabond," Bennett means "a propensity for continuous variation." *Vibrant Matter*, 50.

14. Butler originally proposed the idea of gender as performative in *Gender Trouble,* although the term and what it signifies have been under constant revision and extension by Butler and others since.

15. Albala, *Banquet*, 4.

16. Strong, *Feast*, 75, 85, 118–19.

17. As noted above, in M. F. K. Fisher's cookbook, the pigeon who cries does so for Jonathan Swift: "Here's a pigeon so finely roasted, it cries come eat me," writes Swift in *Polite Conversation* (1738), as Mr. Neverout tempts Miss Notable at a meal. Fisher has uncovered the attraction in Wecker's crying goose—the animal that audibly invites its own consumption makes a tastier tidbit, saucing itself with the addition of sound, the one sense that isn't usually directly addressed by strictly culinary prodigies.

18. Albala calls it propaganda, reflecting on how food choices could convey volumes about colonialist practices, morality, national identity. *Banquet,* 5.

19. Nearly every dead animal in early modern cultural representations gets cast at some point as an image of sacrifice, and thus as tied to the Passion and/or the Eucharist.

20. Albala, *Banquet*, 33.

21. Barad, "Posthumanist Performativity," contrasts the Cartesian "cut," which relies on inherent differences between subject and object, with an "agential cut" that creates a "local resolution *within* the phenomenon of the inherent ontological indeterminacy" (815).

22. *Elinor Fettiplace's Receipt Book*, 334.

23. Wall, *Staging Domesticity,* 338.

24. Strong, *Feast*, 188–97.

25. Wall, *Staging Domesticity,* 335.

26. Day, *Three English Brothers*, A2r.

27. Boehrer, *Animal Characters,* 136–37. In "Dietary Choices," 404, Flandrin notes that the turkey was the sole innovation among fowl in the period, and maintained its gastronomic "status" despite increasing availability (it was easily domesticated).

28. Strong, *Feast*, 181.

29. British Museum, Harleian MS 279 (ca. 1430), 62, lists a "cockyntryche" among the banquet dishes.

30. See Bogost, *Alien Phenomenology*, 66. Bogost coined the term to address how metaphor can function not merely representationally but as a "means to apprehend reality."

31. See Albala, *Eating Right in the Renaissance;* and Fitzpatrick, *Food in Shakespeare.*

32. Albala, *Eating Right in the Renaissance*, 34.

33. Schoenfeldt, "Fables of the Belly," 243.

34. Bullein, *Government of Health*, 26.

35. Boorde, *Compendious regiment*, F1r, F2v.

2

INTRA-ACTIVE PERFORMATIVITY

Rethinking the Early Modern Equestrian Portrait

PIA F. CUNEO

In memoriam: PETER W. FOLEY (1961–2016)

I am convinced that, if we acknowledge the performativity of meaning production—opening ourselves to visual art works as fully embodied sensuous experiences rather than closing them down through reified models of aesthetic or political judgment, fixing them in a matrix of predetermined values, we will find ourselves in a different and more productive relationship with visual culture. We will find ourselves in a relationship that *moves us* (in both senses of the word) rather than securing us in one rather well-worn place.

—AMELIA JONES

Action and response between the species bring about riding as a collaborative practice, where bodies become in sync. And sync is a product of intra-action in that both are changed through a process of training from the meeting between the two—literally flesh to flesh. . . . As such, horse-human communication crosses the species divide through somatic attunements and attentions that are partly about uncovering and discovering what bodies do, and partly about taking control of them, creating and making sense of body kinetics.

—ANITA MAURSTAD, DONA DAVIS, AND SARAH COWLES

In his *Vom Zeumen* (*Treatise on Bitting*) (Gröningen, 1588; fig. 2.1), Georg Engelhard von Löhneysen includes a section discussing the great esteem in which horses have been held throughout history. According to Löhneysen (1552–1622), the highest tribute that the ancient Romans could pay a truly exceptional man was to erect a public equestrian statue in his honor. "They certainly would not have done that," Löhneysen maintains, "if they did not think this animal worthy to honor and grace such an outstanding man."[1]

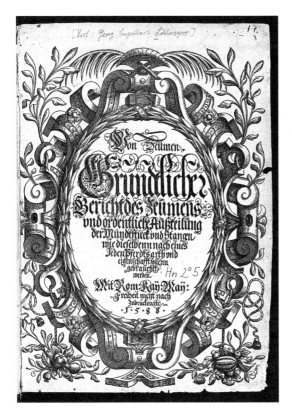

2.1
Title page of Georg Engelhard
von Löhneysen, *Vom Zeumen*
(Gröningen, 1588). Engraving.
Herzog August Bibliothek
Wolfenbüttel: Hn 2° 5.

2.2
Dominicus Custos, *Portrait
of Heinrich Julius*, ca. 1600.
Engraving. Herzog August
Bibliothek Wolfenbüttel: Inv. Nr. I
1736 (Porträtsammlung A 2558).

Since 1589, Löhneysen had served as master of the stable (*Stallmeister*) to Duke Heinrich Julius of Brunswick-Lüneburg (1564–1613; fig. 2.2). Löhneysen dedicated his 1588 treatise to his future ducal patron and employer, and the book was printed in Gröningen, Heinrich Julius's official residence as administrative bishop of Halberstadt.[2]

If his master of the stable knew about the ancient practice and significance of commissioning equestrian portraiture, Heinrich Julius, one of the most highly educated princes in Europe, surely knew the same. Using Löhneysen's text, quoted above, to identify an early modern understanding of that practice, I would like to emphasize that it consisted of two interrelated parts: the commissioning of a statue, and an appreciation of horses. I suggest that when Heinrich Julius commissioned a bronze equestrian portrait of himself from the internationally renowned imperial court artist Adriaen de Vries (1556–1626), he embraced both of these things and was motivated by a desire to emulate the ancient Romans not only in commissioning a statue but also in highly valuing the horse (fig. 2.3).[3] The attitudes toward and practices involving horses at Heinrich Julius's court support this reading. To paraphrase Löhneysen, Heinrich Julius would not have commissioned an equestrian portrait of himself if he did not think that the horse was worthy to honor and grace such an outstanding man as himself.

Heinrich Julius's equestrian portrait of circa 1605 is in excellent company. Anyone surveying a history of art produced in the early modern period will see a colorful parade of horses featured in all media, in both sacred and secular iconographies: saints ride on them, fall from them, cure them, and are martyred by them; men fight, hunt, perform, and pose on them. As a paradigm of its genre, Heinrich Julius's equestrian portrait belongs to a veritable herd of such images that art historians have become very adept at managing. We quickly turn to classical iconography and philosophy, and their early modern afterlives in sixteenth- and seventeenth-century emblems, in order to point to the hermeneutic links established therein between the horse-human figuration and notions of power, control, authority, and morality. The problem is that we make this turn too quickly, too automatically, and too exclusively (in relation to other kinds of sources).[4] In terms of the study of equestrian portraits, we are at precisely that dead end that the art historian Amelia Jones warns us about in the first epigraph above: we have "clos[ed] them down through reified models of aesthetic or political judgment, fix[ed] them in a matrix of predetermined values." We have indeed arrived at that "one rather well-worn place."

In order to escape a hermeneutics of stasis and passivity, Jones advocates that we enter into a relationship with images "that moves us (in both senses of the word)." We can accomplish this by attending to the ways in which both we and they actively produce meaning in a performative manner that hinges on physical experience.[5] Instead of conceptualizing a work of art as an object in which meaning passively inheres, simply waiting for the disinterested and disembodied professional interpreter or art

2.3   Adriaen de Vries, *Equestrian Portrait of Heinrich Julius*, ca. 1605. Bronze. Herzog Anton Ulrich-Museum Braunschweig, Kunstmuseum des Landes Niedersachsen.

historian to uncover it and thus to provide the work with its single, inevitable, true interpretation, Jones invites us to think about the artwork as mediating exchanges between subjects, as an object that activates cascades of interpretation contingent upon the self-consciously invested and physically embodied respondent.

The subject of the animal, however, is neither primary to nor explicit in Jones's work. For further theoretical models, we may turn to the burgeoning interdisciplinary field of animal studies, which has awakened us to the roles that animals play in human history, and to the need to theorize and explicate those roles. Like Jones's work, animal studies, in its broadest sense, highlights weaknesses in the traditional and formulaic interpretations of equestrian portraits that render the horse as a living and familiar being practically invisible. In these interpretations, the horse has only three possible roles to play: as a device—a figure the artist constructs to demonstrate his professional ability; as a symbol—of a state, or of irrational nature; or as a narrative prop—something on top of which a commander-in-chief or a prince logically sits. The horse qua horse does not even exist.

Animal studies helps us to see this blindness and offers us ways to think about the newly visible. Particularly relevant to this chapter is the intersection between animal studies and the fields of social anthropology, philosophy, and gender studies. In the work of scholars such as Anita Maurstad, Dona Davis, and Sarah Cowles, among others, the experience and practice of riding is conceptualized and explored as a physical, collaborative enterprise wherein the bodily intra-action of two different species actively creates an entirely new, mutually comprehensible language, a new way of being in the world. In their use of the word "intra-action," Maurstad and her collaborators draw on the work of the feminist philosopher Karen Barad, who has developed this theoretical concept in order to describe a radical entanglement between subject and object, between matter and meaning, in which each actively constitutes the other rather than existing as an ontologically separate and distinct phenomenon.[6] In arguing that human and horse intra-act, Maurstad, Davis, and Cowles draw upon Barad's concept in order to emphasize how horse and human influence and change each other, how each is necessary for the other's identity, and how together they become more than just a sum of their individual parts. My use of the concept "intra-action" is informed by Maurstad's application as well as my own reading of Barad, as discussed later in this chapter. In contradistinction to art-historical scholarship in which the role of the horse is almost exclusively symbolic, Maurstad and her collaborators' work is built on recognizing the horse as a living, sentient, active being. My chapter insists on that same recognition.

In engaging with Heinrich Julius's equestrian portrait, I heed Jones's call to attend to this work of art not as a static object that passively reflects a single true meaning, but as the instigator of dynamic processes of interpretation in which physical experiences, not just intellectual strategies, play fundamental roles in the intra-action between the artwork and its viewers. In highlighting dynamic intra-action between material and its (visual) consumer as an instigator of interpretation, my work offers parallels to Karen Raber's exploration in this volume of the performance of meat at the early modern table. In my chapter, the key physical experiences in question are those associated with riding; I draw here on the work of Maurstad and others in emphasizing the collaborative nature of this intra-activity that creates and performs meaning and in which both rider and horse exercise agency. Specifically, I argue that Heinrich Julius's equestrian portrait mediates the physical experience of artist, patron, seventeenth-century viewer, and twenty-first-century interpreter, thereby activating performative productions of personal, social/professional, and political meanings.

The Artist

Let us begin with a brief look at the artist, since Heinrich Julius's portrait is the direct result of Adriaen de Vries's physical experiences, even if these were not primarily the experiences of a rider and his horse but instead of an artist and his material. When he probably received Heinrich Julius's commission for an equestrian portrait, de Vries was working at the court of the Habsburg emperor Rudolph II (1552–1612).[7] Rudolph had granted him the title of *Kammerbildhauer*, which meant that, as one of the servants of the chamber (*Kammer*), de Vries belonged to one of the innermost circles of the imperial court and had direct access to the emperor. Rudolph's appreciation of de Vries is further indicated by the number of important commissions he gave the artist.

De Vries was already an internationally acclaimed artist before his imperial court appointment (May 1601), active in Florence in the workshop of Giambologna, in Milan as an assistant to Pompeo Leoni, in Turin as the court artist of the duke of Savoy, and in Augsburg completing prestigious civic commissions. His bronze sculptures ranged from smaller cabinet pieces to monumental life-sized figures, and were commissioned and collected by a wide range of European courts and cities. In particular, de Vries provided highly detailed and exquisitely worked wax models that were given to other artists responsible for the casting process.[8] At Rudolph's court, de Vries worked closely with the German founder Martin Hilliger, who was probably responsible for casting de Vries's model of Heinrich Julius's equestrian portrait in bronze.[9]

Recently, Pamela Smith has drawn attention to what she calls "artisanal epistemology," and she explores the role of the artist's body and senses not only in producing physical objects but also in constructing ways of knowing.[10] She reminds us of the labor and skill involved in production, of the actions and sensations residing in a self-consciously embodied artist who has learned through experience how to use his body and his senses to engage in physical processes to master the material at hand. In creating his wax model for Heinrich Julius's equestrian portrait, de Vries would obviously have activated these physical skills familiar to him from more than twenty years of experience in the workshop. The dexterity of his modeling in wax can be seen in the delicate treatment of the horse's mane and tail; his facility in inventing and rendering idealized naturalism can be seen in the graceful poses and harmonious proportions of horse and rider.

Although I have found no information linking de Vries with active involvement in horsemanship, we do know that his imperial patron kept finely bred horses at the court in Prague. As at other early modern European courts, such as the Wittelsbach in Munich and the dukes of Saxony in Dresden, Rudolph stabled his valuable animals in physical proximity to his art collection.[11] In addition to referring to other kinds of imagery, de Vries may have studied these fine specimens in the imperial stable in carrying out several commissions for equine figures from Rudolph and Heinrich Julius.

The equestrian portrait of Heinrich Julius mediates the physical experience of the hand and body that fashioned it. Part of that experience may have been de Vries's physical access to and firsthand observation of finely bred horses and the high-level equestrian display surely performed at the imperial court. The statuette functions in part as a perpetual performance of de Vries's artistic ability, his technical skill, and his professional identity, but also of his court connections and thus of his social and political identity as well.

The Patron

In commissioning an equestrian portrait of himself, Heinrich Julius may well have chosen de Vries precisely because of the artist's connection with the Habsburg imperial court in Prague. The statuette, inscribed at its base with the artist's name, is not dated, however. Art historians have proposed dates ranging from the 1590s (based on Heinrich Julius's hairstyle) to around 1605 (based on his visits to Prague).[12] Although we are therefore not in a position to assign a precise date to the statuette, its manufacture sometime around 1600 coincides with Heinrich Julius's efforts to establish a personal connection to Emperor Rudolph II. The duke traveled to Prague for the first time in 1598 to enlist the emperor's aid in reining in Heinrich Julius's rogue territorial city of Brunswick. This issue would bring Heinrich Julius to Rudolph's court again in 1602, 1607, and 1610, at which point he actually took up residence in Prague until his death in 1613.

Within this context of navigating and seeking to inhabit court circles, Heinrich Julius's commission to the emperor's own *Kammerbildhauer* was surely significant. It announced not only that Heinrich Julius had access to men close to the emperor but that these men who worked for Rudolph also worked for him. Furthermore, the statuette de Vries fashioned for the duke of Brunswick-Lüneburg is somewhat similar

2.4

Aegidius Sadeler, after Adriaen de Vries, *Equestrian Portrait of Rudolph II*, ca. 1603. Engraving. Rijksprentenkabinet, Rijksmuseum, Amsterdam.

to the engraving the artist contemporaneously designed for the emperor himself: both noblemen are represented as masterfully mounted on a powerful horse posed with elevated forelegs (fig. 2.4). These parallel images suggest a parallel relationship, for example as close allies, between the men portrayed.

Brunswick's intransigence provides another key context for Heinrich Julius's commission. His succession to the Duchy of Wolfenbüttel in 1589 had already brought him into conflict with the government of Brunswick, which was contractually bound by preexisting territorial agreements to declare each dynastic heir of the Brunswick-Lüneburg-Wolfenbüttel line its sovereign lord.[13] But Brunswick simply refused to make this declaration, and Heinrich Julius spent the rest of his life attempting to force the city into submission. A territory's public and continued refusal to acknowledge a prince's authority even in the face of imperial mandates surely constituted a humiliating blow to the rights and prerogatives fundamental to noble identity.

In addition, like many north German noblemen who had embraced Lutheranism, Heinrich Julius had to negotiate conflicting loyalties to Protestant networks, on the one hand, and to his own sovereign lord, the Catholic Habsburg emperor Rudolph II, on the other. Beginning with his first visit to Prague in 1598, Heinrich Julius had

EMBLEMATA. 81

EMBLEMA XLV.

In Adulari nefcientem.

Scire cupis dominos toties cur Theffalis ora
Mutet, & vt varios quærat habere duces.
Nefcit adulari, cuiquamúe obtrudere palpum,
Regia quem morem principis omnis habet.
Sed veluti ingenuus fonipes, dorfo excutit omnem,
Qui moderari ipfum nefciat Hippocomon.
Nec fæuire tamen domino fas. Vltio fola eft
Dura ferum vt iubeat ferre lupata magis.
F iiij Das

2.5
Emblem 45 in Andrea Alciato,
Liber emblematum . . . Kunstbuch
(Frankfurt am Main: Sigmund
Feyerabend, 1567). Woodcut.
University of Glasgow Library,
S.M 45. By permission of
University of Glasgow Library,
Special Collections.

entered into a surprisingly close political relationship with Rudolph that culminated in the Catholic emperor's appointing the Lutheran duke director of the Imperial Privy Council (27 July 1611). Diplomatic documents reveal that Heinrich Julius was viewed with deep suspicion both by fellow Protestants and by court Catholics.[14] Here too, we can imagine that traditional ideas about what constituted noble identity seemed to be in a state of flux. Thus a visible reassertion of that identity might indeed have seemed especially urgent.

What better way to reassert that identity than to commission an equestrian portrait? Drawing from both iconographic and emblematic traditions, the statuette represents Heinrich Julius as the virtuous and powerful prince, despite his ongoing inability to vanquish Brunswick. Indeed, it is rather tempting to interpret the horse's resistance to the rider's influence, signaled by the animal's gaping mouth and striking hooves, as a reference to the duke's intractable subjects. This interpretation becomes even more likely when we consider the text (*subscriptio*) and illustration (*pictura*) in an edition of Alciato's *Liber emblematum* published in 1567 in Frankfurt.[15] In this edition, the book's title was amended by the addition of the word "Kunstbuch," i.e., a resource to be used by artists as a kind of pattern book for figures. In emblem 45, the *subscriptio* refers to Thessaly as a land particularly difficult to govern: "Like a noble stallion, it throws from its back every horseman who does not know how to control it." In the *pictura*, the horse seems to be performing a reluctant *pesade*: he balances on his hindquarters, as the movement demands, but his mouth is open and his forelegs flail, one leg higher than the other, while his rider holds a baton against his hip and looks off to the side (fig. 2.5).[16] The figuration of horse and rider in the Frankfurt woodcut is almost identical to that of Heinrich Julius and his horse in the statuette, and indeed I would suggest that de Vries may well have used this woodcut as a model for his composition. In both the woodcut and the statuette, the horse is having no luck at all in unseating his rider. If we follow the logic of the emblem's text, this must mean that the horseman does in fact know how to control the horse, and thus that the prince does know how to rule his land. In other words, no matter how much resistance Brunswick (like Thessaly) might offer, it would eventually have to submit to its legitimate head of state, Heinrich Julius. The duke would have found the emblem's implications particularly satisfying in the face of a frustrating reality.

But here we have arrived at Amelia Jones's "well-worn place," which understands this equestrian statuette in a primarily static and symbolic way. To move beyond this place, we need to think about how the statuette mediates the physical experiences of Heinrich Julius and his horses. In considering the statuette, we cannot forget that what is figured here, as Maurstad and her colleagues remind us, depends on "the meeting . . . flesh to flesh" and the creation of a unique system of communication based on the physical and dynamic intra-actions between a human and a nonhuman animal who both exercise agency.

Karen Barad conceptualizes agency as "cut loose from its traditional humanist orbit. Agency is not aligned with human intentionality or subjectivity. . . . It is an enactment, not something that someone or something has." Enactments mobilize material practices and also make boundaries—for example, between human and animal—visible. Barad's definition of agency, which embraces the human and non-human alike, and her emphasis on relational being and dynamic enactment, through which "part of the world becomes determinately bounded and propertied in its emergent intelligibility to another 'part' of the world," opens up a space for theorizing the active role of the horse.[17] The animal is not passive matter that is given significance through the human's actions upon him; rather, human/horse enactments mutually constitute and perform the boundary between human and nonhuman.

According to Barad, the difference between the concepts of "intra-action" and "interaction" is crucial for theorizing causal relationships, and causal relationships are at the heart of both riding and the interpretation of art. "Interaction" is grounded in the assumption that two completely separate and distinct entities already in existence, each with inherent boundaries and attributes, come to act upon each other. Intra-activity radically revises that fundamental ontological assumption by positing that mutual enactments are precisely what create entities in the first place. In terms of riding, the horse comes into being as a horse in this figuration, as the human comes into being as a human, each exercising equal agency in the enactment of the other's identity. Similarly, the interpreter and the statuette (as object of interpretation) come into being through their intra-action. The viewer is not in an absolute sense exterior to the work she views but is in dialogue with it and is even constituted by it. Through its subject matter, style, and composition, the work suggests particular responses to the viewer, responses that would arise from the viewer's physical experiences as well as from her intellectual orbit, and that would also serve to create the viewer's subject position on a number of levels, including the social and the political. In turn, the viewer creates the work's status as an aesthetic object, a piece of political propaganda, and so on. This dynamic process of engaging with a work of art and making meaning is consistent with Amelia Jones's vision of performative relationships between artwork and viewer, discussed at the beginning of this chapter.

Furthermore, the work of intra-activity is ongoing and never complete, and the boundaries, properties, and meanings that it creates congeal but are never fixed. Thus intra-action is directly linked to performativity. Barad in fact defines performativity as "iterative intra-activity."[18] Performativity in this sense describes a number of different intra-actions: between horses and riders (Heinrich Julius and other members of the nobility, for example), and between the statuette and its viewers.

What might such enactments, material practices, and dynamic intra-actions have looked like from Heinrich Julius's point of view? Like most noblemen, Heinrich Julius had frequent direct contact with horses and often rode them in court festivals—for example, upon the occasion of his first marriage, to Dorothea of Saxony in 1585, and his second marriage, to Elisabeth of Denmark in 1590. Upon his succession to the Duchy of Wolfenbüttel in 1589, he hired the duke of Saxony's horse trainer, Georg Engelhard von Löhneysen, as his own ducal stable master, a post Löhneysen held for the next thirty-three years. At his first visit to the imperial court in Prague, Heinrich Julius took part, with notable success, in the tournaments on horseback organized there, and Rudolph II honored his skillful guest with affection and a gift of two fine horses. Thus the very basis for Rudolph's friendship with Heinrich Julius, the positive impression the duke made on the emperor at the tournaments, was mediated through horses. In 1605, at a particularly dangerous moment in the duke's siege of his recalcitrant city of Brunswick, Heinrich Julius escaped personally ignominious and politically disastrous capture through his consummate horsemanship, which involved galloping his horse at breakneck speed through a particularly large, dense forest. From his very first residential palace in Gröningen to his very last in Prague, the stable blocks included in these architectural complexes ensured that Heinrich Julius was surrounded by his horses.[19]

Heinrich Julius would have seen, heard, smelled, and touched these animals almost on a daily basis. He also intra-acted with them at especially key moments of transition and consolidation: his marriages, his succession, his introduction to and standing within the imperial court, his exercise of authority. Horses were the means by which Heinrich Julius proved his manhood, bravery, skill, and artfulness to his future wives and their families, to his subjects and his peers, and to the emperor. On such occasions as his flight on horseback from the siege at Brunswick, Heinrich Julius would certainly have been thinking of his horse in terms other than as a passive symbol. His identity as a noble—indeed, his very life—depended not only on his skill as a rider but also on the ability of the horse. Heinrich Julius might not have used the word "agency," but working with a horse at that level necessarily entails a recognition of two bodies, one human, the other equine, responding to and influencing each other.

Thus, when Heinrich Julius looked at his statuette, his vision would have been informed by these physical experiences, as well as by an understanding of histori-cal and iconographic traditions. Some contemporaneous manuals of horsemanship describe a very personal and individual relationship between horse and rider. One of these, written at the duke's own court and dedicated to his sons, is discussed below. Ritual practice at the court of Wolfenbüttel provides further evidence of such an affective and differentiated relationship between horse and rider. As described below, the funeral of a duke featured a horse who processed in the cortege covered in black cloth. According to custom, the horse chosen for this special role was the one known to be the deceased duke's favorite. This practice suggests that individual dukes expe-rienced special bonds with individual horses whom they preferred over others, and that furthermore these preferences were a matter not only of the dukes' own personal and physical intra-actions with the animals but of court knowledge to be activated in funerary rituals. Such texts and practices suggest that the bronze statuette might well have prompted Heinrich Julius to recall moments in the saddle—some precarious, some joyous, some quotidian—and individual horses whose lives had intersected with his own. Whether de Vries intended that the statuette be interpreted along these lines is beside the point. The statuette itself, the figuration of horse and rider, would have activated a relationship with Heinrich Julius, not only as an informed viewer of art but also as a skilled rider of horses. That figuration would be sure to evoke memories of the duke's physical engagement with these animals.

As a nobleman, many of those personal and physical experiences were also deeply embedded in the political. As a rider, Heinrich Julius's intra-action with his horse, their ability to communicate with each other through their bodies, allowed Heinrich Julius to perform brilliantly at court festivals and to prevail in battle, and thus to display his legitimacy as a ruler. His intra-actions with his horses in fact created and enacted his identity as territorial prince. Indeed, both the beginning and the end of Heinrich Julius's life as a duke were marked by the presence and participation of horses.[20] At his funeral in 1613, ten horses processed in the funeral cortege, each one bearing a shield of the duke's individual territories. Heinrich Julius's entire imperium was thus made visible and present by these horses. They were followed in the procession by the so-called horse of mourning (*Trauerpferd*), Heinrich Julius's favorite horse, draped in black and led by Löhneysen. All of the horses followed the body of the duke into the church where he would be interred. Afterward, as was the custom, the duke's heir and successor gave the horse of mourning to the poor and then "ransomed" the horse for the sum of one hundred thaler. Heinrich Julius himself had done the same thing in 1589 at the funeral of his father, Duke Julius, when one of his first official acts as the new duke was to "ransom" his father's favorite horse. This custom in essence provided a demonstration of a new duke's Christian charity in giving alms to the poor among his subjects, but this charity was specifically enacted through the physical exchange of a horse's body.

The Seventeenth-Century Viewer

Where was Heinrich Julius's portrait on view? And who else besides the duke might have had access to it? According to Jochen Luckhardt, the statuette's provenance can be traced back to 1628, where it appears in the inventory of Castle Schöningen, the residence of Heinrich Julius's widow, Elisabeth of Denmark (d. 1626), and then of her daughter-in-law, Anna Sophie of Brandenburg.[21] Luckhardt speculates that the statuette was probably originally housed in the ducal residence at the castle in Wolfenbüttel as part of Heinrich Julius's collections.[22] At Heinrich Julius's death in 1613, it must have passed into the possession of his widow, who took it with her when she moved to Castle Schöningen two years later.

While the statuette's original viewing context cannot be proved conclusively, Luckhardt's location of it in the residential castle in Wolfenbüttel seems both reasonable and likely. Heinrich Julius may in fact have followed imperial precedent in the placement of his statuette portrait. In 1607, closely contemporaneous with the manufacture of the equestrian statuette, Adriaen de Vries modeled a bronze horse for Rudolf II that was placed in the imperial *Kunstkammer* in the palace at Prague, directly beside de Vries's large bronze bust of the emperor, made a few years earlier, in 1603.[23] Heinrich Julius was in Prague in 1607, and as a distinguished and familiar visitor to the court he would probably have been given a tour of the *Kunstkammer*. Placing his own portrait and horse (melded into one figure), produced by the same imperial sculptor, in his own collections in Wolfenbüttel would have drawn another parallel between Heinrich Julius and the emperor. After all, Heinrich Julius was no minor player on the European political stage. Through his second marriage, to Elisabeth of Denmark, he was the brother-in-law of the Danish king and of the king of Scotland. And, like the emperor, Heinrich Julius would have taken distinguished and familiar visitors to his court on tours of his collections. Members of his court and family would also have had physical and visual access to the statuette.

The original audience for Heinrich Julius's statuette, then, must have been small but elite, made up mostly of other members of European nobility. These are also the same circles in which the art of horsemanship was cultivated, practiced, and appreciated. In the second half of the sixteenth century and the early seventeenth, a number of horsemanship manuals were published throughout Europe, most of them written by, dedicated to, and intended for members of the nobility. Such manuals include treatises by Federico Grisone (Naples, 1550; dedicated to Ippolito d'Este), Cesare Fiaschi (Bologna, 1556; dedicated to Henry II, king of France); Claudio Corte (Venice, 1562; dedicated to Alessandro Farnese), and Ottaviano Siliceo (Orvieto, 1598; dedicated to Pietro Aldobrandini) in Italy; Thomas Blundeville (London, 1560, a translation of Grisone; dedicated to Robert Dudley, the earl of Leicester), John Astley (London, 1584), and Gervase Markham (London, 1607; dedicated to various English nobility) in England; Pedro Aquilar (Seville, 1572; dedicated to Philip II, king of Spain), and Pedro Fernandez de Andrada (Seville, 1580; dedicated to Philip II) in Spain; and Salomon de la Broue (La Rochelle, 1593–94; dedicated to various French nobility) in France. Manuals were also published in the German lands: Hans Kreutzberger (Augsburg, 1562; dedicated to Maximilian II), Hans Friedrich Hörwart von Hohenburg (Tegernsee, 1577; dedicated to the count of the Rhine palatinate and duke of Bavaria), Marx Fugger (Augsburg, 1578); and Caspar Reuschlein (Strasbourg, 1593; dedicated to the magistrate of Strasbourg). In addition to his 1588 treatise on bitting, mentioned at the beginning of this chapter, Löhneysen also produced a two-volume treatise on all aspects of horsemanship, *Della cavalleria* (Remling, 1609–10), dedicated to Heinrich Julius's two sons (fig. 2.6).[24]

Many of these manuals indicate that horsemen thought of their mounts as more than just instruments for social and political advancement. Horses are discussed according to their individual characters and preferences. The difficulties involved in the art of riding are constantly stressed, from the physical demands of working with a large and powerful animal to the moral challenges at play: the need to be patient, calm, and clear when training horses of different abilities and temperaments so as not to destroy the individual animal's body or character through acts of cruelty. In the dedicatory section of *Della cavalleria*, Löhneysen quite predictably emphasizes the social and political advantages to be gained by a courtier who rides well.[25] But later in the work he also discusses the horse as a source of joy for his rider, and how morally valuable the horse was to the education of a prince; because the animal does not know flattery or dissimulation, he will throw an incompetent rider from his back

2.6

Title page of Georg Engelhard
von Löhneysen, *Della cavalleria,* 2 vols. (Remling, 1609–10).
Engraving. Herzog August
Bibliothek Wolfenbüttel: 1 Bell.
2° (1).

no matter what title the derriere in question holds. Unlike obsequious underlings, the horse provides a prince with utterly honest feedback and teaches him literally to be "grounded."[26]

These are just some of the attitudes that potentially came into play when Heinrich Julius and noblemen like him intra-acted with their horses, and also when they intra-acted with an equestrian portrait, regardless of whom it portrayed. Noblemen may have known from these horsemanship manuals and from their own experience just how many hours it took for the horse to learn to perform the *pesade*, a movement that Heinrich Julius's horse in the statuette attempts to execute. The *pesade* is a diffi-cult movement that calls for the horse to load his own weight and the weight of his rider onto his hindquarters and to balance there, and it demonstrates both the horse's strength and his submission. We know from Grisone's *Rules of Riding* (Naples, 1550) that this extremely useful movement was gradually introduced beginning already in the early stages of a horse's training, as a method to encourage the horse to lighten his forehand and thus to become optimally maneuverable.[27]

Noble viewers would also know from experience how many hours in the saddle it took for the rider to learn how to cue the horse correctly to perform this movement, and then to remain balanced, erect, and supple while positioned over a thousand pounds of animal surging beneath him.[28] That Heinrich Julius's horse challenges his rider's admirably imperceptible cues does not signal the duke's incompetence—quite the contrary. The horse's resistance, signaled in the statuette by his gaping mouth and flailing forelegs, can be viewed as an expression of the animal's agency and character, his initial response to what would have been a demanding task: lifting his forehand and balancing on his haunches. Far from an automaton mindlessly doing his master's bidding, the horse demonstrates that he has a will of his own and that it is not yet in sync with that of his rider. In the statuette, Heinrich Julius remains utterly unperturbed despite this conflict of wills. Getting a well-trained, docile horse to politely perform a *pesade* is difficult enough, but to work with a spirited stallion who needs to be convinced of a rider's authority, to ride calmly through the animal's explosive disobedience and teach him patiently to respect his rider without breaking the animal's spirit, is the ultimate proof of a supremely skilled horseman and thus a consummate nobleman.

Members of Heinrich Julius's court and family, and distinguished visitors from international circles who intra-acted with the equestrian statuette would have been able to identify with the intra-actions between horse and rider in the statuette from their own personal and physical experiences of horsemanship. Those experiences, in their roles as both riders and viewers, would confirm their own identity as nobility, just as it would deepen their appreciation of Heinrich Julius. Portraying the duke in this iconographically and ideologically freighted pose, a pose inflected with powerfully political resonances from classical antiquity and early modern emblems, manufactured by the hand of the emperor's own court sculptor, who had portrayed his imperial majesty similarly mounted, and viewed in the context of Heinrich Julius's collections, the statuette would have created cascades of meanings for its viewers. Engaging with that audience's intellectual training and physical experiences as diplomats, courtiers, noble relations, and the like, the bronze horse and rider enact the duke's identity as learned prince, imperial ally, magnificent collector, and skilled horseman. Such an identity would certainly inspire loyalty among the duke's subjects and peers. Ensuring that loyalty under politically awkward circumstances, such as the contest with Brunswick and the rapprochement between the Catholic emperor and the Lutheran duke, would be especially desirable.

Evidently, the statuette inspired other meanings for, and intra-acted very differently with, subsequent viewers. By the time of its first mention in the 1628 inventory, it was described as functioning within the ensemble of a table fountain.[29] Located in Elisabeth of Denmark's widow's residence at Castle Schöningen, the statuette seems to have been appreciated more for its decorative, material, and aesthetic qualities than for its expression of the deceased duke's potency. Indeed, at some point the duke seems to have become rather expendable: in its current condition, the figure of Heinrich Julius can be completely removed from the horse's back, allowing for appreciation of the figure of the animal alone, untrammeled by its rider. Although there is no way of telling exactly when this modification of the statuette was made, this moment when the statuette first changed location and function seems a plausible guess. Whether Elisabeth of Denmark was able to engage her own experiences as a rider in intra-acting with the statuette is also unknown. Although many noblewomen were skilled riders, there is no evidence to date, so far as I can tell, of Elisabeth's activities on horseback.[30]

The statuette returned to Wolfenbüttel under Duke August the Younger (1579–1666) when the residence at Castle Schöningen was dissolved, and then made its way to the castle at Salzdahlum as part of the collection of Duke Anton Ulrich (1633–1714). In 1745, these collections became the basis for the Herzog Anton Ulrich-Museum in Brunswick, that once obstreperous city that Heinrich Julius had fought so hard to subjugate. The statuette remained at the museum for two centuries before it became the object of an altogether different kind of performativity: in 1945, it disappeared, only to reappear in 2006, sixty-three years later, as dramatically and mysteriously as it had vanished.

The Twenty-First-Century Interpreter

Lately, I have been looking at equestrian portraits through a viewing framework that is structured precisely by the physical, material, and experiential. I have been looking at equestrian portraits not only as an art historian but also as a dressage rider, as someone trained in and practicing both disciplines. Furthermore, my research for a number of years now deals with early modern horsemanship manuals: texts written—and often illustrated—in order to explain and demonstrate the art of riding. The training exercises and ultimate goals of the riding described in these historic sources are to a large extent still practiced and embraced in the very same way by dressage riders and trainers today. Although the breeding of horses has changed over the centuries, the nature of horses has not: they are still prey animals whose instinct is to flee to survive; they are still animals with a herd mentality who thus seek guidance and leadership; and they still respond to human authority and kindness when practiced appropriately. And, as some details of the tack have changed—for example, the depth of the saddle, the width of the stirrup, the length of the curb—in essence, the tack for dressage has remained astonishingly changeless, even down to the materials used in its construction. As today, early modern attitudes about how to work with horses ranged from strict discipline and the expectation of complete obedience to a more empathetic, playful relationship. In short, there are historically mutable aspects of riding, but there are also aspects—particularly the physical and material—that remain essentially unchanged: horses still have four legs, people still have two, and there are only a limited number of ways in which the two legs can get the four legs to work for them.

The theoretical concepts of performativity and intra-action discussed in this chapter allow for such physical experiences to possess hermeneutic and epistemological legitimacy, and permit them to return to the realm of interpretation and understanding. These concepts also sanction new kinds of relationships with works of art, relationships that are physically dynamic, open to mutual agency, and sensitive to two-way communication processes, including those between object and interpreter and between members of different species.

Instead of interpretation being a disembodied, allegedly disinterested process whereby inherent meaning is simply uncovered by a professional expert trained in art history, Amelia Jones calls for an understanding of interpretation as profoundly contingent and embodied, as a shifting process that involves physical and material relationships between bodies. I have followed her call in bringing my own physical and personal experiences as a rider to my interpretation of the statuette and have allowed it to contribute fundamentally to my experience of this work. Doing so has enabled me to be sensitive to how other riders—Heinrich Julius and other noblemen—may have related to this figuration of man and horse, how their own physical and dynamic intra-actions with horses would have informed their performative production of meaning in intra-acting with the statuette.

Even though the statuette's composition may have been informed initially by general reference to classical iconography, and specifically to Alciato's emblem, its figuration lends itself especially well to an interpretation grounded in the physical practices and experiences of horsemanship. Educated noblemen would certainly have understood the symbolic and metaphorical associations of an equestrian portrait, and these are precisely the associations that art historians return to again and again but seldom move beyond. Performativity helps us see that an early modern viewer like Heinrich Julius might well have associated many other kinds of things with the image. From enacting his nobility on the back of a horse, he would know from experience the responsibilities and the rewards, the frustration and the joy, the labor and the pleasure involved in working with these powerful and beautiful animals. Because many twenty-first-century historians lack physical familiarity with horses and are ignorant of the practices of both historical and contemporaneous horsemanship, they are unable to register the flesh-to-flesh intra-actions between horse and rider, the mutual discovery of what bodies do, so powerfully evoked by the statuette. If we want to understand works of art like this statuette in their dynamic capacity to mediate physical experience and to demand fully embodied interpretation, then it behooves us to attend not only to intellectual, symbolic, and iconographic traditions but also to the physical, material, and experiential performances of human-animal intra-action in art and history.

NOTES

I wish to acknowledge the useful conversations I had with John-Michael Warner and Kate Palmer Albers while writing this chapter.

The epigraphs are from Jones, "Art History/Art Criticism," 46; Maurstad, Davis, and Cowles, "Co-Being and Intra-Action," 326.

1. Löhneysen, *Vom Zeumen*, fol. 2v. In this section, Löhneysen is relying on a slightly earlier text: Fugger, *Von der Gestüterey* (1578), fol. 17v. All translations from the German are mine.

2. Heinrich Julius had first met Löhneysen around 1585 at the court of his first father-in-law, August of Saxony, in Dresden, where Löhneysen gave Heinrich Julius what must have been further instruction in the art of riding. For Löhneysen, see Bepler, "Practical Perspectives on the Court"; and Wade, "Publication, Pageantry, Patronage." For Heinrich Julius, see Lietzmann, *Herzog Heinrich Julius*; Luckhardt, "Kunst am Wolfenbütteler Hof."

3. Herzog Anton Ulrich-Museum, Braunschweig, 52 cm high, signed at the base: "Adrianus de Vries Hagiensis Faciebat." See Lietzmann, *Herzog Heinrich Julius*, 24–25; Luckhardt. "Rückkehr des Herzogs."

4. An early exception to this is Walter Liedtke, who argued convincingly in the 1980s for the relevance of contemporaneous practices of horse-manship to the interpretation of early modern equestrian portraiture. Although some scholars appropriate Liedtke's terminology, their engage-ment with the topic of horsemanship practices remains superficial. See Liedtke and Moffitt, "Baroque Equestrian Portrait," and his fully devel-oped argument in Liedtke, *Royal Horse and Rider*.

5. Jones, "Art History/Art Criticism," 39–42.

6. Maurstad, Davis, and Cowles, "Co-Being and Intra-Action," 323.

7. For de Vries, see Scholten, "Adriaen de Vries, Imperial Sculptor."

8. For de Vries's working method, see Bewer, "'Kunststücke von gegossenem Metall.'"

9. Scholten, "Adriaen de Vries, Imperial Sculptor," 23.

10. Smith, *Body of the Artisan*, 95–114.

11. Scholten, *Adriaen de Vries*, cat. no. 20, p. 166.

12. For a discussion of the dating issues, see Lietzmann, *Herzog Heinrich Julius*, 24–25; and Luckhardt, "Rückkehr des Herzogs," 158.

13. Lietzmann, *Herzog Heinrich Julius*, 32.

14. Ibid., 32–40.

15. The *Liber emblematum* has been digitized and can be searched at http://www.emblems.arts.gla.ac.uk/alciato/emblem.php?id=A67a.

16. The *pesade* and the *levade* are two closely related movements in the training of and per-forming with horses that are probably relevant in these images. The *levade* is a more difficult and advanced form of the *pesade*. In the former, the angle made between the horse's elevated body and the ground is smaller than in the *pesade*, achieved by deeply bent hocks; it is thus more difficult to sustain. Because the horses in the images do not have deeply bent hocks, and because Grisone (1550) describes and discusses use of the *posata* (from which the French term in use today, *pesade*, is derived) in training, I use this term throughout the chapter. See Belknap, *Horsewords*, 258, 316.

17. Barad, "Posthumanist Performativity," 826–27, 817, 821.

18. Ibid., 828.

19. Lietzmann, *Herzog Heinrich Julius*, 12–13, 32–33, 14, 39. For Gröningen, see 18; for Prague, 75.

20. Heinrich Julius's funeral in 1613 is described in detail in *Beschreibung der Verordnung . . . Herrn Heinrich Julii . . . .* (1613). His father's funeral is described in *Beschreibung der Verordnung . . . Herrn Julii . . . .* (1589).

21. Luckhardt, "Rückkehr des Herzogs," 161–62.

22. Luckhardt, "Herzöge als Sammler," 29–32.

23. Scholten, *Adriaen de Vries*, 166.

24. This list includes only the first editions of a sampling of works; many went through several editions during the second half of the sixteenth century and beyond. See Horst, *Great Books on Horsemanship*, 67–337. I have not included books dealing with aspects of treating and curing dis-eases and maladies of horses or books on bitting alone.

25. Löhneysen, *Della cavalleria*, unpaginated dedication to Duke Friedrich Ulrich, Heinrich Julius's elder son.

26. Ibid., 104. In this passage, Löhneysen is again drawing on Fugger, *Von der Gestüterey*, fols. 23v–24r.

27. Luckhardt, "Rückkehr des Herzogs," 166, categorically denies that the horse in the statu-ette is performing a *levade* or any other type of schooled movement: "Around 1600, the rearing up of a horse . . . did not yet have anything to do with airs above the ground trained at the Riding School or with any 'Levade'" (my translation). Grisone's treatise, however, indicates otherwise. The Italian word he uses for the *pesade* is *posata*. See, for example, *Grisone's The Rules of Riding*, 121. Grisone discusses the *posata* beginning in the first section (book 1) and throughout his manual. See Elizabeth

Tobey's remarks about this movement on 123n89 and 550–51. See also note 16 above.

28. For a discussion of the intersection between riding, riding manuals, and noble identity, see Cuneo, "Visual Aids"; see also Bayreuther, *Pferde und Fürsten*.

29. Luckhardt, "Rückkehr des Herzogs," 162.

30. For information on Elisabeth of Denmark, see Wade, "Elisabeth von Dänemark." For information on an eighteenth-century Danish queen in the saddle, see Weiss, "Königin hat (die) Hosen an."

3

PAST PERFORMANCES

Gleanings from the Archives About Early Modern Equine Athletic Performance

RICHARD NASH

A persistent question in the history of horse racing is "did they breed to race, or race to breed?" It is a classic chicken-and-egg question: whether racing as a sport developed in order to measure the relative success and failure of different bloodlines, or whether the development of ever larger and more expensive breeding operations served to promote the aristocratic pleasure of the sport. The rationale offered repeatedly since the reign of Henry VIII was that breeding horses able to carry weight at speed with stamina was essential to national security, as a preparation for times of war; racing tested the effectiveness of such horse-breeding programs. A more skeptical view notes that as time went on, less and less attention was given to this supposed justification of the sport, and sport for its own sake took over as the catalyst for activity. At least one indicator that has drawn very little historical attention suggests that well into the eighteenth century, participants did in fact race to breed. That is, even as they began to pursue notions of breed improvement, as testified in the various studbooks and texts about breeding, both the published manuals and the private trial books that spoke to practices of conditioning running horses for races indicate that racing was seen as a test in which to prove innate ability. Even if the breed might be improved over time, each individual was essentially fixed; born with potential that might differ from that of others, the varying limits of potential were nevertheless all thought to respond to the same conditioning protocols. Trials demonstrated less the developmental progress of an individual than the differences in innate ability that controlled each.

In one of the classic training manuals of the twentieth century, Preston Burch writes, "It must be remembered . . . that horses, like people, are all different."[1] One rarely hears an interview with a thoroughbred trainer today that does not include some cognate of this core principle: "we'll let him tell us" is a favorite sound bite. No two horses are alike. One would be hard-pressed to find anyone today who would disagree with that statement, at least among those who have spent much time with horses. A quick Google search reports thousands of hits on that phrase. The *British Veterinary Journal* of 1890 deploys the phrase as "a truism." Yet that may also be the earliest use of the phrase in print.[2] However common it may already have become when *speaking* of horses to stress their individuality, that emphasis—certainly widespread throughout the twentieth century—rarely appears in published texts from the early modern era. These manuals laid little stress on the importance of recognizing and responding to individual difference; indeed, the variables of exercise and physical conditioning that are likely to be deemed central to preparing a racehorse for competition today (length and speed of gallops, intensity and frequency of workouts and breezes, etc.) played no visible role at all in many of the published manuals that offered guidance for not only selecting but training "running horses."

Scattered references to horses in early modern discussions of rural sport, recreation, and breeding include the sporadic mention of "true bred," or "thoroughbred," though that term did not become a standard breed classification until the early nineteenth century, and since then it has been essentially synonymous with "racehorse." Throughout the seventeenth and early eighteenth centuries, however, the more common term for horses who raced was "running horse." The designation was a metonymic description of performance—horses who raced were running horses, and the activity preceded any reified notion of breed identity. Over the course of the seventeenth century, however, concepts of breed identity emerged, and particularly with respect to running horses, the idea of "improving the breed" became central to a reconception of how people thought about the athletic performance of animals who now came to be thought of as belonging to a distinct breed.[3]

The process of this reconception has potentially wide-ranging theoretical implications for the emergence of modern constructions of human and animal identity, in that performance marks both the suture and the separation between essence and action. Performance lives on the interface of being and doing, where actor and action merge. In the sport of horse racing, the evidence suggests that the developing concept of a breed identity, specifically a dynamic concept of an identity capable of managed improvement, emerges ahead of the concept of an equally dynamic concept of performance, similarly capable of managed improvement. The history of horse racing—and its vocabulary—is tightly aligned with both breed identity and performance, though the former terminology is perhaps more readily available to a lay audience. While almost everyone in the general public has some sense of a breed identity designated as "thoroughbred," constructed from a notion of the possibility of breed improvement, among fans of the sport, "performance" is equally ubiquitous in the literature of the sport, at least since the late nineteenth century.

Peggy Phelan's *Unmarked: The Politics of Performance* (1993) asserts the importance of "liveness" to the study of live performance, contending that "performance exists only in the present."[4] Joseph Roach's concept of "performance genealogies," which "draw on the idea of expressive movements as mnemonic reserves," evokes a more spectral concept of the life of performance, in which performance is not merely that which disappears but also that which contains within its action historical resonance.[5] Both Roach and Phelan, of course, are theorizing artistic, cultural expressive performance in the performing arts, rather than athletic performance. As a field, performance studies has been generally far more interested in the cultural, aesthetic, and political work of aesthetic performance than in the arena of athletic performance; in the instance of horse racing, for instance, such an analytic would be more likely to engage the performative space of the racecourse and the behavior of (mostly human) participants. The chapters in this volume by Marra, Mattfeld, and Weil contribute significantly to that discussion by attending to the ways in which transspecific collaborative performances between horse and human on the dramatic stage catered to a nineteenth-century fascination with equestrian performance in complex and sometimes unsettling ways, staging horse-and-human partnerships in an exoticized and eroticized spectacle that served a wide range of cultural interests. In the ensuing discussion, I try to turn attention away from dramatic performance to the training ground of athletic performance itself, in order to explore how equine athletic performance was conceptualized in the eighteenth century. This chapter invites us to consider how that era's theorizing of athletic performance as an arena of proof, rather than as a developmental training ground, may differ significantly from notions that have been paramount since the late nineteenth century; in doing so, it offers one way to historicize how the performative interface of essence and action changes over time.

In the American context, information about the racing careers of individual horses is carefully recorded and made available to fans and handicappers before every race in a format that has changed little since the late nineteenth century, when the *New York Morning Telegraph* first began publishing the *Daily Racing Form*. In the British context, the closest counterpart to the *Daily Racing Form* might be *Timeform*, which only originated in the mid-twentieth century, or the *Racing Post* (founded in 1986), but before either of these, the *Sporting Life* offered similar information on past racing performance, though not perhaps in the quantitative format preferred in the more contemporary context. Since at least the early twentieth century, the British trade press has tended to refer to this information as "form" or "racing form," from which the *Morning Telegraph* derived the title for its publication, while the American context has referred almost exclusively to "past performances." One of the obstacles that the industry faces in marketing its sport to a wider general public is that it presents information in a seemingly esoteric and arcane code, virtually indecipherable to those who are untrained in the sport's peculiarities. When, in 2015, American Pharoah went to the post in the Belmont Stakes to complete his sweep of the Triple Crown races, fans and bettors would have been looking at the "past performance" record—immediately intelligible to those familiar with the sport's protocols, and almost entirely unintelligible to the uninitiated.

This chapter explores the kinds of evidence available to the cultural historian seeking to reconstruct a more complete history of the emergence of modern horse racing, with special reference to the potential value of manuscript "trial books." While studbooks have understandably dominated such historical work, emphasizing patterns of lineage that are identified with the emergence of a distinct breed of horse, trial books are even rarer and harder to find, and they are less clear in the kinds of evidence they offer.[6] Focusing specifically on three distinct manuscript trial books from the first half of the eighteenth century, this chapter suggests some of the ways in which these records offer a useful supplement to published manuals of the day, in ways that may complicate our formulations about agency in human and animal athletic partnerships. On the one hand, these records document (in ways that human agents were at some pains to conceal and keep private) specific observations of equine athletic performance. In doing so, they also reveal different models of ownership and jockey behavior, including significant patterns of human collaboration in terms of racing "confederacies." Adding yet another level of complexity, the evidence of these books may be read alongside studbooks and sporting art to suggest complex patterns of affiliations between human and nonhuman agents in the development of a sport that promotes the idea that athletic performance tests and proves the value of managed breeding programs.

Jockeys, Confederates, and Private Trial Books

The role of private trials, and of racehorse training more generally, has been relatively understudied for the very good reason that trials and training are among the least recorded activities associated with the origins of the sport.[7] I want to try to sketch at least the general contours of what such records that do remain may suggest about several aspects of the sport's history, in terms of both human activity and the active performance of human-animal interaction that contributed to fundamental changes in the sport's early development. The following discussion is heavily informed by three trial books in particular: that kept for Yorkshire horseman and breeder Cuthbert Routh; that kept by Mr. Ward, who oversaw the training of horses owned and bred by Peregrine Bertie, third duke of Ancaster; and that kept by the as yet unidentified trainer (possibly "Mr. Harrison") who oversaw racing preparation for a confederacy of prominent owners at Newmarket, including Thomas Panton, and apparently centered around the duke of Devonshire.

All three of these books, like the better known early studbooks, were kept as manuscript memorandum books, never designed to be published and not written for a general audience. Routh's book was, in fact, something of an all-purpose memorandum book and, when first described in the nineteenth century, was identified as a "stud book," which was certainly one of its functions. That description, by J. S. Fletcher, identified it as "a fat, comfortable-bodied little tome of parchment binding and hand-made paper, some ten inches tall, six inches wide, and two inches thick, providing a flap to keep the dust out, and a string of faded pink tape wherewith to bind everything securely together."[8] The title, "in a bold, dashing hand, with beautiful letters and old-fashioned capitals," was obviously chosen by someone other than Routh himself, quite possibly Thomas Jackson, who rode and trained for Routh, as it reads *The Stud Book of the late Cuth. Routh, Esq.* Routh himself seems to have used the book as a reversible memorandum book, writing from each inside cover toward the middle, which, as it turns out, contains a large number of blank pages. From the back of the book, his memoranda refer to natural events of some import (descriptions of serious flooding in the region in 1732 and again in 1741, for instance), but more often describing recipes, occasionally for beverages but mostly for medicinal concoctions to serve either his horses or his family. That practice is consistent with many published practical husbandry books, which devote their early pages to matters of buying, breeding, breaking, and training but turn in their later pages to maladies and prescriptions for treatment. A not uncommon marginal notation accompanying such recipes was "Probatum est"; as with the evidence of physical conditioning in the first half of the book, the recipes in the second half were to be proved by trial.

From the first page forward, Routh's book is more of a working ledger, updating the state of his stud at more or less regular intervals, and one can easily imagine that then, as now, the clerical end of stable management was both necessary and probably not relished. The first notations take the form of breeder's certificates attesting to the pedigrees of the horses in his stud. The first so identified is a horse named Creeper purchased from James, Lord Darcy, who witnesses the pedigree. In similar fashion, when Routh later acquired horses, he recited the pedigree, typically if not invariably requiring that the seller attest to the pedigree. While Routh is usually identified as "Cuthbert Routh of Snape Hall, near Bedale, in Yorkshire," in 1718 he acquired the manor of Dinsdale, which had previously been maintained as one of the most important early studs breeding racehorses by Rowland Place, from whom Lord Darcy had acquired his important White Turk for his nearby stud at Sedbury, and it is here that Routh maintained his stud. Creeper was a foal of 1716, and since other entries seem to date from soon after 1718, it seems likely that Routh began keeping his book when he acquired the stud at Dinsdale. Entries continue until May Day 1752, at which time Routh seems to have dispersed his stud—or at least seriously reduced his involvement. In fact, one of the interesting features of Routh's book is that it shows that for a breeder and dealer as important as Routh was, he worked throughout his career from a rather small broodmare band. Interspersed with the other entries of pedigrees, purchases, and sales, beginning in the 1730s Routh also records his trials, not as a separate category of recordkeeping but woven into the fabric of the ongoing management of his small breeding, racing, and sales operation.

The duke of Ancaster's trial book bears some striking similarities to Routh's memorandum book. Measuring 6.25 by 7.75 inches and bound in parchment, this book bears inside the front cover the inscription "23 Novr 1737 [Fr]ed Ward his book."[9] In an apparently different hand, the book records from the front a record of trials conducted from 1719 to 1737. Turned around and read from the back, the book records studbook and pedigree information on the Ancaster stud, both undated and then from 1725 to 1736. Both the Routh and Ancaster trial books record the joint racing and breeding activities of a significant early eighteenth-century stud. The book referred to as the Devonshire trial book appears to be a bit different, though it is structured along similar lines. That book, currently on loan to the National Horseracing Museum in Newmarket, was studied by C. M. Prior in the early twentieth century, when Prior was allowed to make a transcript of it. Prior's transcript begins with the following note:

> The original book in the handwriting of the trainer to William, 2nd Duke of Devonshire came into the possession of Admiral Rous [director of the Jockey Club in the nineteenth century]. He gave it to the Marquis of Hartington and wrote in it the inscription on the opposite page "Admiral Rous presents the old Duke of Devonshire trial book to the Marquis of Hartington, & wishes him to bring out a second Childers" [Childers being the first racehorse to attain national celebrity]. The book is preserved at Chatsworth, and was lent to me to copy by the present Duke. It relates to trials at Newmarket and Odsey.

The duke of Devonshire purchased the estate of Odsey from Robert Chester in 1722 and immediately commissioned William Kent to renovate the cottage and stables and build a Palladian house specifically as a racing lodge near the course for racing and training. When that work was completed in 1724, Devonshire began using the property as a training center during the summer months between the spring and fall Newmarket meetings. While the Routh and Ancaster trial books are quite clearly private, the Devonshire trial book just as clearly documents the trials of a racing confederacy centered around the strings of not only the duke of Devonshire but Thomas Panton and others as well.

That such "racing confederacies" existed we have indirect evidence, though little direct evidence exists of precisely how they operated. Advertisements for several of the early "subscription races"—the precursor of sweepstakes racing—call for owners to subscribe for several years to run a horse of their own "or their confederates," and such arrangements make good sense. Subscription races obligated an owner to pay a fee for several years in order to be eligible to race. But when the number of horses was still quite small, there would be no guarantee that the owner would be able to breed a horse of the right age and sex, and if he did, there was no guarantee that the horse would be suitable to race at the appointed time. Such confederacies presumably predate the advent of subscription races, since records show that during the long tenure of Tregonwell Frampton, trainer of the king's running horses (from the reign of William III through that of George I), Frampton's horses were never once matched against those of Lord Treasurer Godolphin, and only once (at the express desire of Queen Anne) against those of his son, Viscount Rialton, later the second earl of Godolphin. In a similar fashion, the names of owners that appear most prominently in the Devonshire trial book almost never match against one another at race meets, and in some cases horses seem to exchange ownership among parties of the confederacy between racing engagements. So, for example, the trial book documents a trial on "Jan ye 26, 1722/3. Mr. Cotton's Job, 5 years old, & Partner 4 years old, Run over ye Long Corse att 9st each. Partner was as good as Job 3 mile but Job beat him a hundred yards att last." A little more than three months later, the Newmarket match book records: "1 May 1723. Newmarket. Mr. Panton's Partner (wt nine stone) beat Lord Drogheda's Tipler Eight Stone seven pound, four miles, 200 Guineas, half forfeit." Five months later, however, when Partner ran fourth in that October's contribution purse, he ran as "Mr. Cotton's Partner," and at different times subsequently he raced sometimes as "Mr. Panton's" and sometimes as "Mr. Cotton's."

While the Routh and Ancaster trial books clearly integrate their recording of racing and breeding performance, combining the records of trials and stud in the same volume, the Devonshire trial book is specifically geared to a collective record of racing and training performance, independent of (though consistent with) a more wide-spread network of breeding programs. There are no explicit references to pedigrees in the Devonshire trial book, although, over time, one can see successive generations emerging: "Mr. Panton's bay colt out of the confederate filly." Those appearances create something like an interpretive puzzle of their own, as we find, for instance, in 1732, a reference to "Mr. Panton's bay filley out of Ebony," and in the following year, while that filly continued training as Mr. Panton's, there appears "Duke of Devonshire's Chest colt out of Eboney." Was the arrangement between Panton and Devonshire a foal-sharing arrangement in which they took alternating years, or was it one in which one man had first selection among colts and the other first selection among fillies, or some other arrangement? In any case, other records show that Eboney belonged to the broodmare band of which Devonshire was, not unjustifiably, proud. But she herself, like other mares in that band, seems to have descended from the Belvoir broodmare band maintained by Devonshire's near relation the duke of Rutland. The second dukes of Rutland and Devonshire had both married daughters of William,

Lord Russell, viewed by Whigs as the martyr of the Rye House Plot. Thus, through the activities recorded in the confederacy's trial book, one can begin to chart how such a partnership would make significant sense—with the dynastic studs being housed on the dukes' estates and cooperative practices keeping equine family lines within the confederacy, yet sufficiently well distributed to prevent too many female siblings in any one group, and the racing partnerships extending more broadly to include those focused more narrowly on the racing, rather than on the breeding, careers of the animals involved. While the Routh stud is likely to have been a somewhat more commercial and less dynastic enterprise than the Ancaster stud, buying and selling as vigorously as breeding and racing, both the Routh and Ancaster trial records are relatively small when compared to the activities of the significantly larger Devonshire confederacy, whose trial book shows in some years trials of more than a dozen different animals from the same crop, selected from several different studs.

Patterns of Preparation in Routh's Trial Book

Cuthbert Routh maintained a small but very select stud in Durham at Lower Dinsdale on the River Tees that he had purchased from the estate of one of the early significant breeders of running horses, Rowland Place. Routh raced primarily in the north, centering his activity around the most important races at York and Durham and only rarely racing at Newmarket. But his impact as a breeder was considerable, and many jockeys purchased horses from him; notices at the time of his death in 1752 remarked on his reputation in breeding running horses. Routh had married Judith Milbanke, a daughter of Sir Mark Milbanke, a prominent horse breeder, and one of the relatively unusual features of Routh's racing operation was that when he did not sell his horses, they often raced under the ownership of either his wife or one of his daughters. Following the career of one of his more successful homebred horses, Stadtholder, a foal of 1742 according to the memorandum book, is illustrative. In 1730, Routh had sold a filly he bred named Young Nanny to his brother-in-law, Captain Milbanke. Milbanke sold half of her back to Routh in 1735, in exchange for her upkeep, and later sold her outright back to Routh. Routh's memorandum book records no foal from her in 1741, "sent to Potts Roundhead Ap. 16." The foal that resulted from this cover by Roundhead is noted the following spring in the account of the stud: "Young Nanny . . . with her colt foal, a chest wth white face, got by Roundhead, and foaled Ap 13, 1742." The following year the foal is described as "a strong chest colt out of Nanny and Roundhead wth white in his face and a white heel." Routh's book is notably precise in updating descriptions of physical appearance in each iteration, but it is an objective record of existence, making the evaluative adjective "strong" stand out in contrast to the usual record of markings. The following year, when Stadtholder is two years old, the adjective is repeated, and though it disappears in the third year's description, as a four-year-old the horse is described as "a large chesnt colt 4 this grass," followed by his pedigree. The following year, when Stadtholder made it to the races as a five-year-old, Routh appraised the value of his entire stud. The twelve nonthoroughbreds he appraised at £120, or an average of £10 each. His two broodmares and nursing foals he valued at £50 each; his retired broodmare he valued at nothing; a two-year-old gray colt, half brother to Stadtholder, he valued at 50 guineas; and a pair of colts and a pair of fillies, aged four and three, respectively, he valued collectively at £400. Stadtholder alone he valued at 400 guineas, essentially more than the rest of the racing prospects combined.

The first mention of Stadtholder in the "trial" section of Routh's book appears on Wednesday, 19 March 1745 (or 1746—the dating is unclear):

Spun Othello [a seven-year-old horse], my Roundhead colt, and Mr. Scroop's Roundhead, both rising four years old, the 2 miles usual trial for that aged colts. Othello 10st. 5lb. and the colts 9st. 5 lb. each. Othello beat my colt scarce half a neck length, and a hard battle all the way. Mr. Scroop's colt was beat 3-parts of a distance [i.e., 180 yards] at least. The Course was extremely wett and deep, as that ground could be, which must occasion their being so long in running. Per T. Jackson's letter . 4min. 38 sec.

The same two horses again, Apr 1747 when Roundhead beat Othello, 3 miles from beginning to end.[10]

As a four-year-old, in his first trial, Stadtholder kept on even terms with a proven older horse, while in receipt of a stone (fourteen pounds) for two miles; a year later, just before turning five, he outran the older horse for three miles. Four months later, at the York races, he made his debut in the £50 plate (or purse) for five-year-olds, where he defeated "Ld Portmore's Highlander that had beat all the five-years-olds in the South and down to York." The following spring, Routh, who typically raced only in the northern meets, traveled to Newmarket, where Stadtholder once again defeated Highlander, and this time the duke of Ancaster's Badger as well, in the 130-guinea prize for five-year-olds, contested in heats under ten stone weight, in anticipation of the conditions of the royal plate season that began the following month. As a consequence, Routh was able to sell Stadtholder to Lord Tankerville and Mr. Panton, who campaigned him successfully for the remainder of the year, winning three king's plates in the process. Though he had appraised Stadtholder at 400 guineas at the start of the year, after winning the Newmarket prize Routh sold him for 350 guineas. Thus he wound up winning 180 guineas and realizing another 350 with the sale. By any standard, this is an almost textbook illustration of how to breed and develop a successful racehorse. Just as clearly, the comments in Routh's memorandum book indicate that Routh was alert to the horse's potential from the very beginning. In that context, what may be most striking to a modern eye is how generic his preparation and development seem to have been.

Routh commented of that first trial that it was "the 2 miles usual trial for that aged colts," and indeed, the rest of the trial book bears this out. Every spring, Routh would match his young horses, "rising four," two miles in their first trial, and typically would try his five-year-olds three miles and his older horses four miles. The trial book records twenty-three separate trials between April 1735 and March 1749. Of these, eight were at the two-mile distance with which Routh started his horses, five were three-mile trials for five-year-olds, and the remaining ten were four-mile trials. Typically, the racing season began in April (though the earliest race meets occasionally began in March) and ended in October (very rarely extending into November); while Newmarket bookended the racing season with meets in April and October, the culmination of the northern season (so important to Routh's calendar) was the York meet, which coincided with the assizes in August. Ten trials, nearly half of the total, were held between March and mid-May; five more were held in September and October, after the York meeting. Between mid-May and the York meeting, three trials were held, with five more held between December and February.

One recurrent pattern that emerges from Routh's trial book is the relative measurement of speed and stamina that such trials provided. From various trial accounts, it is clear that horses in Routh's trials were asked for speed in the second mile of the trial; as trials extended from two to four miles, the trial became a test not only of speed but of how much stamina remained after speed was tested. In a trial of September 1740 between Trusty and Trumpery, for instance, "it was near run for speed in the 2nd mile, but he beat her at the end of 4 miles, 13 score yards [a distance was 240 yards]." When Trusty was subsequently used in January as a trial partner for Crab, who was nearing the age of five, Crab "run something faster, and out stroked him in ye 2d mile, and provd to have so much steel that he beat T[rust]y at ye end of 4 miles six score yards without the least symptom of trying." Various trials repeat the same pattern of "trying for speed" in the second mile, and then testing for endurance by seeing how well a horse would continue running after being tried for speed.

Routh's trial book meticulously records times for most trials, even though both the infrequency of the trial and the variability of the conditions make it difficult to imagine how Routh valued such times. In the trial of Trusty mentioned above, for instance, Routh records: "T[rust]y was 8m 50sec., but I must make some allowance for a frosty morning, and the Course very slippery, and may safely acct for T[rust]y's *being as good* today as he was 17 Septr last when he run 8m. 45sec." Each trial record generally records the condition of the ground as well ("ground raithr pitted," "ground in tolerable order," etc.).

Time and Trial Horses as Tests of Ability

Like the Routh trial book, the Ancaster book records time consistently, yet it does not generally record the condition of the ground. Sixteen trials recorded between 1719 and 1737 follow a pattern of rough similarity to what is recorded in Routh's book. Six of the trials were clustered in the season of spring grass, from March to mid-May; another seven were recorded in the fall racing season, from mid-September to mid-November, with one in early December, one in late February (effectively an early spring trial), and only one recorded in the summer, in August 1736. Like Routh's, the Ancaster trials progressed to the standard four-mile distance (nine of the sixteen trials were at this distance). Whereas Routh started his young horses around age four with two-mile trials, however, seeking speed in the second mile, the Ancaster trial book records the use of half-mile trials, often at much lighter weights. One other trial distance also appears, though less often: "twice around the sweats" appears to allude to two circuits of the course used for routine gallops (i.e., "sweats"), and from other evidence we gather that this was a distance of something more than three miles. What seems to have been valued most highly in both the Routh and Ancaster trials is the distance by which one horse beat another in these trials, particularly in the longer trials, where the need for speed was followed by a need for stamina.

While both the Routh and Ancaster trial books indicate that times were recorded meticulously, not a single trial in the significantly more extensive Devonshire trial book appears to have been timed. The first page of that book, as mentioned above, records one of two famous trials by Childers, England's first racehorse to achieve national fame; the one recorded in the book is one in which he outdistanced Fox, at that time the most prominent horse in training. But the trial that earned him the name "Flying Childers" was one in which he was reported to have completed the round course in six minutes and forty-eight seconds, a remarkable time that was frequently alluded to as nearly "a mile a minute." Yet not only is there no record of this trial in the trial book; there is, again, no record of *any* timed trial in the Devonshire trial book. All three trial books place great emphasis on the distance by which one horse outperformed another, and nearly as great emphasis on the ease or difficulty with which the horses performed. In all three trial books, but more noticeably in the Devonshire because of the greater number of trials, it becomes clear that trainers relied on having one horse who served (sometimes though not always exclusively) as a "trial horse," setting a standard against which other horses, particularly younger horses, could be measured. A horse named Smart, for instance, at various times owned by Thomas Panton and Lord William Manners, younger brother to the duke of Rutland, shows up only twice in the "Historical List" of races and matches published annually by John Cheny: in a plate race of 1728 and a match of 1733. But in the seven years from 1728 to 1735, Smart shows up in nearly forty distinct trials, at times running trials within a week or two of one another against different opponents. Such horses, often those who were not considered likely to be successful at the highest level of racing but who were sound and consistent, provided useful benchmarks against which one could mark the development of younger, more talented horses.

We have already seen, in the case of Stadtholder, how trials confirmed Routh's initial judgment of the horse's racing potential and consequently justified his entering the horse in the five-year-old plate at York, followed by the unusual step of traveling to Newmarket the following spring in order to maximize Stadtholder's market value. For a small but commercial breeder like Routh, Stadtholder was a major success. The Ancaster trial book reveals a fundamentally different breeding and racing operation. Though still small by modern standards, the Ancaster stud was considerably larger than Routh's, and the homebred operation formed only a nucleus that was continually being augmented by new purchases. Again, however, the trial book demonstrates a similar test of human assessments of horses' ability through private trials. Based at Grimsthorpe in Lincolnshire, the Ancaster stud focused each year on the Wallasey Stakes, its most important target. This race was run on the first Thursday in May, making it the first race of the year in which five-year-old horses were asked to carry full weight (horses, at this time, took their age on the first of May). In addition to its importance on the racing calendar and its unusually high economic value, another reason why this race may have figured so prominently with the duke of Ancaster could have been its political associations: it commemorated the race won by the duke of Monmouth when he organized his western progress as a prelude to Protestant rebellion, and so it carried symbolic significance for the Protestant Whig cause that Ancaster supported. In 1733, the race was transferred from its original Cheshire venue to Newmarket, where it was increased still further in value and became one of the central events in the Jockey Club's effort to consolidate Newmarket's position as a center for national sport.[11]

Between 1728 and 1733, while still run in Cheshire, the race seems to have been the primary target of the duke of Ancaster's racing string, which won the race in 1728 and 1729, finished second in 1730, and then, after being unplaced in 1731, won again in 1732. For good measure, when the race shifted to Newmarket in the spring of 1733, it moved up on the calendar to be run in April, so Driver, who had won it in his first race as a five-year-old in May 1732, won it again in the last race for five-year-olds in April 1733. In each year, the trial book shows that Ancaster would first try his young four-year-olds in a half-mile race roughly a year before the Wallasey Stakes, presumably in order to get an early sense of which horse showed the most potential. There would then be another trial at the four-mile distance in the winter months before the Wallasey, with weights adjusted in accordance with how the horses had finished in the earlier trial. The one anomalous year in this run of success was 1731, when Ball finished eighth of nine in the Wallasey Stakes. But that year the trial book shows that at the four-mile trial in January, when the three colts approaching age five were tried against an older horse, Pert, Ball was defeated: "Pert beat ye Grey Colt 30 yards and beat ball and black Legs a Distance ball beat black Legs 2 lengths." "Ye Grey Colt" appears to have been a son of Sutton's Arabian out of the mare Dainty, and one would ordinarily expect this colt to have been entered in the Wallasey. Since there is no record of this horse's ever racing, it seems likely that in this year something happened (illness or injury) to prevent the horse's making it to the races, and Ball was sent in his place, based on his margin over Blacklegs.

Ordering and Keeping

Peter Edwards, in noting more compassionate attitudes toward the training of young horses in the seventeenth century than had been displayed in earlier eras, remarks on how uniform seventeenth-century manuals tended to be in their doctrines: "While these writers naturally disagreed about specific details, in their general approach they displayed a surprising degree of uniformity. Nearly all rejected the brutal practices of the early sixteenth century, advocating care and consideration as the standard and coercion only as a means of last resort."[12] That general uniformity is even more apparent in the specific instances of advice for the "ordering and keeping of running horses." With the notable exception of Gervase Markham's *Cavelarice* (1607), published works on the topic soon developed a formula that was frequently repeated nearly word for word, whether the work was published under the name of Markham (Markham quickly came to be identified with horse care, in much the way that Bacdeker came to be identified with travel in a later century) or one of his many imitators: Robert Almond, John Halfpenny, Nicholas Cox, A. S. Gent, et al.[13] The formula that quickly developed for these manuals runs something like this: divide preparation for racing into two-week ("fortnight") increments (usually four of them), and discuss the ordering and keeping of horses as it progresses from one fortnight to the next. In each of these discussions, roughly half of the discussion is devoted to diet, with the remaining discussion divided more or less equally between handling and stable care (i.e., "keeping") and actual exercise regimens.

There is, of course, no doubt that each of these aspects of overall care and conditioning is and always has been significant in racehorse preparation, and attention to detail, in even the most quotidian activities, has always been a watchword among the sport's most successful conditioners. But the form that this attention to detail takes in early manuals, and the arguments offered in support of such practices, strikes the modern ear as quaint. Consider the following passage in Halfpenny's *Gentleman Jockey*, which follows one of his more detailed discussions of appropriate exercise:

When he hath drunk (as you think sufficiently) then bring him home gently, without a wet hair about him: When you are come to the stable door, (before which your Groom shall throw all his foul litter continually from time to time) you shall there alight from his back, and by whistling, stretching the horse upon the straw, and raising the straw up under the horse, see if you can make him piss; which if at first he do not, yet with a little custom he will soon be brought unto it: and it is a wholesome action, both for the horse's health and for the cleanly keeping of the Stable.[14]

This particular attention to detail is not unique to Halfpenny but is nearly ubiquitous, and in variant forms can be traced back at least as far as *Cavelarice*. In its various articulations, it is justified as providing health for both the horse and his keeping, as it is better for the horse if he soils his litter as little as possible, and breathe no more than necessary the (strong ammonia) vapor. The habit here advocated complements the main goal of exercise in this system, allowing the body to "void by urine" those unwholesome internal properties that are agitated by exercise.

This in fact is the primary virtue of exercise in early modern training protocols: its function as a catalyst for the excretion of unwelcome (and unhealthy) internal "properties." Whereas we are inclined to think of athletic training in terms of mechanics and physiological development of both the musculoskeletal and cardiopulmonary systems, early modern conditioning paid little attention to that aspect of mechanical development, favoring a quasi-Galenic rationale for practices that anticipate (but are not identical to) our modern notions.

The frequent discussion of "sweats" and "airings" has less to do with mechanical development than with the "wholesome" excretion of unhealthy elements, none of which requires more careful management than "grease." When a horse spends his days turned out to pasture, he grazes peripatetically, walking almost constantly and seldom standing in one place for long. The horse's lymphatic system is adapted to this mode, and the light activity of walking works more or less as a pump, assisting the lymphatic system in its filtration work. When a horse is brought in from pasture to be kept in the stall, he does much less walking, and one consequence is now termed "stocking up," referring to the fluids that gather above the horse's hooves, causing the lower leg to appear greatly inflamed. Though unsightly, this swelling is not inherently dangerous and will dissipate quickly with light exercise, though until the lymphatic system fully adapts to its new circumstances, the horse will again stock up during periods of inactivity. Lacking our understanding of the circulatory system, early modern farriers developed their own explanation for the swollen lower legs. They believed that grass was high in fat, and bringing the horse into the stall in order to exercise him daily raised his heat, which in turn melted that fat into grease, which ran down inside his body. If it collected, it could cause any number of serious consequences, depending on where it collected; the art of managing the healthy excretion of this "grease"—generally by "sweats" and "scowrings"—constituted a chief responsibility of the early modern horseman. Manuals devoted more attention to various dietary treatments and scourings than to descriptions of beneficial exercise. Moreover, because such scourings always ran the risk of weakening and debilitating the animal, there were as many recipes for cordials and restoratives as there were for the various scouring and purging concoctions. John Halfpenny includes this recipe among his cordials:

> If you see that after his Purge, and after you have given him the Hony and Whitewine, he do not fall to his meat, but is still bound in his body, and dungs very small, then give him this Cordial fasting two or three times, and let there be two or three daies betwixt each Cordial giving. It is thus made; Take three pints of stale Beer, course Houshold bread the quantity of half ae penny Loaf, when these two are well boyled together, take it off the fire, and put into it a quarter of a pound of Hony, and a quarter of a pound of fresh Butter, give him all these together as a Cordial lukewarm, then ride him a mile after it, and set him up warm, and tye him up to the Rack for three or four hours after it, then give him a Mash of bursten Oats or Barly, and warm Water with Wheat-bran in it, till the Horse be come to his stomack, and be loose bodied again, which in two or three times giving he will be.[15]

Encountering this recipe in Halfpenny's text in the Huntington Library, I was confronted as well with the trace evidence of its trial in the form of a small hardened mass of beer, honey, and bread stuck to the bottom of the page where it had fallen three centuries earlier: "probatum est."

In contrast to the detailed and remarkably various and contingent protocols and recipes offered in these manuals as aids to properly dieting and dosing the horse in order to eliminate and evacuate the digestive system and bring a horse into optimal physical condition before a race, discussions of workouts and training regimens are remarkably uniform and generic. What variation does exist tends to cluster around a single point: how long it takes to prepare a horse for a race. Even here, the most common advice tends to be that with the proper use of purgatives and scourings, a horse can be made ready in eight weeks—not the six months that some maintain. Indeed, the pattern of "four fortnights" in preparing a running horse becomes more or less the standard, with the first fortnight after a horse has been taken up from grass devoted to exercising the horse with a combination of walking, jogging, and galloping twice daily, at daybreak and again in the evening. Invariably, the emphasis here is on keeping the work demand light so as not to overheat the horse and create problems by melting the grease more rapidly than sweats and scours can evacuate it from the system. In the second fortnight (should no setbacks have been encountered), one may begin to sweat the horse, no more often than twice a week. Sweating may be conducted entirely without exercise by the use of blankets, but more frequently that part of the treatment was preceded by a steady sweating gallop. Both Holcroft and Darvill describe the "brushing gallop," a mode of exercise in which the horse is started at an easy pace and gradually given greater and greater encouragement, until he is being asked for nearly full speed—the "brushing gallop"—generally over an uphill part of the course.[16] Holcroft indicates that the brushing gallop was likely to be followed a day or two later with a sweating gallop, which was conducted at a slower steady pace until the horse was well lathered, which set the stage for the standing sweats and scourings that would follow to carry off the grease broken up by the activity of the previous exercise.[17] Before 1750, however, such exercise is seldom described in any detail except by Markham in *Cavelarice*. That text was so widely imitated in other details that it is likely to have served as a model for much subsequent practice, though it is difficult not to imagine that many advocated more rapid progress than Markham did. Markham insisted on great patience in laying a foundation with gentle work, both to avoid the disorder caused by too quickly melting the grease and also to cultivate a happy and willing spirit in the horse. In the first fortnight, he explicitly warns that the exercise should remain sufficiently moderate as not to produce a sweat: "onelie you must obserue that in all this exercise you doe not make him sweat or put him to any force, as well for feare of his winde as for other inconueniences, but that out of ease, wantonnes and pleasure, hee may both attaine to delight and knowledge, and that also by the moderation of such temperate exercise, he may haue his glut and pursiuenes clensed away, his fat and good flesh better hardned, his winde made more pure, & al his inward faculties better disposed."[18]

For Markham, these workouts were to consist of running a "course" (the standard four-mile distance), but allowing the horse to run up to "three quarters" speed for "twelve score"—the form of exercise that came to be known as a "brushing gallop." Markham then advocated gradually increasing the speed with which the horse is allowed to cover that distance until he is comfortably traveling at full speed. That distance—twelve score yards—is the standard location of the "distance pole"; a horse beaten by more than that distance in any heat was eliminated from competing in subsequent heats. Twelve score yards is also just over one furlong, and as Markham laid out a sequence of training routines, he gradually extended the distance of heats from "twelve score" to "twenty score" to "forty score," and then on up to a mile, and then two miles, until eventually the horse was running the entire four-mile course at full speed. Since most manuals insisted that a horse could be trained for a race in four fortnights, one must assume that either the intensity of the heats or their distance increased more rapidly than Markham recommended.

There is, however, no discussion whatsoever about how to evaluate (or even whether one should evaluate) individual differences in how horses respond to advancing workloads. While great consideration was given to a wide range of physical responses that might manifest individual differences in terms of excreting the grease melted by exercise, that exercise itself was viewed as a formulaic task set for all horses to undertake. Even Markham, who began his training calendar with an emphasis on patience and gentle encouragement, envisioned the regimen culminating in a violent and severe trial: "After that, you shall once in a fortnight make vse of your spurs, and make him runne the whole course thorough vpon the spurs, drawing blood soundly vppon both his fides, and then if you feele that in his course hee doth not faint, but maintaines his speede with a good courage, then you may presume he is a horse of great vertue and worthie estimation."[19]

However much some conditioners may have differed in practice from the regimen advocated by Markham at the beginning of the seventeenth century, the evidence of the trial books suggests that his model remained deeply influential, particularly with respect to seeing physical exercise as serving two complementary purposes: first, raising the body's temperature and by that means and with the agitation of activity breaking up and melting internal fat and grease that could be excreted through sweats and scourings; and second, when the horse had become correspondingly hardened, testing his innate ability to carry weight at speed over distance. With respect to the former function, one needed to observe each individual closely and respond appropriately to often quite various indications as to whether the grease was being excreted and carried away appropriately; with respect to the latter, however, work was ultimately a test of innate ability, a measure of quality and "goodness" that was presumed to be the essential nature of the animal. Implicit in this notion of training was a corollary concept that while individuals varied in terms of ability and potential, such variability was innate, and that the primary function of the trial was to reveal—not develop—that innate talent. If breeders like Fairfax introduced notions of perfectibility and improvement into horse breeding in the seventeenth century, doctrines for training and conditioning individual athletes lagged behind well into the eighteenth century.

NOTES

Special thanks to the wonderful people at Houghton Library, Harvard, for awarding me the Beatrice, Benjamin, and Richard Bader Fellowship in the Visual Arts of the Theatre, and for providing such support and expertise during my time there.

1. Burch, *Training Thoroughbred Horses*, 44.

2. The only use of the phrase I was able to find prior to this instance in the *British Veterinary Journal* was in an eighteenth-century description of the carnival at Florence, where "no two horses are alike" refers to how they are dressed in masquerade; "some are made to resemble stags," etc.

3. Nash, "Gentlemen's Recreation."

4. Phelan, *Unmarked*, 146.

5. Roach, *Cities of the Dead*, 26.

6. Particularly important to this work is the early scholarship of C. M. Prior, especially *Early Records of the Thoroughbred Horse*. See also Nicholas Russell, *Like Engend'ring Like*, especially chapters 4 and 5.

7. Until the description that Thomas Holcroft offered of his work as a stable lad in the 1750s in the early chapters of his memoir of 1816, there are virtually no accounts of daily stable practice. Richard Darvill's *Training of the English Racehorse* (1840) offers a fairly full description of his days as a stable lad in the 1780s. From the earlier era, however, such exercise is seldom described in any detail by anyone other than Markham in *Cavelarice*. See also Oldrey, Cox, and Nash, *Heath and the Horse*, 253–65.

8. Fletcher, "Stud Book of the Eighteenth Century," 214. Routh's book came into the possession of C. M. Prior, and at his death was bequeathed to Weatherby's.

9. C. M. Prior interpreted this as "23 Novr 1737 [di]ed Ward his book"; the last trial entry was from the previous spring.

10. In this era, horses were considered to advance in age on 1 May, so in the spring months between January and that date, a horse was said to be "rising" whatever age he would be after 1 May. In heat racing, the winner of the plate would be the first horse to win two heats. Any horse who finished within 240 (twelve score) yards of the winner was permitted to contest the next heat; any horse outrun by more than that margin was said to be "distanced" and was disqualified from further participation.

11. Oldrey, Cox, and Nash, *Heath and the Horse*, 278.

12. Edwards, "Nature Bridled," 159.

13. Markham's first book of horsemanship, *A Discourse of Horsemanship* (1593), contains a chapter on "the manner to chuse, trayne, ryde and dyet, running-horses," but that discussion is not as detailed or thorough as the later chapter in *Cavelarice* is.

14. Halfpenny, *Gentleman Jockey,* 9–10.

15. Ibid., 193–94.

16. Darvill, *Training of the English Racehorse*, 46; and Holcroft and Hazlitt, *Memoirs of Thomas Holcroft*, 33.

17. Holcroft and Hazlitt, *Memoirs of Thomas Holcroft*, 33–34.

18. Markham, *Cavelarice*, 5.

19. Ibid., 8.

4

"I SEE THEM GALLOPING!"

War, Affect, and Performing Horses in Matthew Lewis's *Timour the Tartar*

MONICA MATTFELD

"I see them galloping! I see them galloping!"

—BLUE-BEARD

In 1811, Covent Garden had "the most profitable season in its history," with the introduction of a unique theatrical extravaganza that told an Oriental tale of forbidden love, epic battles, and exotic kingdoms. Matthew Gregory Lewis's *Timour the Tartar* was a surprising departure for the patent theater, one born out of financial desperation.[1] Known for staging more legitimate forms of entertainment that firmly differentiated between properly dramatic theater and the illegitimate forms of entertainment popular on the other side of the river, Covent Garden's manager, Henry Harris, in his decision to stage "Monk" Lewis's last play, sparked a revolution in London's theatrical landscape. This revolution was not caused by the play's content, which was in keeping with many other popular Orientalized melodramas staged at the time, but by the actors. Performed by John Astley's equestrian troupe from Astley's Amphitheatre, Westminster Bridge, *Timour* was the first play staged at a legitimate theater written specifically for the inclusion of nonhumans as agential actors central to the production's plot. As Lewis recalled, he wrote the play, or the "trifle," as he called it, "merely to oblige Mr. Harris, who prest me very earnestly to give him a Spectacle, in which Horses might be introduced."[2]

By the time *Timour* appeared, theatrical horses were a common sight in the British capital, but they were usually associated with low entertainment and the illegitimate theaters that specialized in animal acts. From their inception in the mid- to late eighteenth century, these establishments, such as the Royal Circus, the Olympic, and Astley's, had fought an ongoing battle for artistic, moral, and legal legitimacy. London's illegitimate theaters developed out of the nation's fairgrounds and pub yards, and they were never able to disassociate themselves from lingering associations of itinerancy, immorality, and social corruption.[3] The theaters' entertainment programs did not help their reputations. Astley's Amphitheatre, for example, was the parent establishment for the later development of circuses around the world. It drew audiences (often a full house) with the latest natural oddity, superhuman feats of strength and agility, acrobats, mechanical wonders, pantomimes, and, of course, horses. Astley's built its reputation on the backs of its horses, and was both loved and reviled because of it.[4] As a result of these associations, Harris was not overly comfortable with his decision to commission Lewis to write an equestrian spectacle—a symptom of this discomfort can be seen in the playbills for *Timour,* which mention the presence of horses only rarely and in passing.[5] However, any associations with immoral and low entertainment were not enough to offset the veritable "hippo-mania" that gripped Londoners in the late eighteenth and early nineteenth centuries.[6] Previous equestrian dramas at Astley's, including the anonymous *Brave Cossac, or Perfidy Punished* (1807), John Astley's *The Arab, or The Freebooters of the Desert* (1809), and especially William Barrymore's *The Blood-Red Knight, or The Fatal Bridge* (1810), had proved amazingly popular, and Harris was quick to take advantage.

While Lewis and many of the critics who viewed *Timour* had "great doubts of the success of these New Performers," that is, the horses, at Covent Garden, and while many decried the degeneration of legitimate theater that their presence implied, the play was a smash hit in a genre that was set to become the most popular in nineteenth-century stage productions.[7] Shown for forty-four nights and revived multiple times in both Britain and America over multiple seasons and in multiple theaters, *Timour* was a guaranteed moneymaker for much of the nineteenth century. Frequently caricatured in the press and onstage, Lewis's trifle also inspired many theatrical burlesques from the Garden's rival establishments. These included George Coleman the Younger's "Tragico-Comico-Anglo-Germanico-Hippodramatico Romance" *The Quadrupeds of Quedlinburgh, or The Rovers of Weimar* (at the Haymarket); Samuel James Arnold's "New Heroic, Tragic, Operatic Drama" *Quadrupeds, or The Manager's Last Kick!* (the Lyceum); and G. Male's *One Foot by Land and One Foot by Sea, or The Tartars Tartared!* (at Astley's Amphitheatre).[8] All poking fun at the men who deliberately introduced horses to the legitimate theaters (and, in the case of Astley's, the men who performed with them), these and the many other hippodramatic burlesques also acknowledged that their and *Timour*'s success was due to those very animals. The nation's press was also quick to point out the novelty. The *Derby Mercury,* for example, called *Timour*'s scenery "splendid beyond description," adding that the plot and dialogue were "extremely puerile; but the introduction and astonishing performances of a number of horses, caused the piece to be received with unbounded applause." Similarly, a critic for the *Morning Chronicle* supposed that, "had the audience been polled upon the subject, we think we may venture to say that three-fourths of them came to see the horses—the horses—and nothing but the horses."[9] Lewis himself acknowledged that the play's success was due "above all to the favour with which the Horses were received by the Public."[10]

Variously interpreted by scholars as signs, metaphors, or representations of human virtues, horses in hippodrama are rarely afforded attention as live animals, even though they were the driving force behind the genre's initial development and ongoing (and controversially unprecedented) success.[11] A handful of studies are exceptions to this trend, but while these innovative and valuable texts, such as Arthur H. Saxon's *Enter Foot and Horse* and Jane Moody's *Illegitimate Theatre in London*, begin the process of opening up the strange world of hippodrama, many limit their focus to general histories of the genre. Others, such as Michael Gamer's "A Matter of Turf," discuss hippodramas in greater detail and connect the genre to wider sociopolitical events in Britain and Europe, and to the equestrian and satirical contexts of London. But Gamer's essay is necessarily brief and does not address the one element that differentiated hippodrama from other genres: the acting animals. Melynda Nuss's work on hippodrama begins to recognize equine actors as live beings onstage; however, because of the work's brevity, the presence and influence of horses on their fellow actors and on the audience has only begun to be explored.

This chapter begins the process of exploring the complex world of romantic hippodrama through the lens of the performing animal. It questions whether animals onstage, as Nuss argues, "always exist outside the theatrical illusion, a spot of realness in a world of fakery"; whether animals, like humans, could adopt a fictitious persona; or whether romantic animal performance was something altogether other.[12] When we take horses seriously as agential beings, as Lewis and nineteenth-century audiences did, what we see in the production of *Timour* is the enactment of military skill and constructions of ideal horseness associated with understandings of what constituted ideal warhorses in general. These constructions, in turn, directly influenced both audience experiences of theater as sublime and many people's views of politics in this period, all the while providing a direct problematization of what was meant by performance on the revolutionary stage.

Animal Performers and Horse-Human Being

Lewis's *Timour* is a standard melodramatic story of good triumphing over evil, of the true rulers taking back their lands from a tyrannical usurper. It begins with Queen Zorilda of Mingrelia's dramatic rescue of her son, the young prince Agib, from the evil clutches of Timour the Tartar (representing Napoleon). Timour has invaded Mingrelia, killed the king, taken Agib hostage, and usurped the throne. In retaliation, Zorilda (representing Lady Liberty) masquerades as an Amazonian queen from neighboring Georgia in order to fool Timour and reenter Mingrelia at his invitation (Timour hopes for a strategic marriage alliance between Mingrelia and Georgia). Zorilda's identity is eventually betrayed by Timour's father, Oglou, who knew Zorilda prior to Timour's overthrow of the throne. As a result, Timour has her consigned to the tower with Agib. Zorilda eventually secures Agib's escape with the aid, ironically, of Oglou, and the play ends with a grand military siege of Timour's tower during which Zorilda also escapes by leaping from the tower window into the moat. Agib in turn mounts a horse and rushes into the water to rescue her. In the meantime, the Georgian cavalry and Timour's Tartars engage in a pitched battle, which ultimately ends with Timour's surrender and the burning of the tower.

In addition to the main plotline, *Timour* also contains a subplot that serves as the melodrama's clearest and most affective statement on ideal morality and lost virtue. Furthermore, while horses were present at multiple points throughout the play— they made a grand entrance while pulling Zorilda's carriage during her entry into Mingrelia, for example, and during the final, climactic battle between the Georgians and Tartars—the subplot also contains the one scene specifically written to illustrate the many and varied abilities of the Astleyan equines. Consisting of a love triangle between Zorilda's maid, Selima, and two Tartar chiefs, Kerim (the one Selima favors) and Sanballat, the subplot contains some of the heaviest chivalric overtones and one of the play's most iconic scenes: the inevitable combat between Kerim and Sanballat over Selima's hand in marriage, in which the horses actively participate. The subplot was where Lewis provided direct stage directions to the horses in the same manner as their human counterparts, and it is where the horses seemingly took an intentional, agential interest in the performed events around them. Frequently removed from the play's main story to be reenacted as a stand-alone piece advertised as "the greatest spectacle" of an already spectacular play, the scene provides us with the most detailed look at Lewis's construction of ideal horseness, insight into his use of nonhuman actors as primary characters in their own right, and a glimpse of the dual human-animal being that was the theatrical horse. His stage directions for the combat are worth quoting at length:

> Scene III: *The Lists—the Circle is formed by Balconies filled with Spectators—On each side is a decorated Throne.—Zorilda, Timour and Selima arrive in a Car of triumph, followed by Bermeddin, Abdalec, and Tartars: They descend; Timour and Zorilda occupy one Throne, and Selima the other.—Agib's Tower appears as in the First Scene.—A Trumpet sounds, and is answered; the Barriers are thrown open, and Kerim and Sanballat enter on Horseback, from opposite sides. They charge with lances: at length Kerim's Horse takes part in the Combat, seizes Sanballat, and drags him to the ground—Sanballat rises, and attributes the victory solely to the*

Horse. Kerim proposes to renew the Combat on foot; the Horses are led away, and the fight begins: Kerim falls, and loses his sword. His Rival rushes to dispatch him, when Kerim's Horse leaps the Barrier, prevents Sanballat from advancing, picks up the sword, and carries it to his Master. Sanballat in fury stabs the Horse, who falls, and expires.[13]

In this scene, Astley's horses performed tasks well outside the realm of everyday equine behavior. They were expected to attack a human without, it seems, the direct influence of a rider; to interpret future events and intervene in order to prevent them; to understand the use of a human tool; and then to know how and when such a tool (a sword, in this case) was needed. The horses in *Timour* performed a level of rationality, interpretation, and awareness, and a level of active, intentional engagement, that was seemingly human in form. However, while doing so, the horses also engaged with period conceptions of horses that were militaristic and akin to, but also radically different from, those witnessed by horsemen and horsewomen outside the theater. *Timour*'s horses were heavily anthropomorphized and thus worryingly human, but they were also idealized and entirely "horse" in form.

One very public and celebratory example of this dual-natured construction of theatrical horses in *Timour* comes from Philip Astley, whose equestrian troupe performed the play at Covent Garden (and later burlesqued it at his amphitheater). Speaking on the subject of the military horse as a retired sergeant of the Fifteenth Light Dragoons, Astley argued at length in his *Astley's System of Equestrian Education* (1801) that

> this fine and spirited Animal participates with man [in] the toils of the campaign, and the glory of conquest; penetrating and undaunted as his master, he views dangers, and braves them. Accustomed to the din of arms, he loves it with enthusiasm, seeks it with ardour, and seems to vie with his master in his animated efforts to meet the foe with intrepidity, and to conquer every thing that opposes itself to his courage.
>
> In tournaments and Equestrian Exercises, his fire and his courage are irresistible. Amid his boldest exertions, he is equally collected and tractable; not obeying his own impetuosity, all his efforts and his actions are guided solely by his rider. Indeed, . . . the pleasures attendant upon his own existence he renounces, or rather centers them in the pleasure and satisfaction of man.
>
> Nothing can be more wonderful than the precision with which he performs every thing that is required of him; resigned without any reserve to our service, he refuses nothing however dangerous or difficult to execute.
>
> He serves with all his strength, and in his strenuous efforts to please, oft-times out-does himself, and even dies in order the better to obey![14]

For Astley, a military charger intentionally sought the din of battle for the benefit of his master. His desires, pleasures, and behavior all came out of a seemingly innate drive to obey all instructions from his master regardless of how dangerous they were. Astley attributed to his horses a level of rationality and intelligence remarkably similar to what was performed in *Timour*. Within Astley's construction of ideal horseness, the horses understand their duty; they intentionally ally themselves with the desires and endeavors of their riders while rationalizing how best to alter their actions depending on the situation in which they find themselves. Within this narrative, there is only a hint of the long and arduous process of training that brought horses to such levels of subjection. Horses, in Astley's view, must become "accustomed" to the sounds of battle, their "pleasures" must be centered around their riders', and vast amounts of time and effort had to be expended to achieve those results (Astley received a royal patent for his unique system of equestrian education).[15] Astley's views were somewhat controversial, and entirely romanticized, constructions of equine behavior unique within the wider equestrian community. While "normative" equine behavior differed substantially among authors on the subject, there were a few core character-istics shared across the equestrian spectrum. Many of Astley's fellow horsemen also understood horses as a species that possessed inherent qualities of strength, nobility, courage, and willingness to obey. However, within Astley's Amphitheatre, such views were heavily idealized. Not only were horses good companions, but at heart they desired nothing more than to live and die for their riders. According to Lewis's stage directions, Kerim's nameless horse was required intentionally to seek out combat and to rush into the fray when his rider needed his assistance. He serves the implicit wishes of his master with all of his might, and (it is implied) knowingly commits the ultimate act of loyalty by dying in order to save Kerim's life, as all good military chargers were to do, according to Astleyan propaganda.

What is somewhat unclear, in both Astley's account of military chargers and Lewis's theatrical construction of "normal" equine behavior, is to what extent the horses on Covent Garden's stage were understood as animals simply following the direction of their human counterparts as opposed to being rational performers in their own right. Animals onstage today provoke equally contested views of the meanings of "animal" and "performance." As Bert States argues, voicing the Cartesian metanarra-tive often associated with acting animals, "An animal can be trained or tranquilized, but it cannot categorically be depended upon" to play a part. An animal cannot adopt a fictitious, alternate self as a consciously performative act. Instead, because the animal does not understand his position as an actor in a play, what we get is trained and mechanical action. We get not "good behaviour, only behaviour." Theatrical animals are simply there, and it is their physical presence onstage that the audience interprets as "natural" and genuine. This behavior, for States, can be used to positive effect, and it frequently results in a situation where an animal "is blissfully above, or beneath, the business of playing, and we find ourselves cheering its performance precisely because it isn't one."[16] The *Dramatic Censor* of 1811 reflected this perception of acting animals in its review of *Timour,* in which the critic applauded the horses for their *"unaffected zeal* and *natural acting"*—in contrast, it was implied, to the adopted and even sensationalized dramatics of the humans.[17]

Acting theory in this period frequently held that some people were suited to acting and some were not. While much of the thespian's art could be taught, there had to be a core of high feeling and bodily expressiveness before someone could be considered an accomplished performer.[18] Those who lacked this natural ability, or those who failed to maintain it, were, for many critics, the source of the poor theater plaguing the nation. As the *New Thespian Oracle* put it, "Nature is the sovereign of all requisites in Acting, but the performers often leave her behind, for some ill chosen, fastidious, and adventitious ornament, which is the very reverse of the natural and the graceful."[19] Human actors must live the emotion on some level before they can accurately or pleasingly portray it. When it came to horses, however, their status as animals complicated such theories. As animals, they were already by nature unaffected. Therefore, whether horses could consciously adopt a fictitious persona was not really an issue for the *Dramatic Censor.* Instead, how the horses *appeared* to behave was of primary concern. On the one hand, they seemed entirely natural in their behavior onstage—they were simply doing what all (idealized) equines as a species did when interacting with a human, and they gave the impression that they were unaffected and natural as a result. In this respect, the horses onstage, because they were incapable of pretense, their actions unfeigned, appeared more virtuous, more trustworthy, more courageous than their human counterparts.

On the other hand, however, equine "naturalness" was an artificial construct created over time and through training (as Astley's royal patent indicates). The horses learned their cues, timing, and actions from a trainer who might or might not be visible to the audience. This epistemological opacity served to blur the lines between the animal witnessed onstage, the construct of "horse" it represented, and the "actual" animal offstage. Were the horses of Astley's Amphitheatre sensational because they were Astley's horses and had been selected for their natural abilities, or because a human had trained them to perform the seemingly impossible? An example of this shifting animal identity comes from Charles Dibdin the Younger. Dibdin recalled in his autobiography a meeting between himself and one of the more famous animal actors of Astley's Amphitheatre. He and the amphitheater's manager at the time, William Davis, were looking for a horse to pull their gig, and Davis thought that Astley's "The Tailor's Horse" would be an excellent choice. This horse was the lead performer in the hallmark Astleyan extravaganza "The Tailor Riding to Brentford," and his "peculiar qualifications" were "throwing his rider, rearing, plunging, kicking, &c., &c."; he was "the very last horse which a timid man would like to sit behind in a Gig." After learning that this horse would be theirs for the day, Dibdin exclaimed, "Oh, let me get out then, . . . he'll be playing his tricks with us and I shall have my Neck broken." Dibdin would have jumped out of the gig had Davis not explained that there was a difference between the equine persona adopted onstage and the performer behind it. Dibdin learned "what I had never imagined, that what the Horse did in the ring, he wouldn't do in the road, unless somebody was near him, and touched him in particular places, and in a particular manner, as was the case in the ring, and which touches were his signals, for playing his different tricks. This pacified me, and I found the Tailor's Horse, when on the road, one of the quietest of his stud."[20]

Dibdin was completely fooled by the theatrical character artificially adopted by the Tailor's Horse. He had never entertained the notion that the horse might be one thing onstage and another off. However, the idea of conscious acting did not even arise here. The Tailor's Horse only did what he was trained to do. In contrast, the *Dramatic Censor* did hint at the possibility of a horse's acting in the more human sense. In raising the question whether the horse's behavior onstage reflected his true horseness or his adoption of a fictitious persona, the *Censor*'s review of *Timour the Tartar* introduced ambiguities that unsettled the firm Cartesian understanding of animals as incapable of performing a part. The horses of Astley's Amphitheatre may have been "natural" actors, but were they in fact "acting"? Astley said that they were carrying out a role of "equestrian agency" that they had been trained to perform and had practiced to perfection.[21] Their preparation for the stage shares remarkable similarities with the rehearsals of their human counterparts, but whether the horses undertook such preparation knowingly, with an understanding of its purpose, remains uncertain. The intentionality of theatrical performance, so central to States's argument, was not, it seems, entirely necessary to romantic understandings of equine thespian ability. For the *Censor*'s critic, the equine actors in *Timour* and other hippodramas were adopting a fictitious history, skill, and learned behavior not in keeping with their own backgrounds, whether intentionally or not. As such, the acting animals of *Timour* certainly introduced uncertainties about what an animal was and could do.

Sublime Performers

Popular and critical uncertainty over what *Timour*'s horses were and could do was frequently manifested in the audience as a feeling of the sublime. Often attributed to Lewis's other gothic stories and plays (such as *The Monk* and *Castle Spectre*), feelings of the sublime were triggered in *Timour* by the Oriental setting, stage decorations, sensational plot, and lighting. Ultimately, however, they were the result of the physical presence of animals onstage. As Melynda Nuss argues in her analysis of *Timour*'s predecessor, George Colman's *Blue Beard, or Female Curiosity*, which also played at

Covent Garden in 1811 but only tangentially included horses, "The sublime, then, is the process of confronting an unrepresentable body, a body that is too solid to ignore but yet too strange to fit into the categories of the mind's understanding. And for the Romantics . . . the animal onstage proved to be the archetypal unassimilable body."[22] Often described in the language of Edmund Burke's theory of the sublime, where an experience was simply beyond the power of language to describe adequately, the experience of seeing *Timour* was "astonishing," "delightful," "extraordinary," and often indescribable.[23] While the physical presence of the horses onstage may not have been enough to evoke feelings of the sublime in an audience accustomed to seeing and interacting with the animals in their own lives and on the streets of London, their performances at Covent Garden as highly idealized beings who seemed innately capable of performing the seemingly impossible definitely was. The "great four-legged characters" "certainly performed extraordinary feats; they scaled walls, leaped through breaches, plunged into the water, and galloped about as if they were quite at home in their parts." Because they were more than "normal" horses, the acting equines had "a wonderful effect" and "enraptured audience[s]" as sublime beings.[24]

Burke argued that horses in general had "nothing of the sublime" because they were "useful" to mankind, but he acknowledged that this was not always the case when it came to the animal. The horse was immortalized in the Bible as a beast "whose neck is clothed with thunder, the glory of whose nostrils is terrible, who swalloweth the ground with fierceness and rage." "In this description," Burke wrote, "the useful character of the horse entirely disappears, and the terrible and sublime blaze out together." When horses harness their sheer physical strength to their owners' wishes, they are not sublime, but when that power becomes independent of human desire, it is overwhelming. "In short, wheresoever we find strength, and in what light soever we look upon power, we shall all along observe the sublime the concomitant of terrour, and contempt the attendant on a strength that is subservient and innoxious."[25]

Other romantic authors used Burke's sentiments, among them Byron in his poem "Mazeppa," to call attention to the affect associated with untamed power, but Lewis had a different view.[26] Lewis's horses in *Timour* were not like the wild Cossack steed in Byron's famous poem or the horse portrayed in the later stage production of "Mazeppa," discussed by Kari Weil in this volume; they were under perfect control during their performances. Instead of untamed power and ungoverned strength, the performing horses recalled the inherent militarism and noble glory of God's biblical animals. They acted the part of the noble charger who independently and intentionally attacked his rivals with terrible fierceness and rage in a theatrical embodiment of military strength. It was Kerim's horse who took it upon himself to "take . . . part in the Combat," who seized Sanballat and dragged him to the ground. He was also the one who intelligently saw the predicament his unhorsed master found himself in at the end of the battle, and took it upon himself to delay Sanballat's attacks while bringing

Kerim's sword to him. Horses like Kerim's were the powerful beings of Burke's sublime; they were more courageous, more noble, more aggressive, and more loyal than any horse outside the theater.

More important, however, such horses also "died" during their performances of the ideal, and in doing so tapped into another, analogous facet of Burke's theory. Witnessing animals onstage could instill feelings of horror and fear in audience members through their own ability to feel sympathy. Burke explains this process of the sublime thus: "For sympathy must be considered as a sort of substitution, by which we are put into the place of another man, and affected in many respects as he is affected: so that this passion may either partake of the nature of those which regard self-preservation, and turning upon pain may be a source of the sublime." Indeed, "we can feel for others, whilst we suffer ourselves; and often then most when we are softened by affliction; we see with pity even distresses which we would accept in the place of our own."[27] For Burke, the ultimate source of pain, and thus of the sympathetic sublime, was the contemplation of death. In *Timour,* the most affecting death occurred in the subplot. Kerim's horse has just rushed into the fray to save his master, with disastrous consequences. "Hold! Hold!—Oh! Coward!" shouts Zorilda, condemning Sanballat for stabbing Kerim's horse, after which the other characters proceed apace: "(*Kerim's desire to avenge the faithful Animal increases his strength. He disarms his Rival, drags him to the Horse, and sacrifices him on the Body: During which all descend. Selima embraces Kerim: Zorilda crowns him: But He takes off the wreath, breaks it, strews the flowers on the Horse, and falls upon Him weeping—Selima hangs over them greatly affected*)."[28] Horses like Kerim's were portrayed as chivalrous beings who would literally sacrifice everything in defense of their master. They were brave and ideally self-sacrificing animals who were rewarded in death for their service with symbols of military might and the sympathetic mourning of those watching. It was the ultimate in melodramatic and sublime experience, and, as mentioned above, it was one of the most frequently reenacted elements of the play throughout the nineteenth century.[29] The death of Kerim's horse, displayed using the "mute rhetoric" of the performing body in pantomime, was arguably the most important and hence most political scene Lewis offered in the play.[30] This was because of what the sublime could do to the person who experienced it. As Burke explained, "For as sympathy makes us take a concern in whatever men feel, so this affection prompts us to copy whatever they do; and consequently we have a pleasure of imitation." Imitation "forms our manners, our opinions, our lives. It is one of the strongest links of society. . . . Herein it is that painting and many other agreeable arts have laid one of the principal foundations of their power."[31] Sympathy and the sublime created imitation, which for Burke resulted in a questioning of the self in relation to the other and in the adoption of (hopefully) improved manners and morals. For *Timour*'s viewers, then, the invitation to imitate came from two types of sources. They could see and thus adopt the sympathy so effectively portrayed by both Selima and Kerim during their moving tribute to their fallen comrade. However, and more controversially, the invitation to imitate could also come from the nonhuman participant in the scene.

Like Bert States, Nicholas Ridout, in his examination of animal performance, argues that animals onstage were natural beings acting "animal," but they were also something more. Ridout explains this phenomenon through the juxtaposition of the "natural" animal body and the cultural space of the theater. For him, the presence of animals onstage, simply by being next to humans in culture, results in their anthropomorphism.[32] Thus thespian horses were by their very presence already disturbingly other. This automatic anthropomorphism was intensified in *Timour* through the horses' performance of the seemingly human. The horses did not simply perform "horse." They performed more than "horse": they performed "horse" as a horse-human. When coupled with their superior ability to act naturally in a way that no human thespian ever could, the horses of Timour were frequently viewed as something worryingly better than the people who viewed them. As Ridout points out for twenty-first-century theater, the animal "does what anyone on stage always has the uncanny capacity to do: it looks back at those who look." In looking back, the animal invites the audience to question who or what is looking, and what that being is thinking/judging about them. This "critical anthropomorphism" means that theatrical animals "disturb us by being just like us, or even . . . better than us in some impossible way."[33] The horses in *Timour* were better than humans; they were uncannily superior beings who were instrumental in the melodrama's reassuring aim of ensuring good's moral and physical success over evil.[34]

This equine model of superior morality was made apparent especially in the death of Kerim's horse. Such a courageous and selfless death in the face of danger was a direct mirror of contemporary portrayals of military masculinity. As I argue elsewhere, the acting horses of the eighteenth century were often viewed and reviewed as animal embodiments of their riders' performed selves.[35] Used extensively by Astley at his own theater in order to enlighten his audience, this slippage between human and animal display included the slippage of sympathy from man to horse. Instead of feeling the pain of a human, which Burke argues was central to the sublime, audiences who came to see *Timour* were expressly invited to feel sympathy for the horse. He was the one who became a holy being upon which the evil Sanballat was sacrificed; he was the one who received tribute for his courage; he was the one upon whom Kerim fell in extreme grief. Kerim's horse was the source of the sympathetic sublime; he was the ideal military charger who upheld the chivalric ideal in which love conquers all and disputes of honor are settled in battle. To see him was to face an uncomfortable invitation to adopt his performed and idealized behavior, morals, and virtues as a horse.

This invitation to adopt the other was often expressed in reviews of *Timour* as negative animality and unfortunately rampant militarism. "Oliver Old Times," for example, wrote to the editor of the *Morning Chronicle* to express his disgust over the increasing mania for everything equestrian, and in so doing aligned the audience with the equine performers they had come to see. "But I will confess to you," he wrote, that "what still more than the mummery astonished me, was, to behold *the shouting and delirious acclamation* that prevailed, and my hearing many grave men and women exclaim, '*Delightful! charming! wonderful!*' and, in a word, curvet round the whole circus of superlatives with as much alacrity as *Bluebeard's* charger."[36] The audience, in their welcomed adoption of the charger's sublime self, were feared to have slipped from human to animal. The sympathetic and equestrian sublime was ideally contagious, but unfortunately, for Old Times, also eminently degenerative.[37] To see the horses of Covent Garden was actively to invite their performed selves, but not the ideal elements thereof. The viewers were delirious, uncontrolled, untamed, and uncivilized in their hippo-manic praise, and as such were also entirely frenzied in their adopted militaristic zeal. "*We are becoming a warlike people*, Mr. Editor," Old Times complained. "We had wars in Queen Anne's time, but then we fought by a *sort of proxy*—at present the case is different, and the military spirit is diffused from the cot to the throne. Thanks to Bonaparte's threats of invasion, *every man* now is *a soldier*, and therefore naturally becomes enamoured of the 'pomp, pride, and circumstance of glorious war'; and among them '*the neighing steed*' of course holds a conspicuous place in his affections— the field of battle is become 'familiar to his thoughts,' and what before he would have turned from in disgust, he now contemplates with pleasure." Britain had always been a nation of strong and courageous men, but with Napoleon at the door, the adoption or imitation of military thought was becoming too much for Old Times. It was no longer controlled or controllable, and of course it was the presence of those "neighing steeds" that was most to blame for this ongoing and self-perpetuating shift to militarism. The audience's adoption of equine animality was worryingly complete. The horses were understood, and heavily idealized, as living embodiments of military glory. Because of the sympathetic sublime working through the theatrical equine bodies, it was "no wonder," Old Times said, "that a body of *such weight* [i.e., hippodrama] should have an influence in turning the scale of national taste."[38]

Politics and Adopting the Horse

While "Old Times" decried the increased military zeal of hippodramatic supporters, the equestrian plays fed upon and sought to increase the enthusiasm and support for Britain's ongoing war with Napoleon. *Timour the Tartar* was no different. Indeed, many contemporary interpretations of *Timour* saw the play as a direct political statement on Britain's involvement in the Napoleonic Wars. According to one critic, "Timour the Tartar seems drawn by the author as a likeness of Bonaparte; vulgarly ambitious, impetuously cruel, the offspring of ignorance and poverty."[39] This "most awful, but at the same time insidious attack on the reputation of BUONAPARTE [sic]" managed to make Lewis's politics eminently clear to the audience within the only literary medium to undergo rigorous censorship that "forbade direct references to the French Revolution."[40] Situating itself in the context of the recent popularity of Orientalized tales, which often placed more emphasis on spectacle than on dramatic energy, Lewis equated the romantic bogeyman with his reckless, usurping tyrant. Firmly effeminized, the character of Timour/Napoleon clearly outlined Lewis's view toward the revolution and war in France. Mirroring contemporary British fears of a French invasion, Timour/Napoleon had overthrown the rightful rulers of the kingdom of Mingrelia/France in an entirely unlawful and cowardly attempt to garner more power. Lewis turned Timour into a national "bogeyman," but in keeping with the melodramatic genre, he was also defeated in a spectacular triumph of good over evil.[41]

As *Timour* makes clear, this defeat could only come at the hands of those who had remained strong and defiant in the face of Timour's tyranny. His defeat could happen only if the nation came to adopt the very militarism that "Oliver Old Times" derided. It was only when the British, those brave Georgians, could "Mount o'er the Walls," bring down the gates, and rescue Zorilda, the rightful ruler and representation of Liberty, that the "Unmanly Tyrant" would fall. Only when the audience adopted the virtues of the Georgians and their horses (one and the same in this play) would Britain remain undefeated and Lady Liberty once again rule. The emphasis on chivalry, military might, and acts of courage and self-sacrifice were usual within the wider genre of melodrama, and, as Jeffrey Cox argues, "melodrama gains its initial power as perhaps the key means of both representing and creating the accelerated culture of perpetual war during the Napoleonic era." In this way, melodrama began to "organize the audience to see the militarized world that they come to inhabit." Indeed, "melodrama" gave "voice to a call for change" while also accepting "the order of home and hearth, church and state."[42] It was an art form that was at once conservative in its emphasis on keeping order and maintaining the status quo but also potentially radical in its power to influence. Therefore, Lewis's third scene was designed to elicit sympathy, the sublime, and hence imitation. The audience was invited to adopt the morals, virtues, and militarism of the play's heroes in order to ensure the final defeat of the real Timour. Napoleon needed to be stopped and, like Kerim's heroic horse, the British people needed to do everything in their power to support the desires of their master—the king.

The horses of Lewis's paradigmatic play were uncomfortable beings situated somewhere between actors, animals, and humans. Their perceived ability to adopt a fictitious persona created uncertainty and fear in audiences. The horses of equestrian spectacles such as *Timour* did not fit within any established categories of "horse," and were often perceived as greater than horses outside the theater environment. They were majestic, special, and other. They were sublime and, as such, they were ideal bodies for the display of ideal virtues and morals. The natural and acting bodies of *Timour*'s equines were the embodiments and representations of the British morals thought so necessary during the revolutionary years. *Timour* emphasized that, like these equines, the British people should be courageous, strong, and willing to die in their quest to defeat invaders. The audience should, and did (as "Oliver Old Times" argues), become as loving of arms, battle, and courageous defense as the military horses they so admired.

NOTES

1. Saxon, *Enter Foot and Horse*, 89.
2. Lewis, *Timour the Tartar*, "Advertisement," 98.
3. See Moody, *Illegitimate Theatre in London.*
4. See Saxon, *Enter Foot and Horse* for further information on Astley's Amphitheatre.
5. See "Playbills and Programs from London Theatres, ca. 1700–1900, Covent Garden, 1811–1830," Houghton Library, Harvard University.
6. *Globe* (London), 30 April 1811, quoted in Gamer, "Matter of Turf," 319.
7. Lewis, *Timour the Tartar*, "Advertisement," 98.
8. For further details, see Cox and Gamer, "Introduction to 'Timour the Tartar,'" 98.
9. *Derby Mercury* (London), 9 May 1811; *Morning Chronicle* (London), 30 April 1811.
10. Lewis, *Timour the Tartar*, "Advertisement," 98.
11. Holder, "Animal Actor," 615; Gamer, "Matter of Turf," 307–8.
12. Nuss, *Distance, Theatre*, 154.
13. Lewis, *Timour the Tartar*, 108.
14. *Astley's System of Equestrian Education*, 10–12.
15. Astley used this imagery, and associated nationalistic discourses of ideal masculinity, in his performances on the illegitimate amphitheater stage with the famous Gibraltar Charger during the 1788 season. See Mattfeld, "'Undaunted All He Views.'"
16. States, *Great Reckonings*, 32–34. See Read, "On Animals," for further examples of Cartesian approaches to animal actors.
17. Quoted in Holder, "Animal Actor," 613.
18. Haslewood, "Secret History of the Green-Room."
19. *New Thespian Oracle, Containing Original Strictures on Oratory and Acting* (1791), in Zunshine, *Acting Theory*, 198.
20. *Autobiography of Charles Dibdin*, 170–71, Victoria and Albert Museum, Theatre and Performance Archives.
21. Playbill, 14 September 1829, scrapbooks related to Astley's Amphitheatre, ca. nineteenth century, 4 vols., Houghton Library, Harvard University, vol. 2, f TS 931.10.
22. Nuss, *Distance, Theatre*, 154.
23. *Morning Chronicle*, 30 April 1811; *Morning Post*, 30 April 1811; *Derby Mercury*, 9 May 1811.
24. *Morning Chronicle*, 30 April 1811; *Morning Post*, 30 April 1811.
25. Burke, *Sublime and Beautiful*, 113, 115. Burke is referring to Job 39:19–25.
26. Leask, "'To Canter with the Sagitarre.'" "Mazeppa" was later adapted by H. M. Milner for the stage, complete with the famous ungoverned flight scene, and became one of the most popular and longest running of the hippodramas produced in England and America.
27. Burke, *Sublime and Beautiful*, 70.
28. Lewis, *Timour the Tartar*, 108.
29. For details, see the Astley playbills housed in Houghton Library, Harvard University.
30. Weaver, *Towards an History of Dancing*, 156. For information on how "mute rhetoric" operated at Astley's Amphitheatre in the late eighteenth century, see Mattfeld, "'Undaunted All He Views.'"
31. Burke, *Sublime and Beautiful*, 80.
32. Ridout, *Stage Fright*, 117.
33. Ibid., 127; see also Weil, *Thinking Animals*, 47.
34. Brooks, "Melodramatic Imagination," 206.
35. See Mattfeld, *Becoming Centaur*.
36. Old Times, "Equestrian Theatricals," 200.

37. See Mattfeld, "'Genus Porcus Sophisticus,'" for information on eighteenth-century "contagious animality" and performing animals.

38. Old Times, "Equestrian Theatricals," 200–201.

39. *Mirror of Taste,* 3:373.

40. Quoted in Moody, *Illegitimate Theatre in London,* 100; Cox and Gamer, "Introduction to 'Timour the Tartar,'" xvii. See Worall's *Theatric Revolution* for a detailed examination of theater censorship at the turn of the nineteenth century.

41. Moody, *Illegitimate Theatre in London,* 100.

42. Cox, *Romanticism in the Shadow,* 55, 58.

5

PEACEABLE KINGDOM

The Place of the Dog at the Nativity Scene

ROB WAKEMAN

The theatrical adage, attributed to W. C. Fields, that warns actors never to work with children or animals might be said to have its biblical equivalent in a line from the Sermon on the Mount: "Give not that which is holy unto the dogs, neither cast ye your pearls before swine, lest they trample them under their feet, and turn again and rend you" (Matt. 7:6). For the audiences of late medieval Europe's biblical dramas—which were as much public exhibitions of communal faith as they were spectacular dramatic entertainment—the prospect of disobedient animal performers trampling on the representation of sacred scripture would be unwelcome.[1] The unpredictability of performing animals and their potential to befoul the sanctity of Christian ritual with eating, urination, defecation, or noise must have worried the plays' producers. Nevertheless, the representation of a peaceable kingdom of humans, animals, and God incarnate is essential to the messianic promise conveyed by medieval "nativity" plays, "adoration of the shepherds" plays, and "adoration of the magi" plays.[2] I will argue that these plays offer an important counterweight to the considerable body of scholarship that focuses on how medieval and Tudor animal entertainments trafficked in blood and violence in order to enforce a boundary between human and animal.[3] Dramatic representation of the eschatology of the peaceable kingdom required that producers of late medieval drama seek animal performers who could be trusted to remain piously pacified.

For the religious and civic institutions that sponsored biblical drama, the use of animals helped foster a sense of community through references to the local agricultural economies in which beasts played an essential part. Through extensive use of anachronism and anatopism, these plays anglicized the landscapes of biblical stories to sacralize local economies, including the animals raised and consumed in them. In politically and religiously divisive times, the settings of nativity plays—which may be said to represent, say, the mangers of the West Riding of Yorkshire as much as those of ancient Judea—are especially powerful for the sense of social cohesion they convey; humble shepherds and noble magi all kneel before the manger. But if the nascent church that gathers to adore the infant Jesus is to represent the nature and constitution of late medieval England's local communities, then that church must be a multispecies flock. The animals are the first worshippers at the trough where the incarnate God is laid. It is on the sturdy backs of the ox and the ass that the community of faith takes shape.

The two Gospel accounts of Jesus's nativity (Luke 2:1–20 and Matt. 1:18–2:23) make no mention of animals, but a rich tradition in the visual arts and theater upholds the image of animals arriving at the manger to pay tribute alongside their human keepers.[4] For productions of biblical drama, the species composition of this assembly varies from community to community, cultural tradition to cultural tradition, and economy to economy, but the use of live animals, while not universal, is often central to the vitality and affective power of the nativity's presentation. The multispecies multitude ballasts the communities that produce these plays, providing a dramatic image of stability and the fulfillment of the messianic prophecies of the Hebrew Bible.

The first living nativity scene in Europe was a tableau vivant erected by Saint Francis of Assisi to celebrate the Advent season of 1223.[5] One of Francis's followers, Thomas of Celano, tells the story of Francis's erection of a *presepe* in the remote Italian village of Greccio, where observers could "behold with bodily eyes His infant hardships; how He lay in a manger on the hay, with the ox and the ass standing by." Thomas of Celano's first *Life of St. Francis* (1229) describes how hay was laid over the ground and an ox and an ass were led to the site: "There Simplicity was honoured, Poverty exalted, Humility commended; and of Greccio there was made as it were a new Bethlehem. The night was lit up as day, and was delightsome to men and beasts." The focus on animals enhances the venerable naked innocence of the scene. Thomas of Celano makes no mention of any attempt to portray Mary, Joseph, shepherds, or magi in the Greccio grotto—only ox, ass, and holy child. The reverence of even poor beasts of burden in this simple scene is meant to be enough to exhort humans to humble themselves in similar fashion (a common theme in Saint Francis's teachings). Animals are not decorative scenery but moral exempla who are invited in to shape and share in the creation of meaning and the formation of community. As a just reward for their devotion, the animals who delighted in the Greccio nativity were given the hay that had been used for the manger. Thomas of Celano concludes his account by describing the miraculous properties of this hay: "And verily so it came to pass, for many animals in the region about which had divers diseases were freed from their sicknesses by eating of that hay," and "a crowd of persons of either sex suffering from various ailments gained their long-wished-for health at that same place." If all flesh is grass, then all flesh—human and animal—that partakes of the Greccio hay is bound together by the image of the nativity. The prospect of the "birth of the poor King" among the animals in the "little town of Bethlehem" creates an aura of humility that suggests that rich and poor, human and animal, are leveled as co-participants in salvation theology.[6]

Dramatic representations of the nativity grew far more elaborate after Saint Francis's early experiment. Although the Catholic Church already had a long tradition of religious drama, the sanctioned vernacular preaching by Franciscan and Dominican friars contributed to the popularization of public adaptations of biblical scenes. From the end of the fourteenth century to the present, these productions shed their austere origins to become elaborate, expensive spectacles that drew massive crowds from the local area and beyond. Production records show that animals continued to perform their part in plays depicting the creation, Cain and Abel, Noah's flood, Abraham and Isaac, the flight into Egypt, the entrance into Jerusalem, and the Antichrist, among others.[7] A 1501 creation-to-Pentecost cycle in Mons (in what is now Belgium) called for reptiles, fish, birds, sheep, cows, horses, mares, rabbits, a goose, two ducks, three doves, and two lambs. Live camels were used in Modane and Bourges in France. The accounts of the 1583 and 1597 Lucerne Passion Play record the use of donkeys, a calf, two sheep, two goats, three kids, two lambs, and a basket of pigeons.[8] In England, as Lisa Kiser has pointed out, the Chester creation-to-doomsday cycle is especially remarkable for its many references to animals. Extant production records confirm the use of live horses in several of the Chester plays, while others draw attention to animals in the Bible through the use of stage properties or humans in animal costume. As Kiser argues, the dynamic relationships of humans and animals in religious drama establish them "as co-enactors of biblical history, in it together for the long run."[9]

No dogs are mentioned in the performance records of biblical dramas, but that does not mean that they did not play a part, as they did in the salvation theology of pastoral England.[10] Dogs frequently appear in iconography, misericordia, paintings, and manuscript illuminations that depict the annunciation to the shepherds. The depiction of dogs in sacred spaces reminds us that their status in late medieval England was far more nuanced than has been conveyed by the broad (and bloody) strokes of performance studies' recent surveys of medieval animals. Lourdes Orozco's useful handbook *Theatre and Animals* has a typical assessment, mentioning only spectacles of torture such as animal baiting, public executions, and staged hunts. Orozco concludes that "these rituals fulfilled the practical and spiritual needs of the community."[11] This view is no doubt influenced by a conventional pejorative view of a rude and uncouth "Dark Ages" that does not account for the rich variety of human-animal relationships that intersected with practically every aspect of everyday life. Theater and animal historians draw support for their broad conclusions from the historical records, but too often this is done without the caveat that the types of documents cited are by their nature already biased against animals. The bulk of the patchwork series of records that have survived from the Middle Ages (criminal depositions, lists of fines levied for improper use of animals, etc.) inherently depict animals in negative contexts. When thinking about the place of animals in the theatrical imagination of late medieval England, we must remember that the account books and session rolls have little cause to document the roles that dogs and other animals played in amateur performance, community-based theater, and civic ritual.[12] We risk reducing the cultural significance of dogs, "the most prevalent and successfully integrated of our animal-others," if we continue to assume that their public torture and humiliation was necessary to the spiritual fulfillment of medieval communities.[13]

Herding dogs working in the fields and performing for entertainment are both subject to and an instrument of what Michael Peterson calls the "animal apparatus" that produces "constructions of social relations between humans and animals." Peterson argues that understanding the meaning of animals onstage requires investigation into how they are made to perform. The performance spaces of late medieval England—such as market squares and banquet halls—already possessed the physical infrastructure that enabled the performance of biblical drama and compelled animals' participation in it. The tools that are used to make animals perform in Peterson's "animal apparatus"—"collars, reins, bits, whips, food"—are the same instruments used to usher beasts along the path from farm to fork.[14] John Caius, in his zoological treatise *De Canibus Britannicus* (1570, translated as *Of Englishe Dogges* by Abraham Fleming in 1576), writes that "the shepherds hounde is very necessarye and profitable for the auoyding of harmes and inconueniences which may come to men by the meanes of beastes."[15] Essential mediators between humans and sheep, herding dogs allow humans to manage much larger flocks while providing protection against product loss.

Shepherds, because they depend on this network of sheep and dogs, are also constructs of the animal apparatus. Those who work with animals, whether agricultural laborers or stage actors, find themselves constrained by the wills of beasts, compelled to follow their lead and respond to their actions. Caius writes that English shepherds were unique in this respect, shadowing rather than leading their flocks across the moors and along the droveways: "For it is not in Englande, as it is in Fraunce, as it is in Flaunders, as it is in Syria, as it is in Tartaria, where the sheepe follow the shepherd, for heere in our country the sheepherd followeth the sheepe. And somtimes the straying sheepe, when no dogge runneth before them, nor goeth about & beside them, gather themselues together in a flocke, when they heere the sheepherd whistle in his fist, for feare of the Dogge (as I imagine) remembring this (if vnreasonable creatures may be reported to haue memory) that the Dogge commonly runneth out at his masters warrant which is his whistle."[16] Caius suggests that the shepherds were not micromanagers but for the most part were content to let their dogs direct the scene and keep order. The shepherd, like the stage performer who works with animals, is more an organ of the collective (a flock, an acting troupe) than its sovereign figure. To work effectively with animals, humans must be able to imagine and inhabit the minds of their nonhuman companions, to meet them on their own terms. As Karen Raber writes:

> When a cowherd, shepherd, goatherd, or fisherman (in any century) moves a flock, he cannot lead from the front (no animal in its right mind follows a predator), but must be able to control and direct the myriad minds of a host of individuals making nanosecond decisions about where to turn, which way to move, often based on stimuli imperceptible to humans. Hence the use of the dog . . . and other supplemental technologies that allow the herder to interact with the "mind" of the group. Ironically, to become effective herders, humans usually have to develop their own extensions of mind, whether animal or mechanical.[17]

Caius describes the cooperative labor of herding dog and handler as a spectacle worth admiring, noting that in his travels along English droveways, he had often "diligently marcked" these displays of agricultural skill: "when wee haue h[e]ard a sheepherd whistle we haue rayned in our horse and stoode styll a space, to see the proofe and triall of this matter."[18] Caius describes a mix of sport and theater in the displays of herding skill on the hillsides of England, or what Donna Haraway might call an "ontological choreography."[19] This thesis is inspired by Haraway's work on the relationship of domesticated dogs to humans. No wonder the descendants of those herding dogs now participate with their human companions in agility competitions!

As an extension of the herder's mind and a tool used to achieve a desired outcome, the working dog must translate and reconcile the divergent desires of both humans and sheep; she must separate friend from foe, stranger from host. It is this collaboration between human and dog that gives the flock its shape, its coherence, and its direction. It should come as no surprise, then, that when England's late medieval communities used dramatic performances to give shape and definition to the communal faith, dogs helped pilot the church's "flock." Dogs played an especially prominent role in the two great comedic "adoration of the shepherds" plays of the early sixteenth century: the Towneley *Second Shepherds' Play* and the Chester *Shepherds' Play*.[20] Both plays depict dogs as instruments used to restore order and obedience to unruly flocks. For example, in the Towneley play, the shepherds describe how they use their dogs to restore to the fold sheep lost in the underbrush near the village of Horbury:

> I have sought with my dogs
> All Horbury shrogs [shrubs],
> And of 15 hogs [yearling sheep]
> Found I but one ewe. (*TSSP,* 656–59)

As the shepherds toil in the fields awaiting the annunciation, this agricultural preamble sets the stage for the nativity scene in which God, humans, and animals join together at the manger. By using dogs to bring the divided flock back together as the herders drive toward Bethlehem, these plays celebrate the domestication of the agricultural landscape and its productive species—the promised instantiation of the peaceable kingdom.

Modern productions have used herding dogs in the Towneley *Second Shepherds' Play* and the Chester *Shepherds' Play* for comedic effect, as the hapless herdsmen find themselves drawn toward the nativity scene. At a *Second Shepherds' Play* performance in 1907 at Leeds University, the human actors were accompanied by a "magnificent collie" who contributed to "the rollicking farce," according to a local newspaper.[21] A herding dog in the field is an essential go-between for humans and their sheep, but the ability to communicate meaning and intention across species is necessarily approximate. The gap between the master's command and the dog's execution of his orders opens up the potential for comedy.[22]

Dottyknoll, the dog in the Chester *Shepherds' Play*, has the most prominent role, slight as it is, of any canine in English medieval drama. The Chester playwright gives Dottyknoll a name (which refers to his distinctively spotted or lumpy head) and dimensionality as an affective presence in the life of Trowle, the shepherds' servant boy. Strictly speaking, Dottyknoll is not a pet, not, as Kathleen Walker-Meikle defines it, an "animal kept for human companionship."[23] He is a working animal with a job to do. But the distinction between pet and working animal is insignificant for the shepherds, since they are not properly human themselves, a point borne out in the bestial insults lobbed back and forth among the shepherds throughout the play. Shepherd and herding dog are *both* laboring beasts, poor creatures that often share the same conventional names in English literature of the period— Coll, Gib, Jack, and so on. Shepherds do not choose to keep dogs, as one chooses to fancy a pet; rather, as Donna Haraway has argued, shepherd and herding dog evolved together and adapted to each other. Boy, dog, and sheep re-create onstage the ancient pseudobiblical Middle Eastern landscape on which the multispecies flock coevolved and created the first systems of animal agriculture.[24]

The Chester playwright's presentation of Dottyknoll breaks down the false distinction between "pet" and "working dog," or between "animal companion" and "laboring comrade." Working dogs were vital for animal husbandry and the management of flocks, but they were also creatures of sympathy for the laboring class. This is evident when Trowle recognizes that he has more in common with his dog than he does with his masters. Trowle indicates the intimacy of this bond, the lack of distinction between dog and laboring servant, when he addresses the audience on behalf of the multispecies flock:

Good lord, look on me
and my flock here as they fed have.
On this wold walk we;

are no men here, that no way.
All is plain, perdee [indeed];
therefore, sheep, we mon [must] go.
No better may be
of beast that blood and bone have. (*CSP*, lines 165–72)

There are no men on the desolate hillsides, only beasts united in their common flesh. The comment is ironic in that all the creatures of the wold—shepherds and their chattel—are awaiting the arrival of the incarnate Lamb of God, who will surpass all beasts of blood and bone. But, for the time being, Trowle is relegated to the fields, where he finds a greater bond with the sheep and dog who walk before him than he does with the landlords and gentlemen who fleece him and exploit his labor.

With Dottyknoll as his companion, Trowle learns to sympathize with and care for animals even as he disparages humans. He waits in the night, apart from the other shepherds, with his stash of salves for veterinary care and his canine companion:

Wot [know] I not, day or night,
Necessaries that to me belong.
Tar-box and tar-ball
you shall [see] here;
nettle, hemlock, and butter abiding [remaining],
and my good dogge Dottyknoll
that is nothing cheeffe [choice] of his chiding. (*CSP*, lines 173–79)

By being with, working with, and sympathizing with dogs, Trowle learns how to view the world. Like Dottyknoll, Trowle refuses to be "cheeffe," or choosy, with his criticisms. Both shepherd and dog bark and bite at anything that disturbs the flock, including lazy shepherds. The comic appeal of the dog is his disrespect of all humans but his master. A shepherd will be able to command his dog, but the dog will be indifferent—at best—to all other comers.

Amid the unjust economic system and insufferable winter weather described by the Chester playwright, Trowle and Dottyknoll await a better future on the bleak and depopulated landscape, virtuously laboring in the hope of economic salvation. While Donna Haraway uses the training of agility dogs as an example of interspecies "co-flourishing," the ancestors of agility dog and dog trainer—that is, herding dog and shepherd—are figured here as examples of *co-languishing*.[25] From their similar subject positions, shepherd and dog attain the same worldview. Trowle says,

If any man come me by
and would wit [know] which way best were,

my leg I lift up whereas I lie
and wish him the way east and westward. (*CSP*, lines 180–83)

Trowle imagines a scenario in which a man asks him for directions ("which way," or path, would be "best" for traveling) and literally tells him to *piss off*. This transgressive gesture conflates the disposition of frustrated rural laborer and ill-mannered working dog. By responding to the slightest intrusion with the threat of urination, Trowle claims the land for his own in the manner of a territorial canine. For Trowle, acting like a dog is empowering rather than debasing. It lets him growl and snarl at his social superiors.[26]

So what should happen to Dottyknoll when deliverance comes to the pasture in the form of an angel announcing the birth of Jesus? The dearth of performance records and descriptions of late medieval biblical drama demands that we examine representations of the scene in the visual arts. The annunciation to the shepherds of the birth of Jesus and the adoration of the shepherds were popular subjects for artists throughout the medieval period and into the early modern era. Herding dogs appear with the shepherds in the fields in almost every depiction of the annunciation, but often the dog is absent from representations of the adoration. This is especially noteworthy if an artist depicted both scenes. A few examples: the Holkham Bible Picture Book (ca. 1327–35) shows a visibly agitated dog in the field with ears pulled back and tail taut at the angel's appearance in the annunciation, but he is not present at the adoration scene by the manger; a frightened dog on the verge of growling is slinking away in the corner of Taddeo Gaddi's 1330 *Annunciation* and absent from his *Adoration*; Hugo van der Goes's 1475 Portinari Altarpiece shows a dog cowering in fear at the annunciation and missing from the adoration. A glazed terra-cotta altarpiece (ca. 1513–20) by Luca della Robbia the Younger shows a sitting dog in the field directing his gaze toward the heavenly host, but he is not seen at the nativity (although a ca. 1460–70 medallion by della Robbia's more famous father does include a shepherd sitting beside his praying master outside the barn); Jacopo Bassano portrays a dog in his *Annunciation* (ca. 1555–60) and multiple noble hunting dogs in his *Adoration of the Magi* (early 1540s), but not in his *Adoration of the Shepherds* (ca. 1545).[27] As Margaret Freeman has written, the herding dog in annunciation paintings and woodcuts "almost always appears in these scenes and often seems aware of the unusual," responding to the appearance of the angel with understandable excitement, frenetic movement, defensive posturing, or barking.[28]

A particularly striking example of the herding dog's marginalized place in the nativity story is Geertgen tot Sint Jans's *Nativity at Night* (ca. 1490), which depicts Mary, Joseph, the ox and the ass, and several angelic figures gathered around the manger and bathed in the infant Jesus's radiant glow. Through the window of the barn, we see the angel appearing to awestruck shepherds. Farthest away of all is a black dog, a shadow at the horizon almost subsumed by the inky night. The unearthly gravity of the two sources of light (Jesus's manger and the angel) draws our eye to holy child and to heaven, and all the figures in the scene are invited to partake in its warmth and message of salvation. But the dog at the farthest margin, difficult to see if unsought, seems unmoved by this message of salvation.

The agitation or the indifference of the dog presents a dramaturgical problem for the manger scene as the kinetic comedy of the shepherds' earthly complaints turns into holy solemnity. If the dog isn't choosy with his barking, then neither angel of the annunciation nor holy family is safe from his rebukes. Some animals might be said to actually contribute to the peacefulness of the nativity scene, as in the case of the reliably patient ox and ass. But not the herding dog: according to Edward Topsell, "there is no creature that will more stirre, barke, and moue noise, then one of these against thiefe or wilde beast."[29] An energetic canine is not to be trusted to stand in silent worship (nor, perhaps, should an audience be trusted to direct their eyes to the image of the holy family when a performing dog shares the stage).[30] The Chester *Shepherds' Play*'s representation of shepherds' bleak laboring lives prior to the annunciation and the harmonious depiction of the adoration demonstrates the different capacities of animals to disrupt or to steady the natural order. A dog's impudence may be appropriate for the physical humor of the play's opening scenes, but as the drama settles into an image of worship, serenity is the order of the day. The living animals at the manger are desirable because of their peacefulness, not their chiding of strangers. Oxen and asses can remain silent and docile, seemingly rapt with devotion, but whether a dog could be trusted with the same is doubtful.

At this point, then, it seems appropriate that the dog should disappear from the text of the Chester *Shepherds' Play*; there is no mention of Dottyknoll once the shepherds are called away from the field to the manger in Bethlehem. What becomes of Dottyknoll—diligent co-worker and loyal companion—when the shepherds embark on new careers as evangelists and anchorites? The early Tudor Christmas carol "Jolly Wat the Shepherd" offers an answer to this dramaturgical dilemma: leave the dog behind to tend to the flock.[31] After hearing the angel singing "Gloria in excelsis Deo," Wat gets ready to leave for Bethlehem, but before he does, he gives instructions to his dog:

> Now must I go there Crist was born;
> Farewell! I cum again to-morn.
> Dog, kepe well my shepe fro the corn,
> And warn well "Warroke [hold]" when I blow my horn!

Wat the jolly shepherd has been given a chance at salvation. But before he is released from his labors, Wat saddles his dog with all of his responsibilities. The vision of the nativity scene is a promise of salvation in a new Eden, where peace has been reestablished—between kings and peasants, between species. But away from the light of the manger that draws our gaze, the labor of animal agriculture goes on. The dog is sacrificed to the animal apparatus so the shepherd can be saved and granted eternal life.

At the end of the Chester play, Trowle renounces the herding life:

> I read we us agree
> for our misdeeds amends to make,
> for so now will I;
> and to the child I wholly me betake [commit myself]
> for ay [forever] securely.
> Shepherd's craft I forsake;
> and to an anker [anchoritic cell] hereby
> I will in my prayers watch and wake. (*CSP*, lines 661–68)

As the multispecies flock gathers together at Jesus's manger, the adoration ultimately subordinates animals to humans just as humans are subordinated to God. The herding dog is pushed to the distant margin, as in Geertgen's *Nativity at Night*. This is a refusal of co-flourishing of shepherd and dog. For Trowle, life as an anchorite will be life closed off from animality, his humanity securely enclosed inside his cell. While the ox and the ass are allowed to perform in the ritual of the adoration, other animals are excluded for practical as much as for theological reasons. In Nicholas Ridout's terms, "non-human animals are just like human performers—not, as some might suggest, because they are part of some deterministic bio-aesthetic web—but because they all work in a theatrical economy characterized by exploitation and the division of labor."[32]

The use of docile animals in the nativity tableau vivant projects an image of pastoral peace. Today, it is common to see churches staging living nativity scenes with oxen, asses, lambs, kids, camels, or other animals who appear to bow humbly before the occasion. Other animals—such as the herding dog—threaten to provoke unexpected audience reactions or to disrupt the established script. Nothing is meant to be uneasy about the nativity scene—it is a promise to rid the world of hardship. But without the shepherds' dog, left behind on the wold, one wonders whether the peaceable kingdom to come will be the product of peace with the animals or of a new apparatus that separates humans from animals, animals who worship at the manger not because of their natural disposition but because of their naturalized place within the agricultural economy.

NOTES

1. The Catholic Church has a long history of worrying about animals disrupting religious ceremonies. See Salisbury, *Beast Within,* 65; Walker-Meikle, *Medieval Pets,* 70.

2. On the place of animals in the eschatology of the peaceable kingdom, see Hosea 2:18 ("And in that day I will make a covenant with them, with the beasts of the field, and with the fowls of the air, and with the creeping things of the earth: and I will destroy the bow, and the sword, and war out of the land: and I will make them sleep secure"), and Isa. 11:6–9 ("The wolf shall dwell with the lamb: and the leopard shall lie down with the kid: the calf and the lion, and the sheep shall abide together, and a little child shall lead them. The calf and the bear shall feed: their young ones shall rest together: and the lion shall eat straw like the ox. And the sucking child shall play on the hole of the asp: and the weaned child shall thrust his hand into the den of the basilisk. They shall not hurt, nor shall they kill in all my holy mountain, for the earth is filled with the knowledge of the Lord, as the covering waters of the sea").

3. Keith Thomas's litany of cruelties to animals in blood sports is frequently cited as evidence of the ghastliness of premodern human-animal relations. Thomas, *Man and the Natural World,* 143–49.

4. The animal iconography of the nativity may draw its authority from the apocryphal Gospel of James (which mentions birds, Joseph's ass, and the shepherds' sheep and kids) and especially the Gospel of Pseudo-Matthew, which mentions the adoration of the ox and the ass as fulfillments of the prophecies laid out in Isa. 1:3 and the Septuagint translation of Hab. 3:2.

5. Saint Francis's Greccio nativity scene is notable for its use of live animals, but the *presepe* or crèche—a miniaturized sculpture or scenic display of the nativity scene using sculpted figures—precedes the Greccio tableau vivant by several centuries. Pope Sixtus III (432–40) may have ordered the erection of a nativity scene in Rome during his papacy. See Berliner, "Origins of the Crèche," 254. On the use of live animals in other medieval tableaux vivants, see Kiser, "Animals in Medieval Sports."

6. Thomas of Celano, *Lives of S. Francis,* 83–85. On the importance of the realism of the living nativity scene and communal participation in the scene, see Rosenthal, "Crib of Greccio," 58; Berliner, "Origins of the Crèche"; and Sinanoglou, "Christ Child as Sacrifice," 496–97.

7. Meredith and Tailby, *Staging of Religious Drama,* 117–22, 133–34; Berliner, "Origins of the Crèche," 260–62.

8. The Lucerne production notes call for an offstage stall to be constructed near the performance site where the animals could be housed for the duration of the daylong performance. Meredith and Tailby, *Staging of Religious Drama,* 117–18.

9. Kiser, "Animals in Chester's *Noah's Flood,*" 30–31. Karl Steel also briefly discusses some exceptional Christian rites outside mainstream doctrine where "some animals might even be honored as co-worshippers, as in the Southern German ritual of the *Umritt,* in which horses were blessed with holy water and ridden into specially designed churches to gaze upon the Host." Steel also details how some early Christian sects embraced non-anthropocentric doctrines, and he gives the example of the fourth-century Acts of Philip, which features the baptism of a goat and a leopard. Steel, *How to Make a Human,* 59, 94.

10. Only a few tantalizing clues allude to performing canines in the later Middle Ages, but they are enough to determine that the dog was not animal non grata on the medieval stage. We do have records from fourteenth-century Yorkshire for traveling performing dog acts (as well as records for performing horses, monkeys, and dancing bears) and references to dogs in later civic performances. Accounts of the Chester Midsummer Watch parade mention spaniels and bloodhounds taking part in the procession. Michael Dobson provides an excellent catalogue of dogs in both professional and university drama of the sixteenth century. There is, of course, Crab in Shakespeare's *Two Gentlemen of Verona* (1590–91). Dobson also cites a King's College, Cambridge account book from 1552 that lists "the considerable sum of 2s. 6d. [that] was paid to 'a household servant of Master Chochely' for bringing hunting dogs to appear in a production of Euripides' tragedy *Hippolytus,*" while a 1572 performance at Peterhouse, Cambridge of "some unnamed plays required the expenditure of 16d. 'for a huntsman for his dogs.'" Dobson cites numerous other examples of dogs on the early modern stage: the lover's hound in *Il Pastor Fido,* a 1586 Italian pastoral tragicomedy by Giovan Battista Guarini; the dog belonging to the hapless Puntarvalo in Ben Jonson's *Every Man Out of His Humour* (1599); the mythological hunting dogs who join in the spectacle of Thomas Heywood's *Silver Age* (1616). Robinson, *Fifteenth-Century Stagecraft,* 50;

Baldwin, Clopper, and Mills, *Cheshire, Including Chester*, 461; Dobson, "Dog at All Things," 116–17.

11. Orozco, *Theatre and Animals*, 14. Related to this point is Michael Dobson's suggestion that the "development of dog-training for entertainment rather than bloodsports seems to have lagged behind that of the training of other species until well into the eighteenth century," which reflects the class bias of the historical records. Dogs were of course trained for many things besides blood sport before the seventeenth century, including the amusement of their keepers. The lack of professional and permanent acting companies before the late sixteenth century makes it impractical that a dog would be trained solely for the entertainment of an audience, but this in no way should foreclose the possibility that an actor's dog would be capable of entertaining an audience. Dobson, "Dog at All Things," 119.

12. In most cases, we know that live animals were used in many of these performances only because account books list prices for the food that was purchased to feed the animal performers. There was no need to list food purchased for dogs, since dogs were generally fed leftovers from human meals.

13. Williams, "Inappropriate/d Others," 95.

14. Peterson, "Animal Apparatus," 34.

15. Caius, *Of Englishe Dogges*, 23.

16. Ibid., 24.

17. Raber, *Animal Bodies, Renaissance Culture*, 17. See also Donna Haraway, who, following Edmund Russell, describes herding dogs as "macrobiotechnologies," both the instrument and demonstration of "the ways in which human beings have shaped evolution" and the ways in which human-dog relationships have "changed both themselves and other species [such as sheep]." Haraway, *When Species Meet*, 56.

18. Caius, *Of Englishe Dogges*, 24.

19. Haraway describes such interspecies relationships as "ontological choreographies" that organize or "script" the "dance of being" through which "bodies, human and non-human, are taken apart and put together." Haraway borrows the term "ontological choreography" from gender and women's studies and science studies scholar Charis Thompson's work on assisted reproductive technologies. Haraway, *Companion Species Manifesto*, 8.

20. All citations from the Towneley Plays are from Stevens and Cawley, *Towneley Plays*, and all citations from the Chester cycle are from Lumiansky and Mills, *Chester Cycle,* both cited hereafter parenthetically in the text as *TSSP* and *CSP*, respectively. I have modernized the spelling. At present, it is impossible to date the

performance of the *Second Shepherds' Play* with any precision, but recent evidence strongly suggests that it is from the late fifteenth or early sixteenth century and nearly contemporaneous with the Chester *Shepherds' Play*. Formerly called the Wakefield Mystery Plays and long assumed to be a creation-to-doomsday cycle along the lines of the Chester or York Cycles, the Towneley Plays (Huntington MS HM1) are now generally thought to be a collection of biblical plays from various locations in West Riding, Lancashire, and Westmorland, collected sometime during the reign of Queen Mary (1553–58). Although Corpus Christi plays in Chester date to 1422, the first reference to the Chester *Shepherds' Play* in the historical record does not occur until 1516. For the dating of the Towneley and Chester plays, see Palmer, "'Towneley Plays'"; Palmer, "Recycling the Wakefield Cycle"; Clopper, "Development of the Chester Cycle."

21. Quoted in Robinson, *Fifteenth-Century Stagecraft*, 2–3.

22. According to Caius, a herding dog learns to respond "either at the hearing of his masters voyce, or at the wagging and whisteling in his fist, or at his shrill and horse hissing bringeth the wandring weathers and straying sheepe, into the selfe same place where his masters will and wishe is to haue them." Caius, *Of Englishe Dogges*, 24. As Richard Rastall notes, the pipes mentioned in the Chester *Shepherds' Play* could easily double as dog whistles. Rastall, "Music in the Cycle," 118.

23. Walker-Meikle, *Medieval Pets*, 1.

24. The domestication of dogs (i.e., the divergence of dogs from wolves) occurred at least fifteen thousand years ago in eastern Asia. Sheep and goats were the first animals domesticated for human consumption; the ancestor of all modern domestic sheep breeds, the Asiatic mouflon, originated in southwest Asia eleven thousand years ago. See Haraway, *Companion Species Manifesto*, 27–29. See also Chessa et al., "History of Sheep Domestication," 532; Gifford-Gonzalez and Hanotte, "Domesticating Animals in Africa."

25. Haraway introduces the concept of interspecies co-flourishing in the *Companion Species Manifesto* and develops it further in *When Species Meet*, especially chapter 5, "Cloning Mutts, Saving Tigers: Bioethical Angst and Questions of Flourishing," 133–57.

26. Trowle's marking of his territory, irrespective of the prerogatives of his superiors, might fruitfully be compared with that of Crab, the dog in Shakespeare's *Two Gentleman of Verona*, who urinates on or near his betters. As Erica Fudge writes, "Thus, lacking reason, self-control, and civility . . . a pissing dog comes to stand for everything

that a human is not, and cannot be." Trowle's rude gesture is thus a confirmation of his similitude to the animals with whom he lives rather than to the landowners whom he serves. Fudge, "Dog Is Himself," 198.

27. Hunting dogs frequently appear in representations of the adoration of the magi as well as in representations of nobles on pilgrimage to see the infant Jesus in Bethlehem, as in Pinturicchio's 1501 *Adoration of the Shepherds*. In the seventeenth century, dogs become more frequent in representations of the adoration, perhaps reflecting the increasing cultural status of pets and their rising place inside the home. Notable examples of dogs adoring Jesus at the nativity include Palma Vecchio (1523), Pieter Pourbus (1574), Fray Juan Bautista Maíno (1612), Juan Ribalta (1616), Rembrandt (1646), and Bartholomé Esteban Murillo (1650).

28. Freeman, "Shepherds in the Fields," 114.

29. Topsell, *Historie of Foure-Footed Beastes*, 158.

30. As Brigitte Resl has written, the zoological treatises and husbandry manuals of the later Middle Ages reflect the ways in which "the exegetical approaches of the earlier medieval period were being supplemented and superseded by experience. In the eyes of humans, animals had evolved into more complex beasts in the later Middle Ages." By 1607, Edward Topsell was saying that oxen "are by nature meeke, gentle, slow, and not stubborne," and describing asses as "very tame, not refusing any manner of burthen although it breake his backe: being loaded it will not out of the way for any man or beast, and it only understandeth the voice of that man, with whom it is laboured, knowing also the way whereunto it is accustomed." Resl, "Animals in the Middle Ages," 26; Topsell, *Historie of Foure-Footed Beastes*, 65, 35.

31. Quiller-Couch, *Oxford Book of Ballads*. The earliest extant recording of this carol is in Richard Hilles's commonplace book (which contains many carols and songs) at Balliol College, Oxford MS 354 (which dates to 1536).

32. Ridout, *Stage Fright*, 110.

6

PERFORMING PAIN

The Suffering Animal in Early
Modern Experiment

SARAH E. PARKER

Galen (ca. 131–ca. 201 C.E.) was one of the most famous medical practitioners of the ancient world. He was summoned to Rome as personal physician to the emperor Marcus Aurelius, and his discoveries about medicine held sway for hundreds of years after his death. At this time, medicine was a competitive business. Doctors not only competed for patients; they were also philosophical competitors, positing rival ideas about the workings of the human body. Their debate was public and was usually recorded in written treatises and displayed in public demonstrations structured like formal debates. Thanks to the record left behind in Galen's extant writings, it is clear that he often incorporated anatomical demonstrations into such public debates. In these performances, rather than take center stage himself, Galen developed a form of rhetoric in which he allowed the truth of his argument to occupy the focal position. In other words, the experience of performance was defined by the interaction between Galen's argument and the animal who occupied the central position as the body where proof of that argument would become manifest.

Galen's model of experimental proof, where the researcher presented his argument as speaking for itself through the animal body on display, reemerged in the medical schools of sixteenth-century Italy and, through the influence of William Harvey's training at the University of Padua, made its way to England and the eventual formation of the Royal Society. While the performative vivisection of animal bodies was undeniably fundamental to the physiological discoveries that Galen and later researchers like Vesalius, Fabricius, Harvey, and other members of the Royal Society would make, it is important to note that the performance of such vivisections persisted even after a discovery had been acknowledged in the field and published. The repeated performance of a vivisection to prove an argument legitimized the researcher's authority by insisting on a relationship between the audience's act of witnessing the experiment and the vivisected animal's conformity to the experiment's predicted outcome. According to this model, the animal was understood to have a kind of voice, but that voice only confirmed the accuracy and authority of the person designing the experiment. The records that describe these experiments rarely reflect a sensibility toward the animal experience outside that role. But the authors sometimes leave traces of another kind of experience for animals occupying this performative and demonstrative role, the experience of pain. This chapter recovers those traces in order to offer some suggestions about the early modern development of a sense that animals were capable of suffering pain.

Galen: Creating Fame Through Animal Performance

As one of the most prolific authors of the ancient world, Galen made deliberate use of the power of publication. He wrote hundreds of treatises on topics in medicine, surgery, and philosophy, and throughout these writings he worked carefully to develop an authorial persona that would promote his fame as a medical expert and convince his critics that his ideas were sound. In his work *On the Natural Faculties*, for instance, he took a strong stand on philosophical debates about the nature of the living organism to argue for the Hippocratic position that nature (*physis*) governs the faculties or powers (*dynamis*) of the organism, therefore requiring a holistic approach to treatment rather than treatment focused on isolated parts. In making this argument, he attacked a group of physicians known as the Asclepiadeans, the followers of Asclepiades (ca. 124–40 B.C.E.). Asclepiades was influenced by the atomic theories of Democritus and opposed the Hippocratic medical model, which understood health and illness as the effect of an overall balance or imbalance of the four humors. Galen's *On the Natural Faculties* rejects this view in defense of humoral theory. The work illustrates both Galen's highly developed use of rhetoric to launch colorful attacks on his opponents and his use of animal vivisection to prove his positions.

In the first book of *On the Natural Faculties*, which focuses on the definition of terms and the issue of nutrition, Galen attacks Asclepiades's denial of the kidney's role in the secretion of urine. Galen argues that Hippocrates's understanding of the kidneys' role in the production of urine may be proved "not merely from the way in which his opponents are at variance with obvious facts, but also from the various subjects of natural research themselves—the functions of animals." The most effective way to prove an argument is to state the obvious (or what Galen describes as obvious in order to ridicule his opponents) and to use the body of an animal in demonstration. Galen uses this method in his discussion of the kidneys and elsewhere. His first example draws on what he considers the clear markers of pain exhibited by someone suffering from a kidney stone. He says, rather sarcastically, "I do not suppose that Asclepiades ever saw a stone which had been passed by one of these sufferers, or observed that this was preceded by a sharp pain in the region between kidneys and bladder as the stone traversed the ureter, or that, when the stone was passed, both the pain and the retention at once ceased."[1] Galen argues that his opponent lacks basic observational skill even when it comes to the pain experienced by a suffering patient. The implication is that not only do the Asclepiadeans refuse to form opinions based on observation rather than theory, but they do not even notice the suffering of their own patients. The tone of Galen's accusation, however, is not primarily moral but intellectual. He attacks the Asclepiadeans not for being cruel or indifferent to suffering but for being unobservant. Pain can be useful to the physician because it indicates that something in the body is amiss, and this helps the attentive practitioner understand the workings of the body and thus improve his practice.

Galen's understanding of suffering as a clue to the workings of the body, rather than as an experience demanding an empathetic response, extends to his discussions of animal experimentation. To prove his argument that the kidneys send urine to the bladder through the ureters, he claims that he was "therefore, further compelled to show them [the Asclepiadeans] in a still living animal, the urine plainly running out through the ureters into the bladder." The experiment involves opening the peritoneum of an animal, tying the ureters, bandaging the animal and letting him go, and then reopening the animal to show that the bladder is empty and the ureters "quite full and distended—in fact almost on the point of rupturing"—and then releasing the ligatures to show the bladder filling with urine.[2] After the animal has been opened twice in the service of this demonstration, Galen goes on to describe tying yet another ligature around the penis of the animal before he has a chance to urinate, in order to show that movement of the urine in the reverse direction is not possible. The animal is then permitted to urinate, but Galen's demonstration continues. He ties one ureter and not the other to show how the ligatured ureter fills with urine; he goes on to cut the ligatured ureter, so that the onlookers can witness the urine spurting out of it. Finally, he cuts both ureters, bandages the animal again, only to cut him open a final time to show how the abdominal cavity has filled with urine because of the severed ureters.

This long process would certainly be effective in proving Galen's argument about the urinary system, and he invites anyone not present at one of his public demonstrations to "test this for himself on an animal."[3] But aside from the usefulness of the animal body for proving an argument, Galen gives no indication that he or his onlookers witnessed the experience of pain in the animal on display. Instead, *On the Natural Faculties* represents the animal as a blank presence that serves only as a medium for the proof of Galen's argument. The generic status of the animal is evident in the fact that Galen uses the Greek word *zōon*, which refers to any kind of animal or living being in the most general sense, and does not specify what particular kind of animal would serve best for such a demonstration. Furthermore, when Galen points out that it is easy to observe the changing location of acute pain in a person suffering from a kidney stone, he uses the verb *algeō*, which refers to a feeling of bodily pain or suffering, but his discussion of the animal experiment uses no verbs describing pain.

Galen's text does contain, however, an elliptical reference to pain, an etymological link between the animal body in service of scientific proof and the performance of pain. In Galen's invitation to his audience to "test this for himself on an animal," he uses the verb *basanizō*, which originally meant "to rub on the touchstone" and came to mean "to put to the test, to prove," or "to investigate scientifically." When used with reference to a person, the verb referred to a cross-examination, including questioning under torture.[4] In this latter sense, it was used in reference to animals by the Sophist Philostratus (ca. 170–ca. 247), who flourished in the half century just after Galen's death. Philostratus's *Life of Apollonius of Tyana* recounts many (probably fictional) stories about the life of the Pythagorean philosopher. At one point in the story, Apollonius is conversing with a king who invites him on a hunt in a park stocked with animals for that purpose. The philosopher declines and gives as his reason the condition of those animals, which he describes as both "enslaved" (*douloō*) and "mistreated" or "tortured" (*basanizō*).[5] While it is unlikely that Galen would have been familiar with this particular use of *basanizō* in reference to the suffering of animals, since it first appeared after his death, it is nevertheless significant that a term indicating a protoscientific notion of proof or evidence also refers to the suffering involved in producing that evidence. The animal body that serves as the touchstone for proving the validity of an argument about physiology is also a suffering body.

The experimental animal's ability to speak both as the proof of an argument and as a suffering body appears more clearly in Galen's most famous vivisection experiment, a demonstration performed on a pig to prove the relationship between the nerves and the brain. In the ancient world, philosophers and doctors engaged in an ongoing and heated debate over which organ of the body was the seat of intelligence. Aristotle and his followers believed that it was the heart, but Galen argued that the nerves and the spinal cord originate in the brain, making it the locus of both movement and cognition.[6] In order to prove that the nerves extending from the brain control the movements of the body, Galen performed a vivisection on a pig in which it was essential that the pig squeal throughout the demonstration. The pig's voice was crucial to this demonstration of the nervous system so that, in a dramatic climax, Galen could announce that he was going to cut the laryngeal nerve controlling the vocal cords, which would make the pig fall silent. Galen recounts this demonstration in *On Anatomical Procedures* and *On Prognosis*, and he gives a thorough description of the laryngeal nerves in *On the Usefulness of the Parts of the Body*. As in the urinary system demonstration described above, the animal body plays a central role in both Galen's proof of his argument and in the performance itself, which established his authority on questions of medicine and philosophy.

Galen's account of this demonstration is not concerned with the experience of the animal but rather with the effect of the performance on the audience's opinion of his own talents as a philosopher. At one point during the demonstration, Galen tells of a witness who expresses the views of the skeptical school, calling into question any knowledge based on sensory observation. Galen haughtily dismisses this man's philosophical view and leaves the room, refusing to continue his performance before an unsympathetic audience. Only after other members of the audience condemn the skeptical spectator and beg Galen to continue does he agree to resume his demonstration. Galen's somewhat egotistical behavior in this famous scenario illustrates how animal experimentation came to be established as a performative practice. The importance of Galen's role in this episode is clear, since the experiment clearly cannot continue if he refuses to perform it. Yet the role of the animal is also fundamental, in that the audience must accept the authority of evidence manifested in the animal body. The skeptical spectator disrupts the performance because he refuses to accept the performative role that the animal body plays in the Galenic understanding of legitimate scientific evidence.

Vivisection in Sixteenth-Century Italy

Galen's style of medical research experienced a decline in the medieval period in Europe.[7] With the advent of the Renaissance in Italy came a renewed interest in the study of anatomy.[8] While Galen was seen as a predecessor to be surpassed, his writings also found an eager audience among learned medical practitioners, especially in Italy, and his extant works were translated into Latin and published by a number of presses.[9] One edition in particular, a publication of what was believed to be the complete Galenic corpus at the time, includes a specific reference to Galen's famous experiment on the pig. Its title page announces the subject of the book, and this information is framed by a series of pictures depicting significant events in Galen's life and practice (fig. 6.1). The vivisection of the pig's laryngeal nerves occupies a central place in this layout, taking up the entire lower banner. The only scene that is perhaps more prominent is located in the parallel banner at the top of the page, which shows Galen attending the sickbed of his most famous patient, the Roman emperor Marcus Aurelius. It is significant that the publisher gives Galen's experiment on the pig such pride of place. The title page would also have served as an advertisement for the book, since such paratextual materials were one of the main strategies that publishers employed to attract a market for their books.[10] This choice suggests that

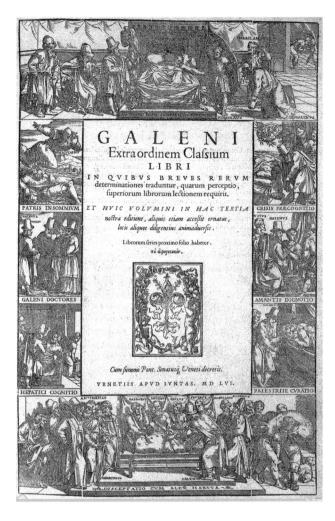

6.1

Title page of Galen, *Opera Omnia* (Venice: Heirs of L. A. Junta, 1556). Wellcome Library, London.

Galen's sixteenth-century publisher anticipated that the experimental model would appeal to Galen's readership at a time when medical researchers were performing such experiments with an eye to improving upon the knowledge of the ancients.

Histories of medicine have tended to focus on the early modern dissection and study of the human body, but many anatomical studies and most physiological research relied on the bodies of animals.[11] The focus on human anatomy stems largely from attention to Andreas Vesalius, widely acknowledged as the most important anatomist of the Renaissance. Vesalius insisted that he had succeeded in making new anatomical discoveries because he performed primarily human, rather than animal, dissections. In the preface to his masterwork, *De humani corporis fabrica* (1543), he critiques Galen's research on animal bodies: "I am quite certain . . . that he himself [Galen] had never cut open a human body and furthermore that, deceived by his apes (although he did chance upon two human skeletons) he frequently and quite wrongly finds fault with the ancient physicians who actually did their training by dissecting

6.2

Title page of Andreas Vesalius, *Andreae Vesalii Suorum de humani corporis fabrica librorum epitome* (Basel: J. Oporini, 1543). Wellcome Library, London.

human material.''[12] Though Vesalius was a great admirer of Galen and clearly imitated him, the early modern surgeon has been remembered in the history of medicine as the figure who challenged Galen's authority and noticed that many of Galen's errors resulted from the fact that he dissected animals rather than humans.[13]

Vesalius made major contributions to the study of human anatomy, and yet it is important to keep in mind that animal dissection and vivisection still played an essential role in the development of scientific knowledge in the early modern period. The title page of Vesalius's seminal work introducing corrections to Galenic anatomy and physiology, *De humani corporis fabrica*, and the publication of an *Epitome* in the same year, illustrates both the performative nature of anatomical demonstration and the role that animals played in such performances (fig. 6.2). Rather than relegate illustrations to the frame, as the publisher of Galen's *Opera Omnia* opted to do, *De fabrica*'s frontispiece is entirely dominated by a magnificent and complex woodcut depicting the anatomist as the central character in a performance. The rounded architectural structure of an intimate anatomy theater embraces a throng of observers who engage with this performance in a variety of ways. While some look on attentively, others are caught up in conversation, and still others direct their attention toward a variety of distractions. The most obvious sources of distraction are a monkey and a dog in the foreground. These animals pull various audience members' line of vision away from the demonstration at the center, drawing the viewer's attention to the animal figures as well. Though Vesalius performs his anatomical dissection on the body of a woman, the presence of the dog and the monkey anchoring the lower, foundational corners of the woodcut illustrates the importance of animal anatomy to *De fabrica*'s study of the body. Vesalius was deeply involved in the production of the images for his book, and the deliberate inclusion of these animal bodies in this complex and dynamic frontispiece illustrates that even the figure most closely associated with the rejection of animal anatomy believed in the importance of studying animal bodies.

De fabrica's frontispiece also demonstrates the extent to which Vesalius preserved Galen's focus on the performative role of the anatomist. The places where such dissections were held were called theaters, and the professors who lectured in them often took advantage of the performative opportunities such spaces provided.[14] While the attention of several spectators is diverted by the dog and monkey, the woman's body on the table at the center holds the rapt attention of most onlookers. Just next to her stands Vesalius himself, his hand gesturing toward her body. He is the only figure who looks directly out, and his gaze draws the viewer (and potential book buyer) into the performance of his anatomical demonstration. *De fabrica* seeks to re-create this performative experience for the reader by continually repeating Galen's invitation to his readers to try this for themselves. The original *De fabrica* would probably have been too large and expensive to serve as a manual that a student of anatomy could consult in the course of conducting a dissection, yet Vesalius clearly assumes that his readers are using the book for the practical study of dissection. Furthermore, the *Epitome* of the work published in the same year allows the owner to perform a kind of paper dissection by cutting and pasting woodcuts of organs on a figure.[15] In other words, while Vesalius criticizes Galen for his mistakes in using animals for his research, he nevertheless adopts his predecessor's rhetorical device of offering the animal or human cadaver as proof of his argument.

This rhetorical practice also characterizes *De fabrica*'s final chapter, on vivisection. Nearly all of the work focuses on human anatomy, and it is divided into seven books on different topics related to the various categories of anatomy (ligaments and muscles, veins and arteries, the brain, etc.). A closing chapter titled "Some Remarks on Vivisection" appears as a coda to the seventh book, on the brain, and seems an odd conclusion to the entire work. The chapter contains some generalized remarks on vivisection along with gruesomely practical advice on when it might be useful to the student of anatomy and physiology. Vesalius maintains the book's focus on dissection, and he insists that students master dissection before they move on to working with live animals, "for there is no point in trying vivisection unless one is a skilled dissector of the dead." He does admit, though, that vivisection can be especially useful for the study of what would come to be called "physiology," the "action and function of parts" in a living animal.[16] The relationship between vivisection and physiological demonstration means that the animals under Vesalius's knife take on a more active role in several of the procedures that he describes in this chapter.

The chapter on vivisection is divided into subsections that follow the overarching order of *De fabrica* to show the student of anatomy which areas of knowledge are best served by vivisection. For example, Vesalius does not encourage readers to conduct vivisections in order to learn about the bones and ligaments, since these are "apparent even in dead animals" (263). The subsection "Examining the Heart and the Parts That Serve It" is the most developed portion of this chapter, since observing the function of the heart, lungs, veins, and arteries is much more difficult in a dead body. Vesalius specifically states that these vivisections are "done as part of the more drastic vivisection that I normally present in schools" (269), meaning that they were often conducted in an educational context with an audience of students. A passage describing the procedure gives a sense of the hands-on role of the anatomist in the performance and his ambiguous connection to animal performance:

> In order to see the natural movement of the lung as it follows the thorax, cut away the cartilages of two or three middle ribs on one side, make incisions along the intervals between these ribs, and break off each rib by bending it outward. This makes an area through which you can inspect the lung on the undamaged side; for the membranes that partition the thorax in dogs are quite transparent and it is easy to examine through them the part of the lung that is still following the movement of the thorax and, after piercing carefully through the membranes, to see how this part of the lung as well ceases to move. . . . In addition, as you perform this operation it is a good idea to grasp the base of the heart and quickly tie off with a single tie all the vessels that come forth from it, then cut away the heart below the tie, undo the bonds that are holding the animal down, and allow it to run; we have seen dogs treated in this way run for some distance, and cats even further. (268–69)

This passage highlights the various kinds of manual dexterity an anatomist needed, from the brutal action of breaking away the ribs of a living animal to the delicate piercing of just the right number of membranes to observe the functioning organs without damaging them. The ability to follow a procedure like the one outlined here would prove the virtuosity of the anatomist and earn him the admiration of his audience. This description's focus on the skills of the anatomist is interrupted by the image of the dog (or cat) who has, until now, been restrained on a board, leaving no record of her experience of these events apart from manifesting the truth of the body. Vesalius's suggestion that the anatomist loosen the ties holding down the object of his experiment, usually a dog, introduces a trace of the animal's experience into the scenario. The image of this creature, who has had her ribs cracked away to reveal her still-beating heart and breathing lung, suddenly breaking away at a run until she finally dies is, as the translator John Carman puts it, "somewhat alarming . . . to present day eyes at least" (ix). The animal's performance in this scenario is unclear, since Vesalius does not explain exactly what her instinct to run at this point demonstrates beyond, perhaps, the heart's impressive capacity to keep an animal alive even under excruciating duress.

Vesalius's narrative maintains a noticeable distance from the experience of the animal at the center of this cardiovascular demonstration. His indifference makes it all the more surprising that he hints at his own—possibly heretical—belief in the similarity of human and animal cognition in the very next section on the brain:

In examining the brain and its parts there is nothing to be gained by vivisection, since here, whether we like it or not, we are required by theologians of our own day to deny that dumb animals have memory, reason, or thought, even though the construction of their brain is the same as that of the human one. Hence the anatomy student who is versed in dissection of the dead and not infected by any heresy will understand what a mess I should find myself in if I were to say anything about the vivisection of the brain, much as I should like to do so. (269–70)

Vesalius's refusal to engage in (or at least to publish) a discussion of comparative anatomy in his study of the brain is a tantalizing omission. His address to "the anatomy student who is versed in dissection of the dead" implies that he is speaking elliptically to an insider audience of other researchers who know very well that the brains of humans and animals are remarkably similar, despite religious doctrine's insistence on the strict boundary between them.[17] Vesalius's use of preterition here calls attention to the incongruity between the dogmatic insistence that memory, reason, and thought are exclusive to humans and the obvious similarity between the structure of human and animal brains. Just a few lines after his description of the dog or cat running in panic and horrific pain from the vivisection table, her thoracic cavity split open to reveal her heart and lungs, Vesalius seems to suggest that animals might be capable of many of the same experiences as humans. Of course, this does not stop the voracious researcher from pursuing his project, and it is important to recall that dissecting cadavers would also have required the kind of distance that Vesalius displays in his chapter on vivisection. The passage on the brain nevertheless hints at an early modern sensibility about the experience of animals that may have been shared by other authors similarly hesitant to risk offending the church.[18]

Vivisection from Padua to England

The period between Vesalius's *De fabrica* and William Harvey's discovery of the circulation of the blood witnessed the development of a pedagogical model in Padua that made regular use of dissection and animal vivisection. As Cynthia Klestinec has argued, the late sixteenth and early seventeenth centuries tend to be overlooked in the history of anatomical study, even though this was a seminal period for establishing the use of anatomy as a pedagogical tool. When Harvey arrived at Padua in 1600, he encountered a learning environment that encouraged students to gain hands-on experience in surgery and dissection. Vesalius's successor was his former pupil Realdo Colombo, a teacher who prioritized the close and intimate inspection of the body undergoing study. He made ample use of both vivisection and anatomical dissections conducted before a small audience of students. These intimate anatomical demonstrations, which focused on teaching, differed from demonstrations like the one featured on the title page of *De fabrica*. Such large performances were public and civic events where politicians (rather than students) tended to sit closest to the cadaver.[19]

Colombo's accounts of vivisection seem to suggest at least some attention to the experience of the suffering animal in these anatomical demonstrations. His major anatomical publication, *De re anatomica*, memorably describes the vivisection of a pregnant dog. Colombo observes that the dog reacts angrily when he harms her puppy, which he has just pulled from her womb, and that she licks the puppy tenderly while snapping at anything else put in front of her. In this account, a group of clergymen praise the canine mother's caring instincts and relate the actions of the dog to those of the Virgin Mary. As Maehle and Tröhler point out, this seems to contradict the church's strict division between human and animal cognition. They also specify that Colombo sometimes referred to the dog as "the poor dog," or "the unhappy dog," only to correct himself by calling the dog happy for her role in providing new insights and discoveries about the body.[20] In Colombo's performances, the suffering animal appears with more clarity than we have seen up until this point, but Colombo is careful to channel that suffering into the anthropocentric goals of anatomical demonstration. Whether the animal is demonstrating the divinely blessed inclination toward maternal affection or affording the researcher a new step in his path to discovering the secrets of the body, animals perform in the service of the philosophical and scientific goals of their human dissectors. The animal experience persists only in the narratives left by these researchers, and so animal performance is made to fit with those rhetorical ends.

William Harvey, the English doctor and researcher who is most famous for his work on the circulatory system, studied medicine at Padua under Girolamo Fabrici, who was responsible for helping to found the first permanent anatomical theater in Padua. Harvey learned a great deal from Fabrici, particularly the refined techniques necessary to successful anatomy. And while Fabrici was not himself a notable practitioner of vivisection, he did believe in comparative anatomy, the importance of studying animals in order to learn more about humans.[21]

Harvey's devotion to comparative anatomy and his frequent use of vivisection stand out in his work on circulation. While the demonstrations described above featured the bodies of large animals, like dogs, cats, and pigs, Harvey's studies of circulation explored a much wider array of creatures, thanks to the recent introduction of the microscope: "I have likewise observ'd, that there is really a heart in all animals, and not only (as *Aristotle* says) in the greater sort, and such as have blood, but likewise in lesser, and such as have none, as those that are crusted without, or have shels [*sic*], as house-*Snails, Crabfish, Crevises, Shrimps*, and in many others, nay in *Wasps, Hornets*, and in *Gnats* by an optick glass made for the discovery of the least things, in the upper end of that place which is called their tail, I saw the *heart* beat & shewed it to others."[22] Harvey's interest in crustaceans and insects introduces another kind of animal performance in which the creatures that had hitherto been unavailable to study because of their small size are suddenly made visible to the human eye. This perspectival shift brings the problem of animal experience into an entirely new realm. If Vesalius was nervous about admitting that human and animal brains are similar, what did it mean that Harvey could prove something about the human heart by looking at gnats and shrimp? These new reaches of comparative anatomy made it more difficult to describe human experience as radically different from animal experience.

Harvey's use of comparative anatomy drew the human into closer proximity to a wider variety of animals, even as he more drastically removed the animal's experience from his accounts of vivisection. For example, Harvey did not specify what animal should be used for the vivisection that shows the motion of the heart, but he went into great detail about what the heart of a dying animal revealed:

> So the *heart* first leaves beating, before the *ears*, so that the *ears* are said to out-live it: the *left ventricle* leaves beating first of all, then its *ear*, then the *right ventricle*, last of all (which *Galen* observs [*sic*]) all the rest giving off and dying, the *right ear* beats still: so that life seems to remain last of all in the right. And whilst by little and little the *heart* is dying, you may see after two or three beatings of the *ear*, the *heart* will, being as it were rowsed, answer, and very slowly and hardly endeavor and frame a motion. But this is chiefly to be observed, that after the *heart* has left beating, and the *ears* are beating still, putting your finger upon the *ventricle* of the *heart*; every pulsation in perceived in the *ventricles*, just after the

same manner as wee said the pulsations of the *ventricles* were felt in the *Arteries*, a distension being made by impulsion of blood.[23]

The experience of this unspecified animal is almost completely imperceptible in Harvey's focus on the heart as an organ that seems isolated from the body that houses it. The heart's capacity to demonstrate animation perceptible to the anatomist's touch even as the creature's life slips away almost makes the organ appear capable of performance independent of the animal.

Distancing the Dissector

Harvey was a private man wary of the controversy generated by his publication on the circulation of the blood, but his attention to experiment led the more public and performance-minded founders of the Royal Society to adopt him as a kind of figurehead for their philosophical project.[24] In the dedicatory epistle to the Royal College of Physicians that opens his 1628 publication of the *Exercitatio Anatomica de Motu Cordis*, Harvey discusses the importance of proving his conclusions through experiments performed before a community of peers. While the presence of an audience had also been important to the anatomical studies of sixteenth-century Italy, the theatrical setting in Padua was pedagogical, featuring an instructor lecturing to students or performing for a wider audience of nonexperts. In Harvey's work, peers who were intellectual equals had to corroborate new ideas. When the Royal Society formed in the 1660s, they drew on Harvey's model, retroactively reading his work as Baconian.[25]

The Royal Society's motto, *nullius in verba* (take no one's word for it), emphasizes the importance of firsthand, eyewitness knowledge. Animal performance plays a key role in the formation of this kind of knowledge. For example, in an article published in the Royal Society proceedings in 1666, Richard Lower explained an experiment to test the role of the diaphragm in the process of respiration. He described his technique for severing the nerves that control the diaphragm of a dog and how this made the "Dog *draw his breath exactly like a* Wind-broken Horse."[26] He compared the dog's reaction to the severed diaphragm nerves to a pulmonary disease that afflicts horses and is characterized by laborious breathing. The article specified that Lower had already attempted the experiment in private before performing it for the Royal Society. What is interesting about this case, and about the structure of the Royal Society more broadly, is that Lower's private experiment is not sufficient. It must be tried in private, tested (often multiple times) for an audience of peers, and only then published. On certain occasions, the audience would have extended beyond Royal Society members, as special guests were frequently invited to experimental demonstrations. In this way, even a relatively minor experiment such as Lower's would have met with a sizeable audience, and the performance of his dogs in each repetition of the experiment made up a necessary component in the Royal Society's conception of what qualified as legitimate knowledge. In other words, members of this august group would have witnessed the suffering animal multiple times and in a variety of experiments. Laurie Shannon, borrowing a term from Thomas Browne, describes this phenomenon in performative terms as "disanimation," in which "the traumas of vivisection and the vacuum tube take place as theatrical spectacles with routinized scripts."[27] The Royal Society valued a Baconian insistence on the importance of a community of witnesses in order to establish scientific truth, and this communal structure lends itself to the performative model of a theatrical space. The noise and mess that these experiments would have created, and the interest and curiosity that their spectators would have felt, sit somewhat uncomfortably with the distanced accounts that appear in the *Philosophical Transactions of the Royal Society*, which leave little trace of the suffering animal body at the center of these spectacles.

Repetition makes up an important element in each of these instances of animal experimentation, from Galen's performances for his mixed audience of supporters and skeptics, to the pedagogical goals of Paduan anatomy, to the notion of scientific proof among peers of the Royal Society. In each instance, the animal body seems to be at the center of attention, but the real focus is typically on the reputation and status of the researcher conducting the performative experiment. The vivisected animal whose squeals are silenced, whose heart slowly loses its capacity to beat, and whose breathing becomes permanently labored, is often overlooked or obscured in the celebratory tone of these historical records.

Joseph Wright of Derby's painting *An Experiment on a Bird in the Air Pump* (1768) illustrates an eventual shift in this dynamic (fig. 6.3). Wright represents the air pump that Royal Society member Robert Boyle invented to prove the existence of a vacuum. The pump was used on numerous occasions to demonstrate that a bird, a puppy, or some similarly small creature would perish if deprived of air. This experimental demonstration continued well beyond the number of times that it might have been necessary to prove this fact, in part because of the dark fascination that it held. Wright's painting captures the air pump's disquieting appeal as it relocates the experiment from the institutionally sanctioned chambers of the Royal Society to a private household. The man who controls the air pump looks more like an itinerant charlatan than a reputable scientist, and his audience is a well-to-do family. Each figure shows a different level of curiosity or disinterest, from the young man in the foreground, gazing with rapt attention at the demonstration, to the lovers at the left, more fascinated by each other than by the spectacle. Only the young girls show clear signs of concern. As the most illuminated figures in the painting, these two distressed daughters stand out, and they are decidedly worried about the fate of the bird. The

6.3   Joseph Wright of Derby, *An Experiment on a Bird in the Air Pump*, 1768. Engraved by Valentine Green. Mezzotint (first state). Victoria and Albert Museum, London, 29445:1.

written reports of vivisection and dissection leave only the most fleeting traces of the animals who suffered for the sake of performative pedagogy and physiological research, but Wright's painting suggests that sharing animal experimentation with a broader audience may be what eventually led, in the eighteenth century, to the beginnings of a movement to protect the rights of the animals who are made to perform in the service of scientific discovery.

NOTES

1. Galen, *On the Natural Faculties*, 49, 51.
2. Ibid., 59.
3. Ibid., 61.
4. Liddell and Scott, *Greek-English Lexicon,* s.v. "basanizō."
5. Philostratus, *Vita Apollonii,* in *Flavi Philostrati Opera,* 1:38. The Pythagoreans practiced vegetarianism and were opposed to all killing.
6. In his article "Galen and the Squealing Pig," Gross gives an overview of this demonstration and shows that Galen's experiment may have been the first proof that the brain controls movement and thought.
7. On the one hand, it is important not to overstate this point. As Katharine Park has convincingly argued in *Secrets of Women*, bodies (especially women's bodies) were opened and examined in the medieval period. However, there was a notable turn to a more experimental model that resembles Galen's methods in the Renaissance. Nancy Siraisi's *Medieval and Early Renaissance Medicine* gives an overview of this transitional period (78–114), and Andrea Carlino's *Books of the Body* describes the history of Galen's influence and attempts to explain why it took anatomists nearly two centuries of direct observation to begin to discover his errors (3).
8. See Roger French on the renewed interest in anatomical study and also vivisection in the Renaissance. See also Wear, French, and Lonie, *Medical Renaissance*. On the revived interest in vivisection, see Shotwell, "Revival of Vivisection."
9. R. J. Durling's bibliographical work on the Galenic corpus in the Renaissance is the authority on this matter. See also Clara Domingues's doctoral dissertation on the same subject.
10. See Remmert, "'Docet parva pictura,'" on frontispieces in early modern scientific publication. More generally, see Smith and Wilson, *Renaissance Paratexts.*
11. Karen Raber, in *Animal Bodies, Renaissance Culture*, discusses the tendency to relegate animal studies to a prehistory of veterinary medicine despite the fact that animal anatomies were widespread and fundamental to anatomical histories (32). Shannon, in "Invisible Parts," also addresses the focus on histories of human anatomy.
12. Vesalius, *On the Fabric of the Human Body,* book I, lii–liv.
13. Andrew Cunningham's *Anatomical Renaissance* shows that early moderns who claimed to reject the errors of the ancients were at the same time deeply influenced by, and hoped to revive, the ancient study of dissection. It is important not to overstate Vesalius's critique of Galen, since he also saw himself as perfecting a technique begun by his ancient predecessor.
14. As Cynthia Klestinec has argued in *Theaters of Anatomy*, the visual model was only part of the theatrical feel in early modern anatomical demonstrations. Music and the auditory experience of hearing a lecture were perhaps even more fundamental than the visual experience. All of these would have combined to create a theatrical effect for the audience.
15. The *Epitome* is discussed in O'Malley, *Andreas Vesalius of Brussels*, 183. The Cambridge Digital Library has digitized their extraordinary copy of this book in the Treasures of the Library collection, and it is accompanied by an informative annotation by Sachiko Kusukawa, available at https://cudl.lib.cam.ac.uk/view/PR-CCF-00046 -00036/1. This digitized edition includes images of the *Epitome*'s paper dissection (images 39–49).
16. Vesalius, *Fabric of the Human Body,* books VI and VII, 265, 263 (hereafter cited parenthetically in the text). The term "physiology" was coined by Jean Fernel in his *Universa Medicina.*
17. Jessica Wolfe's chapter in this volume offers a more extended discussion of the complex natural philosophical questions that surround the classification of nonhuman entities, specifically insects.
18. In his "Apologie de Raimond Sebond" (in the second book of the *Essais*), the essayist and philosopher Michel de Montaigne was bold enough to imagine animal experience and postulate the possibility that animals experience cognition. Laurie Shannon offers a reading of Montaigne's essay in *Accommodated Animal.*
19. Klestinec, *Theaters of Anatomy*, 10, 41, 14. See also Cunningham, *Anatomical Renaissance.*
20. Maehle and Tröhler, "Animal Experimentation," 18, 19. The demonstration is described in Colombo, *De re anatomica*, 256–59.
21. As Klestinec points out, Fabrici did not perform vivisections as frequently as Colombo and Harvey did, and he even aroused the ire of his students one year by omitting the typical and popular vivisection at the end of an anatomical demonstration. Klestinec, "Medical Education in Padua," 218, and *Theaters of Anatomy*, 79.
22. Harvey, *Anatomical Exercises*, 18.
23. Ibid., 14.
24. On Harvey's concerns about the controversy generated by his work, see George Ent's preface to Harvey, *Anatomical exercitations*. On the use of Harvey as a figurehead for the Royal Society, see Thomas Sprat's *History of the Royal Society.*
25. Roger French has shown convincingly that Harvey was not a Baconian but was shaped instead

by his education in Padua and the influence of Aristotelianism there. This did not prevent the founders of the Royal Society, especially according to Thomas Sprat's account of that body, from identifying Harvey with the new approach to natural philosophy they adopted based on Baconian philosophy. French, *William Harvey's Natural Philosophy*.

26. Lower, "Making a Dog draw his Breath," 544.

27. Shannon, *Accommodated Animal*, 21. Shannon's term recalls Cartesian mechanism, which was gaining philosophical ground in England at this time, as Marjorie Nicolson shows in "Early Stage of Cartesianism." Cartesian comparative anatomy, however, was meant to highlight the divide between humans and animals. See, for example, Descartes, *Discourse on the Method*, 141.

7

CIRCUS MINIMUS

The Early Modern Theater of Insects

JESSICA WOLFE

In 1579, according to the eyewitness reports of John Stow and Raphael Holinshed, one Mark Scaliot, a London blacksmith, crafted a miniature lock, key, and gold chain of forty-three links, "to the which chaine the locke and keie being fastened, and put about the fleas necke, she drew the same with ease."[1] Accounts of the spectacle, drawn from Stow and Holinshed, continued to circulate for more than a century, and Scaliot's performance is still cited in both popular and scholarly histories as a prototype for the flea circuses that cropped up across Europe and America during the later eighteenth and nineteenth centuries, in which meticulously trained fleas pulled chaises and hearses, staged reenactments of duels and naval battles, donned historical costumes, and—at the Tivoli (Copenhagen) flea circus of William and John Torp, which closed only in 1974—rode tricycles.[2]

This chapter does not provide a genealogy of the flea circus from Elizabethan England down to the fairs and pleasure gardens of Victorian London and Coney Island, itself a worthwhile and fascinating subject. Instead, I investigate the philosophical roots and branches of Scaliot's flea circus, as distinct from later manifestations of the phenomenon, in light of the precarious and contested place accorded to insects in early modern natural philosophy, and in light of the related early modern conception of insects as peculiarly *theatrical* creatures, performers who enact "liveliness" or "life-likeness," even though, or perhaps precisely *because*, they are not habitually imagined to be fully alive.[3] Like Todd Borlik's work in this volume, this chapter is interested in the theatrical sensibilities of early modern insects, but whereas Borlik interprets the imagined affinities between insects and fairies, with the shared challenges they pose to notions of scale and their joint capacity to interrogate "who, or rather what, counts as an actor," I instead focus on the communal and reciprocal relationship between insect and machine bodies whose intersections, keenly investigated by seventeenth-century natural philosophers, have reemerged as a focal point of posthumanist scholarship that studies the cross-fertilization between the supposedly living and the supposedly nonliving: the "becoming animal of technology" and the "becoming technical of the insect."[4]

At least in the imagination of those who first documented it, Scaliot's performance showcase the blacksmith's fine metalworking skills more than the physical prowess or tractability of his insect crew. And as writers churned out description after description of Scaliot's impressive ability to craft a chain, lock, and key that (along with the attached flea) together weighed "but a graine and a halfe," their accounts situated the spectacle neatly in a genre passed down to Renaissance culture from Pliny, namely, the catalogue of *miniatura*—tiny carvings of ivory ants, a chariot so small that a fly might cover it with her wings, chains made of glass, poems carved into cherry stones, and even a new form of shorthand invented by the calligrapher Peter Bales—that pays tribute to the artist's subtle skill as well as to the acute eyesight of the audience.[5]

In the seventeenth-century catalogues and "technematophylacia" (collections or repositories of technical knowledge) in which accounts of Scaliot's flea circus appear, many of the miniature objects lauded for their intricacy are insects, or rather objects crafted to resemble insects: Scaliot's account of a flea "with a golden chain about her neck" and kept in a dainty box; the uncannily lifelike iron spider described by Joannes Walchius, "exactly made to the form and proportion of a Spider, and . . . made to imitate his motions"; and above all Regiomontanus's iron fly, a tiny airborne automaton crafted by a late fifteenth-century German mathematician and immortalized a century later by Du Bartas:

> O divine wit! that in the narrow womb
> Of a small Flie, could finde sufficient room
> For all those Springs, wheels, counterpoiz, and chains,
> Which stood in stead of life, and spur, and rains.[6]

Each of these spectacles features a puzzlingly hybrid actor whose motions confound a key rung of the scale of nature—the one demarcating the lowest of animal forms from what lies beneath—and thus muddies the contested and shifting boundary between living and nonliving, not simply by combining trained animals with mechanical spectacle, but also by featuring creatures that are in themselves equivocal. If insects are performed, theatrically, by miniature machines in early modern culture, it is because insects themselves are imagined to *be* machines, or at least to be *like* machines, contraptions that merely *seem* to be alive, or that might *come* alive, or that hover, much like the puppets, automata, and speaking statues that populate the Renaissance stage, in some indeterminate middle ground between aliveness and not-aliveness: "machinists," to cite Jakob von Uexküll's distinction, if not in fact machines.[7]

Scaliot's *circus minimus* is no exception, in part because we cannot be entirely certain—any more than modern audiences were able to determine that the performing fleas at Tivoli were real and not mechanical—that Scaliot's fleas aren't likewise the product of the blacksmith's art, made of iron and not living walls of jet. That uncertainty is exacerbated when we place Elizabethan descriptions of Scaliot's flea circus alongside the only other contemporary account I have found of such a spectacle, Thomas Moffett's description of a flea circus staged in 1586 by Gawen Smith, an engineer and inventor known principally for his failed projections to erect a lighthouse on Goodwin Sands and to invent a boat that would travel from Dover to Calais and back within twenty-four hours.[8] Including his account in a descriptive catalogue of objects that illustrates how "little caskets hold our richest goods" and "greatest worths in smallest things appeare," Moffett praises Smith's flea circus as a feat of artistic verisimilitude, wedging his description of it between the miniature iron castings made by the ancient sculptor Theodorus and the iron fly crafted by the "Ingenious Germane" Regiomontanus:

Nay, for to speake of things more late and rife,
Who will not more admire those famous Fleas,
Made so by art, that art imparted life,
Making them skippe, and on mens hands to seaze,
And let out bloud with taper-poynted knife,
Which from a secret sheat he ranne out with ease.
The[n] those great coches which the[m]selves did drive,
With bended scrues, like things that were alive?[9]

What Moffett is describing is not a living flea circus at all, but rather a mechanical spectacle crafted with the same kinds of "springs" and "scrues" and "rowells" employed by Regiomontanus—or, to invoke a more present-day analogue, Mattel, Inc.'s 1965 "Flea Circus: The Magnetic Action Game You Itch to Play," in which the "fleas" are in fact tiny magnets. To further enhance the verisimilitude of his mechanical fleas, Smith appears to have incorporated into the spectacle a common Renaissance stage trick, in which fake blood was hidden in a sheath, bladder, or the empty hilt of a knife and then released at the opportune moment to simulate a gory wound or amputation.[10]

Returning to Scaliot's flea circus, we confront the problem that it is not at all clear where the blacksmith's art ends and the equally intricate artistry of nature begins. The apposition of Scaliot's tiny locks and chains to the equally miniscule flea attached to them creates a kind of *paragone* between art and nature as each competes with the other to fashion the most minute and complex artifacts while simultaneously confirming the Aristotelian maxim (here paraphrased by Francis Bacon) that "*the nature of every thing is best seene in his smallest portions.*"[11] This refrain, when echoed by Moffett,

Wilkins, and Powell in their catalogues of natural and artificial *miniatura*, places insects and machines in a peculiarly intimate relation to each other, highlighting an analogical rapport also on display in Scaliot's and Smith's flea circuses, which despite the rather different status of their insect actors—the former probably living fleas and the latter almost certainly not—dramatizes a kinship between insect and machine that is rooted in some fundamental anatomical and ontological questions about the status of insects. These questions would emerge, over the course of the seventeenth century, to occupy center stage through the lens of the microscope.

One dimension of the perceived kinship between machines and insects, and especially the flea, resides in their shared amplification of power or force. The feat performed by Scaliot's fleas—pulling objects far heavier than the insects themselves—showcases skills of physical prowess distinctive to fleas, namely, their extraordinary jumping and pulling power. A flea can pull seven hundred times its own weight; it can jump seven inches into the air and up to thirteen inches horizontally. The human equivalents, for a six-foot-tall person, would be 160 and 295 feet, respectively. Inasmuch as machines were largely understood during the Renaissance, following Vitruvius's definition, to be assemblages of wooden or metal parts "chiefly efficacious in moving great weights" and thus in augmenting the limited powers of the human body, the flea's superhuman powers can help fashion the creature into a kind of living machine, one whose strength might enhance or supplement the human hand in a manner similar to a pulley or lever.[12] In his own account of Scaliot's flea circus, Moffett highlights the aspect of the spectacle that brings it closest to the circus strongman shows of the nineteenth century, reporting that "this Flea so tied with a Chain, did draw a Coach of Gold that was every way perfect, and that very lightly; which much sets forth the Artists skill, and the Fleas strength."[13] For Moffett, Scaliot's strongman flea embodies all the topsy-turvy promise that the "weak things of the world" will "confound the things which are mighty," thus explaining why, in *Silkewormes and Their Flies*, his catalogue of admirably detailed or skilled small creatures and devices shifts registers, turning to a consideration of how David, that "little shepeard with a pibble stone," somehow managed to defeat the "huge and mighty" Goliath.[14]

Moffett's account of Scaliot's flea circus in turn shapes some of the earliest and most formative descriptions of actual fleas, creatures whose anatomical features are explained by comparison with their mechanical replicas. Henry Power, whose microscopic observations of insect bodies were printed in 1664, one year before the first publication of Hooke's *Micrographia*, begins his first observation by depicting the natural armament of the flea, weaponized by nature "thus *Cap-a-pe* like a Cuirazier in warr," but quickly shifts to a recapitulation of Moffett's report of the flea circus, pairing it with a firsthand recollection of a similar spectacle involving flea-drawn chariots at "Tredescants famous recondiroty of Novelties," and then returning to a consideration of the flea's marvelous strength: "so great is the mechanick power which Providence has immur'd within these living walls of Jet."[15]

Yet when seventeenth-century microscopists such as Power and Hooke compared insects to "Watches," "curious Engines," and "little Automatons," they did so not simply to underscore the sophisticated and intricate anatomical design of creatures capable of lifting and pulling objects that far exceed their own body weight, but also to draw attention to the ways in which the structure and operation of insect bodies threw into uncertainty the natural philosopher's capacity to distinguish between living and nonliving bodies.[16] The kinds of experiments that Hooke, Power, and others conducted upon insects with their microscopes opened up for serious scientific investigation questions previously relegated to the more playful arena of Scaliot's flea circus or sixteenth-century curiosity cabinets, which displayed illusionistic wire insects as well as *Schüttelkasten*, or shaking sieves, boxes containing papier-mâché models of beetles and other insects that blended into the soil at the bottom until the box was agitated and the bugs would suddenly seem to come to life, twitching and shaking somewhat like the Mexican jumping beans of my 1970s youth, and seedpods inhabited by the larva of a small moth that twitches when warmed by the hand.[17] Like automata, as Horst Bredekamp has argued, the lifelike replicas of "lesser living creatures" in the Renaissance *Kunstkammer* dramatized the "transition from an inert natural material to an animated body" and vice versa, in the process probing and shifting the relationship between animate and inanimate.[18] The insects perched on the tabletops, dishes, and flower petals of late sixteenth- and seventeenth-century still lifes and cabinet paintings perform a similar function, poised for imminent flight or looking as though they have just alighted, their potentiality for motion signaled by the delicacy of their wings or the lightness of their bodies.

Let us turn now to a second set of implications implicit in this early modern habit of analogically yoking together insects and machines. In his *Religio Medici* (1643), Thomas Browne rejoices in the beauty and order of nature by praising the finger of God as a master of the *multum in parvo*: "Ruder heads stand amazed at those prodigious pieces of nature, whales, elephants, dromedaries, and camels; these, I confess, are the colossuses and majestick pieces of her hand; but in these narrow engines there is more curious mathematicks; and the civility of these little citizens more neatly sets forth the wisdom of their Maker. Who admires not Regio Montanus his iron fly beyond his eagle; or wonders not more at the operation of two souls in those little bodies than but one in the trunk of a cedar?"[19] Echoing Du Bartas, whose *Semaines* would later provide a template for the *Pseudodoxia Epidemica*, a sort of hexameral epic in prose, Browne also replicates Moffett's unfavorable comparison between "Neroes Colossus five score cubits high" and the tiny horse-drawn chariot constructed by Theodorus, the latter deemed more impressive for its capacity to achieve such verisimilitude on a very small scale: "So liuely made, that one might see them all / Yet was the whole worke than a flie more small."[20] What is even more striking about Browne's anthem to insects in the *Religio*, however, is its odd slippage from *actual* insects, implicitly compared to "engines" on account of their equally diminutive and complex structures, to mechanical insects (Regiomontanus's iron fly), and then back again, the passage ending with a consideration of how nature manages to squeeze two souls (rational and sensitive) inside the tiny body of an ant or fly.

Browne's blurring of insect and machine has two effects: it illustrates the potency of his metaphor comparing insects to "narrow engines" as more than just a similitude, and it dramatizes, through that powerful metaphor, a key question regarding the status of insects that would continue to vex Browne throughout his career as a naturalist while also shaping contemporary representations of insects by early microscopists such as Hooke and Henry Power. Although the *Religio* offers up a rather tidy metaphysical distinction between plants and insects—the former have only one soul (the vegetative) while the latter have two—Browne knew all too well that this distinction did not stand up to the evidence offered by Aristotle, whose *De anima* repeatedly mentions the problem that some plants, as well as some insects, "go on living when divided into segments," as a means of calling into question aspects of Plato's theory of the tripartite soul.[21]

For Browne, a naturalist eager to classify the order of nature but also a lay theologian who loved to lose himself in the "wingy mysteries" of faith, Aristotle's observation presented a double challenge.[22] It illustrated that insects may be closer to plants than they are to animals, a dilemma solved for some seventeenth-century naturalists by the intermediate category of zoophytes, or plant-animals. It also suggested that a single insect, because it may be bisected and continue living in two discrete parts, might not have a sensitive soul after all, and indeed might not be an individual or (to use the preferred Scholastic term) a *suppositum*—an individuated substance complete in its species, or with complete *quidditas*—in the same way that a person or a dog is.

In the *Pseudodoxia Epidemica*, Browne addressed this problem through an arrangement of material that made the status of insects ambiguous, or demonstrated their resistance to normative classification schemes. In an otherwise rather sensibly organized work that plots the scale of nature upward from "Minerall and Vegetable bodies" (book 2), to animals (book 3), human nature (book 4, the amphibious middle of the text), human art (book 5), geography and cosmography (book 6), and finally religion and the supernatural (book 7), insects are the one set of creatures who don't seem to fit in any fixed place. Browne placed his observations on insects in three separate chapters of two different books: the final chapter of book 2 (*PE* 2.7), which over the course of four successive revisions between 1650 and 1672 folded in material from what was originally contained in the previous chapter to create a rather miscellaneous chapter ultimately titled "Of some Insects, and the properties of severall plants," and *PE* 3.27 and 3.28, both a hodgepodge of observations about various kinds of insects mixed in with discussions of storks and pelicans, chicken eggs, the torpedo fish, and the vegetable lamb of Tartary, and both heavily revised by Browne in 1650, 1658, and 1672. By scattering material on insects across two books devoted, respectively, to minerals and plants and to animals, by repeatedly revising and rearranging the material in those chapters, and by giving them titles—*PE* 3.28 is simply called "Of some others"—Browne tacitly acknowledged that when it comes to insects, the categories established by the structure of the *Pseudodoxia* are inadequate and must be forsaken. One of the insects under investigation in the *Pseudodoxia*, the dead-watch, makes a "little clicking sound," and its eerily mechanical noise is the cause of "terrifying apprehensions" among the superstitious.[23]

That insects throw philosophical questions about individuation and aliveness into disarray only strengthened their kinship with machines for seventeenth-century naturalists and philosophers, since both kinds of bodies and the motions performed by them challenge Platonic and Aristotelian definitions of life as self-motion, the principle that to move oneself immediately, and as the principal cause of one's own motion, is the proper office of life.[24] Either repudiating or misinterpreting the traditional definition of *intrinsecus motus* from Aristotle's *Physics* and its commentary tradition, René Descartes redefined the concept of self-motion in order to posit that all animal bodies are a mechanism or assemblage of parts whose internal motions—digestion, respiration, nourishment—are no different from those of automata, since "these functions follow from the mere arrangements of the machine's organs every bit as naturally as the *mouvements* of a clock or other automaton follow from the arrangements of its counterweights and wheels," neither of them prompted by vegetative or sensitive soul, but rather, according to Descartes, by the "mere disposition of the organs" and by a heat that agitates corpuscles, setting them into self-propelled motion.[25]

Early opponents of Descartes's physics and metaphysics were especially alarmed at the way in which his doctrines turned "sensible Creatures" into "Artificial Engins," devaluing or effacing the characteristics that might distinguish inert objects and plants from animals. Some of them pushed back against the Cartesian analogy between animal and machine by invoking Vitruvius's distinction between two kinds of machine, the οργανον (engine or prime mover) and the μηχανη (machine), the latter moved not by its own accord but by a prime mover. In his *Primitive origination of mankind* (1677), Matthew Hale accepted the Cartesian position, arguing that "Animal Nature is like an Engin that hath a greater composition of Wheels, and more variety of Wheels" than "Vegetable Nature," which he likened to a "curious Engin" that "hath but some simple and single motions, like a Watch that gives the hour of the day." Yet Hale also, a paragraph later, protested against

> that Opinion that depresseth the natures of sensible Creatures below their just value and estimate, rendring them no more but barely Mechanisms or Artificial

Engins; such as were *Archytas* his Dove, *Regiomontanus* his wooden Eagle, or *Walchius* his iron Spider: that they have no vital Principle of all their various Motions but the meer modifications of Matter . . . no other form or internal principle of Life, Motion, and Sense but that which is relative and results from the disposition, texture, organization and composition of their several Limbs, Members, or Organs.[26]

For Hale, engineers who crafted automata in the form of insects were somehow complicit in the reclassification of insects *as* automata, as if the rendering of a living creature in the form of a machine—precisely what Smith's 1586 spectacle did with its mechanical fleas—set into motion an analogical logic that slid all too easily from the witty figuration of a stage trick to the literalness of a philosophical truth. Kenelm Digby, one of Descartes's earliest English readers and one especially eager to reconcile Cartesian mechanism, with its eradication of the vital or organic functions of the soul, with atomism, Aristotelianism, and an eclectically Catholic metaphysics worked out a similar distinction in his 1644 *Two Treatises*, which provides an extended contrast between two kinds of machine—one a device that raises up water from the Tagus River to the palace at the top of Toledo, and the other the mint at Segovia, a kind of assembly line in which each stage is a "distinct complete engine" yet also "a serving part of the whole"—in order to illustrate the distinction between two different kinds of living bodies, those that possess "one continuate substance" and those whose parts are "notably seperated one from the other" and then "artificially tyed together." While plants, according to Digby, resembled the hydraulic device invented in the mid-sixteenth century by Juan Turriano in Toledo, all its parts working continually in unison, "sensible living creatures" conformed to the model of Segovia's Casa de la Moneda, designed in the 1580s by Juan de Herrera under the direction of King Philip II.[27]

While the microscope reveals that insects belong, anatomically, to Digby's latter category, revealing to the human eye an intricately interconnected assemblage of tiny parts, it also lays bare the machinelike structures and operations of insects in a manner that exacerbates, rather than resolving, the question of whether insects are alive at all. In the previous chapter in this volume, Sarah Parker demonstrates that the presence of blood during early modern vivisections was linked to sentience and the capacity to feel pain, and insects provide an especially vivid illustration of this theater of "disanimation." Consider the confusion that animates Power's discussion of the circulatory system of insects, which begins by observing that just as perfect animals (those that reproduce sexually) display an "incessant motion of their Heart, and Circulation of their Bloud," so too "in these puny *automata*, and exsanguineous pieces of Nature, there is the same pulsing Organ, and Circulation," but then proceeds to question the correspondence just established between insects and other animals, observing that in insects, "the whole Organ," by which Power means the single dorsal blood vessel that constitutes the insect's open circulatory system, "seems too little to have any parts at all."[28] Although prevailing medical opinion in the 1660s held that "the Motion of the Lungs was necessary to Life upon the account of promoting the Circulation of the Blood," a hypothesis tested out by Hooke, Richard Lower, and John Mayow, among others, the visible evidence of a insect's beating heart does not, for Power, constitute proof that the insect is alive in the most basic sense of that term.[29] Peering through the translucent skin of one particular insect, Power remarks that "you might most lively see the pulsation of her Heart for twelve or fourteen hours, after the head and neck was separated," an experiment aimed at testing the capacity for anterior regeneration in certain insect species that Aristotle had noted as a challenge to Platonic theories of the tripartite soul.[30]

Both Power and Hooke repeatedly liken the anatomical structures of insects to mechanical assemblages, often to emphasize their intricate composition out of small parts but also to voice uncertainty about the aliveness or not-aliveness of insects while conducting experiments that might strike today's readers as early modern versions of Schrödinger's cat, either alive or dead (but not both at once). Guided by the question of whether insects belong properly to the *classis* of animals, and by the question of which physiological process or organ—circulation, respiration, or motion; the heart, lungs, or brain—might be the ultimate guarantor of life, Power and Hooke examine living insects under the microscope but perceive creatures that more closely resemble Gawen Smith's mechanical fleas, Walchius's spider, or the lifeless but lively bugs of the *Schüttelkasten*. The mouth of the butterfly, according to Power, can "winde and coyl it self up by a Spring" on account of a "spiral or cochleary contrivance," while the eyes of the bee appear "drill'd full of innumerable holes like a Grater or Thimble." Hooke relies on corresponding similes to describe the eyes of the fly: "like a lattice drilled with abundance of holes" or "cover'd with golden Nails."[31]

When Hooke promises to reveal to public view the "inward motions" that are "perform'd by the small Machines of Nature," his language calls to mind the arena of the stage, a theater of actors "manag'd by Wheels, and Engines, and Springs" whose bodies create the kind of ontologically equivocal spectacle likewise designated by the spectrum of meanings implicit in the early modern term "motion," which denotes voluntary locomotion or change of posture by a sensible animal body but also the involuntary, mechanized movements of a clock, puppet, or perpetual-motion machine.[32] It is patently unclear to Hooke whether the "quick spontaneous motion" of flies' wings belongs to the former category or the latter.[33] Approaching the objects of their investigation thoroughly steeped in the implicit correspondence between insects and machines, Hooke and Power compare the circulatory system of the louse to "a Pump" and "pair of Bellows," and the "curious blue shining armour" of the blue fly to "a polish'd piece of steel," figurations that raise the question of whether organic anatomical structures imitate art or vice versa, and also the question of where the crossroad between nature and art, and between living and dead, in fact resides.[34] The uncertain answers to those questions are likewise reticulated in their repeated use of the word "lively" to describe the delicate appearance or quick motions of insects under the microscope, a term that suggests not aliveness per se but rather a quality of objects that seem alive or possess verisimilitude, a power of dead things—statues, paintings, puppets—that are uncannily forcible or vivid.

The entomological experiments conducted by Power and Hooke reinforce the uncanny and liminal quality of insects, but also their theatrical powers. As they cut off the heads of bees to see if their hearts will still beat, or prick lice with needles to discern whether blood emerges and when life departs, they assume the part of Gloucester's indifferent gods, killing flies "for their sport," and simultaneously perform the more tragic roles of so many Lears and Othellos, straining to see if "breath will mist" the mirror, if the feather might stir, or if a body on the cusp of death might still possess motion and life:

Ha! no more moving?
Still as the grave . . .
. . . I think she stirs again. No.[35]

For the seventeenth-century naturalist, the challenge of discerning whether insects are alive or dead arose from the exiguity of their forms, as well as the much-disputed question of where, in the body, physical life resided and how legible the signs or manifestations of that life were. Yet the way that both Power's *Experimental Philosophy* and Hooke's *Micrographia* describe that challenge assumes a distinctly theatrical, often tragic, tenor, as Power hunts for signs of "vivacity" in flies that appear at one moment "desperate and quite forsaken of their forms" and in the next "revoked to life" by the "virtue of the Sun or warm ashes."[36] Power can sound downright wistful about the sudden and irrevocable disappearance of life in his specimens: the locust, he observes, is "kill'd with the least touch imaginable," purpling his nail in the blood of innocence like the cruel mistress of Donne's "The Flea." Yet Power also refers, repeatedly, to the little stage plays enacted by his dissections as a "very pleasant spectacle," an attitude shaped by the theatrical conventions and practices of the early modern stage—the tragic ways of killing Shakespearean women and then watching, attentively, for lingering signs of life, but also the dramatic feats of Scaliot's fleas and the comically macabre stage tricks outlined in treatises on actorly legerdemain, which instruct in jokes such as "How to seeme to cut off a mans head," how to cut an object in two and then make it whole again, how to thrust bodkins and other sharp objects into one's own head without genuine or lasting harm, and how to "kill a Hen, chicken, or Capon and give it life againe," the last trick effective thanks to the extreme posterior placement of the bird's brain in its head (and the careful placement of the performer's knife).[37]

In two analogous experiments, Hooke intoxicates some flies and then an ant in wine, the results illustrating how the creatures may seem to die but then become "reviv'd" once removed from the liquor: "I gave it a Gill of Brandy, or Spirit of Wine, which after a while e'en knock'd him down dead drunk, so that he became moveless . . . till at last, certain bubbles issuing out of its mouth, it ceased to move. . . . I suffered it to lye above an hour in the Spirit; and after I had taken it out, and put its body and legs into a natural posture, remained moveless about an hour; but then, upon a sudden, as if it had been awaken out of a drunken sleep, it suddenly reviv'd and ran away."[38] Although more sensitive readers might grimace as Hooke intoxicates the ant a second time, only to permit it once again to "recove[r] life and motion," the narrative patterning of his account echoes the passage from life to death and back again typical of dramatic comedy and romance—the revivification of Hermione's statue in *The Winter's Tale*, the resurrection of Thaisa's not-quite-dead-yet corpse in *Pericles*, or the even more farcical resuscitation of Rafe in Beaumont's *Knight of the Burning Pestle*, who appears in the play's final scene sporting a "forked arrow" through his head, only to act out the most melodramatic of deaths and, moments later, recover unscathed, dying and rising in a scene that mocks the power of theater to kill off and then resurrect its actors at will.[39] Killing off insects and then reviving them with the cavalier indifference of an engineer flipping a mechanical switch, Hooke and Power were spectators at a miniature theater in the round, a *circus minimus* whose insect actors were alternately stifled and stirred, enchanted and disenchanted, their little lives rounded with a sleep, but then released from their bands back into the world of the living.

NOTES

1. Holinshed, *Third Volume of Chronicles*, 1299; Stow, *Annales of England*, 1164. Holinshed comments, "A thing almost incredible, but that my selfe (amongst manie others) have seene it, and therfore must affirme it to be true" (1299). For later accounts of Scaliot, see Purchas, *Purchas his Pilgrimes*, bk. 1, chap. 8, p. 840; Powell, *Humane Industry*, 12, 182–83; Stubbe, *Legends no histories*, 5; Wanley, *Wonders of the little world*, 225; Burton, *Versatile Ingenium*, 1–2; Winstanley, *New help to discourse*, 141; Evelyn, *Numismata*, 163.

2. Later examples include the London flea circus of a watchmaker named Mr. Boverick, who in 1742 advertised a show featuring a flea pulling a chaise; the early nineteenth-century Italian performer Louis Bertolotto, mentioned by Dickens and Emerson, famous for dressing up fleas as historical figures in a show billed as an "Extraordinary Exhibition of the Industrious fleas"; the Parisian Monsieur Roberts's tame flea circus of the 1940s; Roy and William Heckler, who presided over Hubert's Flea Circus in New York; and the father-and-son team William and John Torp at Tivoli Gardens in Copenhagen, whose fleas rode tricycles and pulled carriages.

3. For similar arguments, see Gross's *Puppet* and his earlier *Dream of the Moving Statue*.

4. Parikka, *Insect Media*, 26, in turn discussing Wise, "Assemblage," 84. For other posthumanist discussions of insects, including Uexküll's studies of the *Umwelt* of the tick, see Agamben, *Open: Man and Animal*, 40–45; Buchanan, *Onto-ethologies*, chapter 1.

5. Holinshed, *Third Volume of Chronicles,* 1299; Stow, *Annales of England,* 1164; Pliny *Natural History* 7.21. A notable exception is Stubbe, who calls Scaliot's feat "an unusual improvement of *the Powers of Mankinde*" to tame "our Rebellious and vexatious *Fleas." Legends no histories,* 5.

6. On the spider, see Walchius, *Decas fabularum humani generis,* 244; also mentioned in Powell, *Humane Industry,* 185. For catalogues of miniature marvels, see Wilkins, *Mathematicall magick,* 2.3, pp. 171–74; and Powell, *Humane Industry,* 180–87. On Regiomontanus's iron fly, see Du Bartas, *His devine weekes and works,* 168 (week 1, day 6).

7. Uexküll, *Foray into the Worlds,* 45–46. Parikka, *Insect Media,* 15–16, discusses some nineteenth-century scientific theories that serve as analogues to these insect-machines, including the theory that spiders shoot and arrange their threads via electricity, and that moths are capable of wireless telegraphy.

8. On Gawen Smith's proposal to erect a lighthouse and establish a ferry service, see *Calendar of House of Lords Manuscripts,* 7.1:191, and Hebb, "Profiting from Misfortune," 112.

9. Moffett, *Silkewormes and Their Flies,* 34–35.

10. Rid, *Art of jugling,* E3v; Hocus Pocus, *Anatomy of Legerdemain,* D3v, E3v. On these tricks, see also Butterworth, *Magic on the Early English Stage,* 97.

11. Bacon, *Advancement of Learning,* bk. 2, p. 64.

12. Vitruvius *De Architectura* 10.1, p. 173: "Machina est continens ex materia coniunctio, maximas ad onerum motus habens virtutes"; compare Bacon's preface to the *Novum Organum,* which likens his scientific method to the moving of a "vast obelisk," a task virtually impossible with the "naked hands" but made effortless with the proper use of "instruments" or machinery. Bacon, *Novum Organum,* 40.

13. Moffett, *Theatre of Insects,* 2.28, p. 1101.

14. Moffett, *Silkewormes and Their Flies,* 36; 1 Corinthians 1:27.

15. Power, *Experimental Philosophy,* observation 1, pp. 2–3; compare observation 22, p. 25, on the ant's "Herculean strength of its body, that it is able to carry its triple weight and bulk."

16. Hooke, *Micrographia,* observation 44, pp. 193–94.

17. On *Schüttelkasten* and the wire insects displayed at Schloss Ambras, see Bredekamp, *Lure of Antiquity,* 47–48.

18. Ibid., 48.

19. Browne, *Religio Medici,* 1.15.

20. Moffett, *Silkewormes and Their Flies,* 34.

21. Aristotle *De anima* 1.5 (411b19–20); compare *De anima* 2.2 (413b18–22).

22. Browne, *Religio Medici,* 1.9.

23. Browne, *Pseudodoxia Epidemica,* 2.7.1 (ed. Robbins, 1:153).

24. See Aristotle *Physics* 8.4.

25. Descartes, *Treatise on Man* and *Discourse on the Method,* both in *Philosophical Writings,* 1:108, 1:136.

26. Hale, *Primitive origination of mankind,* 48.

27. Digby, *Two Treatises,* 1.23.4–6, pp. 205–8.

28. Power, *Experimental Philosophy,* "Some Considerations, Corollaries, and Deductions," 58–60. The observation anticipates Uexküll's discussion of whether insects such as the tick are living organisms or merely a "reflex republic . . . which has no hierarchically superior center." *Foray into the Worlds,* 77.

29. Hooke, "Account of an Experiment," 539–40.

30. Power, *Experimental Philosophy,* observation 26, p. 30; compare observation 2, p. 4: "if you divide the Bee, you shall . . . see the heart beat most lively."

31. Ibid., observation 5, p. 8, and observation 2, p. 3; Hooke, *Micrographia,* preface, Gr.

32. Hooke, *Micrographia,* preface, Gr. On the term *motion,* see Bacon, *New Atlantis,* 33, 42: "Engines . . . to set also on going diverse Motions"; "divers curious Clocks; / And other like Motions of Returne: And some Perpetuall Motions." Compare Jonson, Epigram 97, "On the New Motion," in *Workes,* 797–98, in which said motion is successively a puppet, a puppet master, a perpetual-motion machine, and a courtier so artificial that his "clothes have over-leavened him."

33. Hooke, *Micrographia,* observation 38, p. 173.

34. Ibid., observation 54, p. 212; observation 42, p. 184.

35. Power, *Experimental Philosophy,* observation 6, p. 9; Shakespeare, *King Lear,* 4.1.36–37, 5.3.267; *Othello,* 5.2.96–98.

36. Power, *Experimental Philosophy,* observation 3, p. 6.

37. Ibid., observation 28, p. 31. At observations 10 and 11, pp. 14–15, Power twice uses the phrase "a very pleasant spectacle" about dissecting two spiders, repeating the phrase again at observation 13, p. 18; Hocus Pocus, *Anatomy of Legerdemain,* E2v, F2v–3r; Rid, *Art of jugling,* E3r–4r.

38. Hooke, *Micrographia,* observation 49, p. 204.

39. Beaumont, *Knight of the Burning Pestle,* 5.5.276–77.

8

SHAKESPEARE'S INSECT THEATER

Fairy Lore as Elizabethan Folk Entomology

TODD ANDREW BORLIK

They have a little head, and a mouth not forked but strong and brawny, with a very short neck, to which one Mark, an Englishman (most skillful in all curious work), fastened a chain of gold as long as a man's finger, with a lock and key so rarely and cunningly [made], that the flea could easily go and draw them, yet the flea, chain, lock and key were not all above a grain weight. I have also heard from men of credit, that this flea so tied with a chain did draw a coach of gold that was every way perfect, and that very lightly, which much sets forth the artist's skill and the flea's strength.

–THOMAS MOFFETT, *THEATRE OF INSECTS,* CA. 1589

The Admiral's Men and the Children of the Chapel were not Shakespeare's only rivals in the competitive world of London show business. A menagerie of performing animals, from bears such as Harry Hunks to horses like the famed bay Morocco, also entertained the play-going public in Elizabethan London. When Wenceslaus Hollar mislabeled the Globe the Bear Garden (and vice versa) in his panoramic view of the city, he unwittingly anticipated current critical efforts to undo the distinction between animal play and human performance. Over the past decade, Erica Fudge, Bruce Boehrer, Andreas Höfele, Karen Raber, and Laurie Shannon (among others) have established that Shakespeare's ethological imagination raids the animal kingdom for analogies with human behavior.[1] Yet the teeming realm of six-legged creatures has, for the most part, scurried and flitted beneath the ken of animal studies.[2] In the modern environmental movement, wildlife conservation likewise tends to focus on "charismatic megafauna," consigning the diminutive world of insects to neglect, boyish amusement, or fear-mongering sci-fi films. One might assume that in a mainly agrarian society like Shakespeare's England, people would have regarded creepy-crawly things with disrelish if not outright loathing. To be sure, there are ample biological reasons for entomophobia: insects often dwell amid slime and filth; many

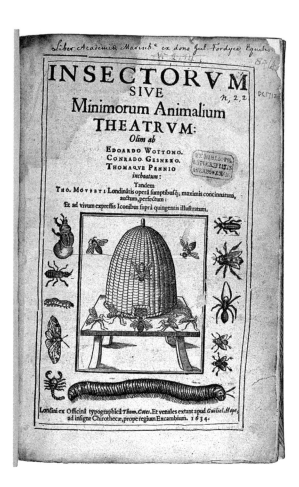

8.1

From Thomas Moffett,
*Insectorum sive minimorum
animalium theatrum* (London,
1634). University of Aberdeen,
f5957 Mou.

species bite, sting, or compete with humans for biomass resources; they reproduce at staggering rates; to human eyes they appear emotionless and implacable; social insects act like superorganisms in ways that undercut the growing sense in early modern Europe of the sanctity of the individual, etc.[3] In *A Midsummer Night's Dream*, however, Shakespeare conjures a miniature realm of Lilliputian creatures who incite wonder rather than disgust. Situating Shakespeare's fairies alongside early modern writings on insects, this chapter reveals that a fascination with the dramatic life of arthropods existed long before modern nature documentaries. Insect exhibitions like the one described in the epigraph above would, this chapter argues, have provided an imaginative catalyst for Shakespeare's Queen Mab. Although insect societies like the bees in *Henry V* could be allegorized as performing the "act of order" (1.2.189), the insectoid fairies that actually appear onstage in the *Dream* instead seem to incarnate what Schiller called the "play instinct."[4] Like the macro photographic lenses used in such films as the 1996 documentary *Microcosms*, Shakespeare's insect poetics tinkers not only with the audience's sense of scale but also with anthropocentric notions of who, or rather what, counts as an actor.

Theseus's account of the poet assigning "airy nothing / A local habitation and a name" (5.1.16–17) uncannily captures how many early moderns might have dismissed the task of the entomologist. Unbeknownst to most readers of the *Dream*, entomology was an emergent discipline in Shakespeare's day. In the late 1580s, Thomas Moffett (also spelled Moffet, Muffet, Moufet) was editing and expanding a landmark work of Renaissance natural history: *Insectorum sive minimorum animalium theatrum* (*Insects, or The Theatre of the Smallest Animals*, better known today by the condensed title of the 1658 English translation, *The Theatre of Insects*).[5] Like a sixteenth-century Horton, Moffett tried desperately to get his contemporaries to hear the "Who" of the insect world. To skeptics who regarded them as superfluous pests, Moffett devised a clever rebuttal: insects are the actors of the animal kingdom. Moffett huffed with impatience that his countrymen would travel long distances and pay good money to see large beasts "brought upon the stage": "Yet where is Nature more to be seen than in the smallest matters, where she is entirely all? For in great bodies the workmanship is easy, the matter being ductile; but in these that are so small and despicable, and almost nothing, what care? How great is the effect of it? How unspeakable is the perfection?" (viii). While larger animals are rather scarce and can flee humans with ease, the ubiquity and comparatively small size of insects allow for more sustained observation; one may watch them as a spectator in the top level of the Globe's galleries would watch a play, "as from a high watchtower" (ix). As Moffett's title boldly proclaims, insect behavior thus amounts to a quasi-dramatic spectacle unfolding in gardens, meadows, and forests throughout England.[6]

The engraving on the title page further invites the reader to interpret the *Theatre of Insects* in an almost literal sense: the insects arranged symmetrically upon the platform seem to be in the midst of a performance, resembling actors upon the raised scaffold of the Elizabethan thrust stage (compare the famous DeWitt drawing of the Swan). The small opening at the bottom of the woven hive (or skep) even looks like the discovery space in the tiring-house façade (see fig. 8.1). In *The Alchemist*, Ben Jonson mentions "the Fleas that run at tilt / Upon a table" (5.1.25–26) in an inventory of the popular lowbrow entertainments he despised. So it seems a fair assumption that Moffett's title is indebted, as Eric C. Brown argues, to the "actual performances of insects themselves, on the stages, and in the streets of London."[7] Encompassing feats of prodigious strength and agility, exhibitions of colorful attire, and recitals involving music and dance, insect performance represents a neglected species of Elizabethan street theater.

Fittingly, the *Theatre of Insects* contains one of the earliest descriptions of a flea circus. In the passage reproduced in this chapter's epigraph, Moffett recounts how a blacksmith named Mark Scaliot harnessed a finely wrought gold chain to a flea, who then towed a miniature carriage. A report of this flea appears in the *Annals* of the esteemed historian John Stow, who claimed to have witnessed the performance himself in 1579.[8] Stow's eyewitness account is reproduced more or less verbatim in the 1586 edition of Raphael Holinshed's *Chronicles*, a book that Shakespeare knew intimately.[9] Scaliot's flea seems to have become rather notorious; a 1619 text lists the flea as one of five marvels widely "held to be the most strangest accidents in the *Chronicles*."[10] Others would replicate Scaliot's feat, as flea coaches remained a popular sideshow entertainment throughout the early modern period. The Restoration-era naturalist John Tradescant dazzled guests with a coach-toting flea, and included the flea chain in his celebrated *Wunderkammer*. In *The Microscope Made Easy* (1744), Henry Baker claimed to have examined with his microscope "a chaise (made by one Mr. Boverick, a watchmaker) having four wheels with all the proper apparatus belonging to them, turning readily on their axles . . . all formed of ivory and drawn along by a flea without any difficulty."[11]

To a Shakespearean, Moffett's description of the flea pulling a coach inescapably recalls Mercutio's monologue describing the fantastical equipage of Queen Mab. Mercutio pictures "a small grey-coated gnat" (1.4.65) in the driver's seat, while Mab's wagon is "drawn by a team of little atomi" (1.4.58). According to the *OED* (which cites this passage as the first usage), atomy (pl. atomi) here means a "diminutive or tiny being, a mite."[12] In other words, atomy functions as a generic name for the smallest of insects. In Peter Woodhouse's 1605 poem *The Flea*, the word "atomye" is applied to this particular species.[13] Moreover, fleas, Moffett reminds us, are especially prone to "molest men that are sleeping" (1101), just as Mab's carriage gallops over the bodies of dreamers "as they lie asleep" (1.4.59). The performance of Scaliot's flea, then, is an analogue and the probable inspiration for one of Shakespeare's most beloved poetic rhapsodies. The various dreams Mercutio anatomizes may betray the subconscious desires of the dreamers, but the somatic trigger for these dreams is the flea's nocturnal assault upon the sleeping body. This chapter takes this anecdote as a springboard for an inquiry into the peculiar affinity between fairy lore and entomology. With its vibrant miniatures of anthropomorphic insects and arthropomorphic humans, *A Midsummer Night's Dream* can be seen as a bio-mimicry of Moffett's insect theater.

In highlighting the commensurability of insects and fairies, this chapter situates itself in a niche between animal studies (with its fixation on "charismatic megafauna") and Robert Watson's ingenious reading of fairy enchantment as an intimation of hormonal surges.[14] While endocrinology was not yet dreamed of in sixteenth-century natural philosophy, entomology was a nascent discipline in Shakespeare's day. By placing the fairy under the critical microscope at a slightly higher magnification, the correlation between these magical wee folk and insects comes into shimmering focus. Approaching Shakespeare's fairies as an attempt to capitalize on contemporary interest in performing insects raises questions not only about the precarious distinction between living and inanimate (as expertly probed in Jessica Wolfe's contribution to this volume) but also about theatrical agency: did early moderns consider drama a uniquely human endeavor? Or is Moffett's title to be interpreted in a literal sense? With their love of spectacle and mischief, the insectoid fairies in *A Midsummer Night's Dream* challenge *Homo ludens*' monopoly on histrionics, supporting Johan Huizinga's claim that "animals have not waited for man to teach them their playing."[15]

Historians of fairy lore often accuse Shakespeare of Disneyfying the fairies.[16] Admittedly, the fairy, as we in the modern West know it today—a mixture of sugar, spice, star-capped wands, and gossamer wings—is largely an Edwardian confection. But Titania has as much in common with Tinkerbell as she does with her premodern avatars. The wee folk of European folklore were quasi-demonic beings who abducted children, punished lazy servants and rewarded industrious ones, and lured mortals into twilit realms where a single night of revelry might last a human decade. The fairies in *A Midsummer Night's Dream* are, the custody dispute over the changeling notwithstanding, "spirits of another sort" (3.2.389). Shakespeare's droll portraits of these puckish creatures allowed J. M. Barrie and his ilk to associate them with the innocence and imaginative play of prepubescent girlhood. By sanitizing them of their malevolence, *A Midsummer Night's Dream* pries open a Pandora's box that loosed the maudlin antics of Peter Pan upon the world. Rather than revisit this twice-told cultural history, this chapter examines the fairy through the lens of natural history. While postcolonial critics have duly observed the parallels between the fairy realm and India, an ecocritical approach to the *Dream* might seize upon the fairies as an imaginative transfiguration of early modern people's intimacy with insects.[17] One of the fairies in Titania's retinue is christened Moth, which could mean either a dust mote or the winged creature now classified among the Lepidoptera. Another is named Cobweb, suggestive not only of insubstantiality but also of the spider and her spinning. The splicing of fairies with butterflies in Victorian paintings and illustrations does not, as we shall see, represent a drastic mutation but a successive stage in Shakespeare's metamorphosis of the fairy. Rather than twee caricatures of girlishness or diabolical baby snatchers, the fairies emerge from the chrysalis of Shakespeare's poetry as a cross between anthropomorphic insects and arthropomorphic humans. The ass-headed Bottom may not be the only transspecies performer in this play. In attempting to represent the seemingly unrepresentable microcosm of insects, *A Midsummer Night's Dream* not only complicates facile notions of performance as a uniquely human endeavor but also, I contend, dramatizes the limitations of human spectatorship over the natural world while pretending to overcome them.

The congruence between Shakespeare's fairies and insects becomes more evident when Titania's followers are herded into a lineup with their ancestors. In medieval romances, the wee folk are not quite so wee. In the fifteenth-century *Huon of Bordeaux*, for instance, from which Shakespeare lifted the name Oberon, the fairy king stands three feet tall, much too large to crawl under an acorn shell. So why did

Shakespeare cast a shrinking spell on the fairies? Perhaps, as Katharine M. Briggs contends, Shakespeare was following a West Midlands tradition that mythologized fairies as flower spirits. If so, Shakespeare's Warwickshire upbringing would have put him in an ideal position to spy the resemblance between fairies and insects.[18] Titania voices concern for the flowers when she orders some of her fairy entourage to protect the "muskrose buds" (2.2.3). The First Fairy, meanwhile, describes the cowslips as the queen's "pensioners" (2.1.10). "Pensioner" can imply servant but also signifies one dependent upon the bounty of another. The bounty the flowers receive from the queen turns out to be not a financial reward but a dewdrop. Although fairy lore provides an etiological explanation for atmospheric condensation rather than pollination, the verse bespeaks an understanding of the intimate connection between arthropods and angiosperms. In John Day's early seventeenth-century poem *The Parliament of Bees*, Oberon serves as the hive's overlord.[19] Shakespeare similarly describes Ariel as insectlike and a flower-feeder in *The Tempest*:

> Where the bee sucks, there suck I
> In a cowslip's bell I lie. (5.1.88–89)

Titania likewise beds down for the night upon

> a bank where the wild thyme blows
> Where the oxlip and the nodding violet grows,
> Quite overcanopied with luscious woodbine,
> With sweet musk-roses, and with eglantine. (2.1.249–52)

Perhaps it is not by chance that the flowers in Oberon's posy happen to be among those beloved by pollen-bearing insects.

Intuitively, it makes perfect sense that a preliterate culture prior to scientific entomology would have recorded its observations about the enigmatic underworld of insects in the form of fantastical narratives. Anthropomorphized insects can be found in many world cultures long before the time of Aesop.[20] Ants and bees have highly organized social structures, and it would not require an overactive imagination to compare these to the class divisions in premodern European society, as the Archbishop does in *Henry V*. Their nests resemble the fairies' subterranean kingdoms, their frenetic movements the fairies' love of dancing, their bioluminescence the *ignis fatuus* with which fairies like Puck "mislead night wanderers" (2.1.38), and their bites or stings the "pinches" with which fairies punish slovenly housekeepers. This is not to imply that *all* fairy lore is merely a form of enchanted entomology. Fairies are not monolithic creatures. Early modern accounts of them—derived from snippets of popular folklore, classical mythology, medieval romance, trials of witches

8.2
Henry Fuseli, *Titania and
Bottom*, ca. 1790, detail. Tate
Britain. Presented by Miss Julia
Carrick Moore in accordance
with the wishes of her sister, 1887.
N01228.

or cunning women, and demonological treatises—display a great deal of regional variation. Yet no attentive reader of Shakespeare's comedy can, I think, deny that he consistently conveys the scale of the fairy world through detailed miniatures of the six- and eight-legged creatures with whom humans have coexisted for millennia. Instead of fabulous ethereal beings spun ex nihilo from the poet's overheated imagination, the fairies of *A Midsummer Night's Dream* attest that Shakespeare cast an attentive eye on the insect world.

This correspondence has (inevitably) been remarked upon before. In his sonnet on ants, John Clare dubs them "deformed remnants of the fairy days"—a line quoted by A. S. Byatt in her scintillating *Angels and Insects*.[21] By and large, however, literary critics have neglected the importance of the insect world to Shakespeare's fairies. Visual artists, by contrast, have compensated with exquisite portraits of Shakespeare's fairies as transspecies chimeras. Perhaps the most celebrated paintings inspired by *A Midsummer Night's Dream* are those of the Swiss-born artist Henry Fuseli. Not coincidentally, Fuseli was a "keen amateur entomologist," and his fairies derive some of their exotic charm from his studies of insects.[22] In *Titania and Bottom* (ca. 1790), tiny winged creatures flit in and out of the shadows. An impish Moth stares back at us in the lower left portion of the canvas, his head spliced with the wings and abdomen of his namesake (fig. 8.2). Robert Huskisson's 1847 painting depicts Shakespeare's fairies battling ants and fleeing in terror before a charging snail. Amid the psychedelic welter in Richard Dadd's *The Fairy Feller's Master-Stroke* (ca. 1855–64) stand a butterfly-winged Oberon and Titania, their arrival heralded by a trumpet-playing dragonfly (fig. 8.3). Lepidoptera swarm in the undergrowth of another painting Dadd executed of Shakespeare's fairy monarchs. Insectoid fairies also flutter through the pages of Arthur Rackham's 1908 edition of the *Dream*, one of the masterworks of Edwardian book illustration. Collectively, these images are a testament to the profound intimacy between insects and fairies in Shakespeare's poetry. Visual artists have

8.3
Richard Dadd, *The Fairy Feller's Master-Stroke*, 1855–64, detail. Tate Britain. Presented by Siegfried Sassoon in memory of his friend and fellow officer Julian Dadd, a great-nephew of the artist, and of his two brothers who gave their lives in the First World War, 1963. T00598.

been so drawn to this particular play—like moths to the proverbial flame—largely because it depicts a bug's-eye view of the world in a way that could be represented only awkwardly onstage. Capturing this microcosm seems a task more suited to the artist's brush than to the playwright's pen or actor's pantomime.

Insects creep and flutter through many of Shakespeare's plays besides *A Midsummer Night's Dream*. Yet Shakespeare tends, for reasons that seem self-evident but are worth scrutinizing, to narrate their behavior rather than to stage it. Unlike the other animal performers examined in this collection, insects are not available in the same way as dramatis personae. To belabor the obvious, miniscule thespians, such as Scaliot's flea, would be invisible to any spectator sitting more than a foot away. The carriers at the roadside inn in *1 Henry IV* can tell us that they have been horribly flea-bitten during the night (2.1.16), but we have to take their word for it. When the Archbishop delivers his homily on order in *Henry V*, the Lord Chamberlain's Men did not trot out an ersatz beehive on the Globe's stage. An insect has a memorable if unenviable cameo in *Coriolanus* when the young Martius shreds a gilded butterfly with his teeth. Again, however, the scene is reported rather than enacted, as it is safe to assume that Shakespeare's company did not employ a butterfly wrangler.[23] The fly scene in *Titus Andronicus* stands as a notable exception. Unlike Martius's butterfly, the fly is imagined to be physically present onstage. Such moments present formidable challenges for directors, as Eric C. Brown has observed: "Ought a performance to maintain a stable of expendable *Drosophila* understudies? . . . And how literally can one take the directive of Hugh Evans, 'And twenty glow-worms shall our lanterns be'" (5.5.77)?[24] The performance history of these plays suggests that the respective answers to these rhetorical questions are probably no, and not so literally. Though some productions pipe in a buzzing noise through the sound system, the fly itself has to be imagined. Paradoxically, it is the smallness of the fly in *Titus* compared to the butterfly in *Coriolanus*, its invisibility, that allows for its "appearance" in the scene.

In the nondramatic fairy poetry of Michael Drayton and Robert Herrick, magnifying the diminutive world of microfauna does not pose a problem. As a playwright, however, Shakespeare would have immediately grasped the difficulty of reproducing insect performance in an Elizabethan playhouse. The fact that the fly scene occurs only in the 1623 Folio text of *Titus* would seem to betray an anxiety about the verisimilitude of insect theater. Perhaps it was a later addition, inserted to spice up a now familiar play. Alternatively, the scene, as written, may have been deemed too outlandish, and therefore as expendable as the fly's life. If so, Marcus's stab presents an onstage correlative to the editor's cut. The fly scene in *Titus* could be regarded as an experiment, perhaps not entirely successful, in incorporating insect theater into a play. Shakespeare conducts a similar experiment, but with an important twist, in *A Midsummer Night's Dream.* Thanks to the shaping fantasies of the poet's pen, the audience gains access to a microcosm in which human actors can impersonate insect-sized creatures.

In order to make insect theater viable onstage, a playwright basically has three options: the first approach, of which *Titus* is a rare example, is to have actors pretend they are in the presence of an unseen insect. A second, subtler method would be to manipulate verbally the audience's sense of scale. Viewers listening to the Queen Mab speech, for instance, imagine themselves contracted to the size of a gnat. Mercutio's lyric fantasy conjures an insect theater that capitalizes on the Elizabethan delight in the miniature. Mab resembles the fly in *Titus*, however, in that both are visible only in the theater of the mind. *King Lear* presents a variation of this strategy. It radically inflates the distance between audience and actors so that humans, like birds glimpsed from Dover cliff, "show scarce so gross as beetles" (4.5.14). The blind Gloucester, no longer biased by relative size, can perceive humans as "flies" (4.1.37). His subsequent groveling in the earth enacts his earlier insight about Tom o' Bedlam, who "made [him] think a man a worm" (4.1.34). Gloucester is, in effect, performing a worm. The upshot is not to elevate insects to the ontological dignity of humans but to demote humans to the status of overgrown vermin.

If *Lear* dwindles humans down to insect size, a third, somewhat more daring tactic to make performing insects perceptible would be to do the opposite: enlarge arthropods to human size. An example of this approach in Renaissance drama would be Ben Jonson's *Volpone*, in which people are flies not to the gods but to one another. Mosca's flylike behavior, buzzing about the stage to prey on his victims, confirms his belief in the stark parallels between humans and insects: "All the wise world is little else, in nature, / but parasites and sub-parasites" (3.1.12–13). Unlike the fly in *Titus*, Mosca is visible to the audience, but only by virtue of assuming human form. In Jonson's Aesopian theater, Mosca performs the moral character of his namesake.

In *A Midsummer Night's Dream*, Shakespeare combines the second and third approaches. At times, his poetry describes rather than shows the fairies creeping under acorn cups, spearing bumblebees, and plucking wings from butterflies. Shakespeare shrinks the fairies of English folklore down to the size of insects, and the audience recalibrates its perceptions accordingly. Apart from his entomological imagery, Shakespeare also achieves a shrinking effect through his prosody. As Diane Purkiss observes, the fairies' octosyllabic couplets "extend the effect of miniaturization to the verse form itself."[25] But the illusion is not conjured only with words, as it is in Mercutio's Mab speech. Moth and Cobweb, like Mosca, appear onstage. Primed by Shakespeare's verse, the audience succumbs to the fantasy that humans can impersonate insects. Revealingly, one of the first modern plays to attempt this, the Čapek brothers' *Insect Play*, may have been inspired by Max Reinhardt's expressionist production of *A Midsummer Night's Dream*.[26] In 1595, however, Shakespeare's company could not have relied on the elaborate costumes and set designs featured in expressionist theater. To compensate for the difference in scale, it seems likely that Shakespeare would have enlisted the child apprentices in the Lord Chamberlain's Men to discharge the fairy roles. If so, the name Moth (which recurs in *Love's Labor's Lost*) includes a pun on the small stature of the performer. In support of this contention one might point to Mistress Page casting her "daughter, [her] little son, / And three or four more of their growth" as fairies to torment Falstaff in *The Merry Wives of Windsor* (4.4.47–48). John Lyly's *Endymion* (ca. 1588), a play performed by the Children of Paul's, similarly refers to fairies as "fair babies."[27] In Elizabethan fairy plays, the small stature of the child player serves as a visual metonymy for the diminutive size of these mythical beings. It is worth recalling, however, that Shakespeare's fairies are not child-sized but insect-sized. Not even the most premature infant can be shoehorned inside a cowslip bell. To assume that the child's stature conveys the miniature scale of the fairies limned by the poetry seems a failure of the imagination as ridiculous as mistaking Snug the Joiner for a real lion. Having children impersonate microfauna is flagrant anthropomorphism. So Shakespeare inevitably distorts the alterity of the insect world and insect embodiment in the process of making it visible.

There is, nevertheless, a significant difference between imaginary insects like the fly in *Titus* and impersonated insects such as Mosca or Shakespeare's fairies. When the animal performer is "imaginary," its agency is severely curtailed. The behavior of real insects is simply too unpredictable to use them as performers in a conventional stage play. Butterflies and bees are not as tractable as dogs, bears, or horses. Shakespeare permits the fly in *Titus* to flit across the stage because its invisible presence could be conveyed through dialogue or pantomimed by the actors' gestures. Its "performance" is entirely pre-scripted. There is something comforting about this scenario: the unruliness of the nonhuman world becomes tame and predictable. On the downside, scenes with imaginary animal actors are thereby robbed of much of what gives theater its excitement: its seeming spontaneity, which allows for the possibility that things can go wrong.

By "blowing up" insects to human size, a playwright can—through speech and affective gesturing—convey some of the impetuous energy and wildness of the non-human. In contrast to the fly in *Titus*, Mosca and Puck possess a conspicuous flair for improvisation. Mosca commends himself for being so "limber" (3.1.7), exalting in his ability to "be here, / And there, and here, and yonder, all at once" (3.1.26–27). With his talent to adapt himself to all situations, Mosca is a consummate actor. The difference from *Titus* could hardly be more drastic, as Charlotte Scott has noted: whereas the invisible fly in *Titus* presents the insect world as incommensurate with theater, the flylike Mosca epitomizes the art of acting itself.[28] Like Mosca, Puck can connive, play pranks, make mistakes, and extemporize. When he stumbles upon the mechanicals' rehearsal in the woods, Puck resolves to become "an actor, too" (3.1.74), not unlike those spotlight-loving insects who sometimes dive-bomb performers in Shakespeare in the Park. He takes an evident delight in causing mayhem: "those things best please me / That befall prepost'rously" (3.2.120–21). Of course, the antics of these characters are also scripted in the play text. But in contrast to "imagined" animals, these insec-toid humans possess an agency and even a self-conscious theatricality that insists that play is not an exclusively human pastime. Indeed, the *Dream* represents theater not as an outgrowth of the adult rational mind but as a manifestation of the subrational delight in play exhibited by children and animals. Shakespeare's entomological drama can thus be seen as "collapsing the difference between theater and play, and inscribing the theater, too, as an analogously insective space."[29]

As Shakespeare understood, the physical disparity between insects and humans that makes insect theater problematic could foster contempt and disqualify insects from ethical concern. It is not surprising that the vast majority of his allusions to insects occur as reported dialogue. What does arch an eyebrow is the sympathy Shakespeare expresses for creatures whom many of his contemporaries regarded as puny, noisome vermin. Far from excusing "wanton boys" (*Lear* 4.1.37) like the butterfly-shredding Martius, Shakespeare equates gratuitous cruelty toward insects with savagery. When Marcus stabs the fly, Titus explodes with rage and imagines it "buzzing its lamenting dirges" (3.2.62). The acquittal of Marcus on the technicality of the fly's blackness points to a troubling confluence between Eurocentric racism and anthropocentric bigotry. But this does not negate Titus's denunciation of Marcus as a "murderer" (3.2.54), or his tribute to the fly as a fellow creature with its own biological ties of kinship and a capacity for suffering.[30] A similar moment occurs in *Measure for Measure* when Isabella ruminates on the epistemology of insect pain:

The poor beetle that we tread upon
In corporal sufferance finds a pang as great
As when a giant dies. (3.1.77–79)

This passage beautifully captures the green ethos of the analogical world picture. Size is arbitrary; mankind is not, contrary to the famous maxim of Protagoras, the measure of all things. By denying the equation of bulk with dignity, Isabella undermines the priority of the macrocosm over the microcosm. Crucially, however, the mimetic limitations of theatrical performance would threaten to restore the primacy of the macrocosm. There is, in other words, a link between a playhouse's capacity to portray animal subjectivity onstage and the ethical status of the nonhuman. The claim that Shakespeare draws on fairy lore to dramatize insect agency thus has significant ecocritical ramifications.

Shakespeare spliced together his insect fairies at a time when the disciplinary divide between the sciences and the humanities was not so pronounced. Revealingly, the same Thomas Moffett who compiled *The Theatre of Insects* also composed an Ovidian poem about silkworms. Entitled *Of the Silkewormes and Their Flies*, it features a lengthy retelling of the Pyramus and Thisbe legend that may have influenced the wedding masque in *A Midsummer Night's Dream*.[31] The poem makes repeated mention of the technical term for the *Bombyx mori*'s cocoon: a "bottom." It is probably not by chance that a weaver with the name Bottom plays the role of Pyramus, whose life is figuratively imagined as a "thread of silk" (5.1.336). As in *Lear*, aesthetic distance (here created by the inept play within the play) insectizes the human performer. Conversely, the insectoid fairies seem almost human. Nowhere does Moffett equate silkworms with fairies. Yet by metamorphosing Pyramus and Thisbe into butterflies, his poem parallels Shakespeare's makeover of the fairies as microfauna.

In the opening of the Čapeks' 1921 *Insect Play*, a lepidopterist brushes aside a tramp's plea not to capture some butterflies while they are playing: "Playing, you call it. I'm afraid you haven't the scientific mind, my friend."[32] When Shakespeare created his anthropomorphic insects, the "scientific mind" did not shun such poetic flourishes. *The Theatre of Insects* contains several memorable descriptions of insect play. Although Moffett often glosses it in didactic terms, he also makes it clear that their play is not staged solely for the edification of human onlookers. His chapter on bees reports that they "fly abroad for their pleasure" and "play together oftentimes and tickle one another" (899); he even describes them as arranging duels "in jest, for exercise and recreation," like the fencing exhibitions staged in Elizabethan playhouses and in the plays themselves. Similarly, gnats gather before sunset to "play up and down in the open air" (956). Insects can even, like Montaigne's cat, treat humans as a source of amusement: fleas, according to Moffett, "play [with] and tickle men" (1102).

Moffett also descants on the "music of grasshoppers" (991–92), hails the beauty of the spider's "Dedalian art" (1069), and commends the "rich robes" (974) donned by the butterfly. By imagining insects deriving pleasure from their own dress, music, and antics, Moffett endows them with the same theatrical sensibility as humans.

With the advent of the mechanistic philosophy developed by Descartes and his followers, such behavior could more easily be dismissed as mere instinct, devoid of any meaningful volition. Such attitudes encouraged mechanical engineers to design machines that mimic biological organisms. As with many modern flea circuses, some performing insects in the Renaissance were actually automata, as Jessica Wolfe observes in her chapter in this volume. The fifteenth-century polymath Regiomontanus, for example, is reported to have constructed an iron fly. The fact that a watchmaker harnessed the coach-pulling flea recorded in *The Microscope Made Easy* invites suspicion that it was mechanical as well. In Baker's 1744 text, the reader's wonder is excited less by the flea than by the watchmaker's "apparatus" and the intricacy of its design as revealed by the microscope. After the late seventeenth century, the craftsmanship of the human engineer, rather than Dame Nature, increasingly commands admiration.[33] In contrast, the pre-Cartesian accounts of Scaliot's flea tend to divide their praise between, as Moffett phrases it, "the artist's skill and the flea's strength." In *Virgidemiarum* (1598), Joseph Hall applauds a "smith at Uulcan's forge up brought" (leaving Scaliot unnamed), while also hailing the flea as a "tamelesse steed [that] could well his wagon wield / Through downes and dales of the vneuen field."[34] Hall's description of the flea as "tamelesse" implies that its behavior is spontaneous, not the result of human training or engineering. Moffett likewise pays parenthetical tribute to Scaliot as "most skillful in all curious work," but he fixes the spotlight more squarely on the superhuman brawn of the flea. Shakespeare arguably takes this even further. Instead of being built by a human blacksmith, Mab's chariot is "made by the joiner squirrel or old grub" (1.4.69). The passage is another example of Shakespeare's enchanted entomology; "grub" here probably alludes to the larva of the nut weevil, likened to a carpenter because of its burrowing into hazelnuts. By eliminating a human contriver or trainer entirely, Shakespeare credits nonhumans with the same artistic impulse and fondness for spectacle that underlie human drama.

There is, however, a significant caveat with this reading. In what remains of this chapter, I would like to complicate my initial thesis by arguing that the fairies are not merely personifications of insects; they also perform human dominion over the world of microfauna. The cultural belief in purposive creation allows Shakespeare to imagine another species whose existence confers upon insects what we would now call an ecological niche. But that niche disturbingly replicates the subordinate one that larger fauna occupied in relation to humans. In fact, Shakespeare's portrayal of Queen Mab, Titania, and Oberon raiding the insect world and converting its raw materials into the vestments of their pomp and majesty bears a striking resemblance to the actions of the

Tudor monarchs, who sought out crimson and purple silks (derived from cochineal, sea snails, and silkworms) for their regalia. In blending Warwickshire flower fairies with the cult of the fairy queen at Elizabeth's court, Shakespeare parodies the actual depredations upon insects committed by the early modern trade in luxury goods.[35]

Of course, many more insects are killed each day to keep them from our food or homes. Domestic space is carved out from the wild and exists in a state of perpetual siege. Insects are often the first scouts across the battle lines. In particular, they were (and still are—as the recent resurgence of bedbugs demonstrates) feared for their assault upon the sleeping body. In *A Midsummer Night's Dream*, the fairies intone a spell to ward off creepy-crawlies from Titania's bower:

> Weaving spiders, come not here;
> Hence, you long-legged spinners, hence;
> Beetles black, approach not near;
> Worm nor snail do no offence. (2.2.20–23)

It is, I think, significant that fairies in early modern England were associated with domestic management that would keep the house free from pests. Shakespeare acknowledges this tradition in the epilogue, when Puck appears wielding a broom "to sweep the dust behind the door" (5.2.20). In hindsight, Arthur Rackham's illustrations of Cobweb about to skewer a bumblebee and of a skirmish between slingshot-wielding fairies and caterpillars appear a saccharine premonition of the chemical warfare the twentieth century would declare against the insect kingdom (fig. 8.4). The technological feats of Elizabethan miniaturists like Mark Scaliot anticipate those of modern scientists who can now tamper with nature on a molecular level. If we think of organic chemistry as a displacement of magic by science (that is, as applying arcane knowledge to intervene in biological processes), it would be tempting to gloss fairy magic as a fictional antecedent of modern pesticides. Just as the average Elizabethan knew little about the process involved in manufacturing red dye from scale insects, the lethal effects of modern pesticides are often invisible to the human eye. In asking his audience to visualize humanoid creatures combatting insects, Shakespeare's fairy lore exposes some of the concealed violence licensed by humanity's disregard for microfauna.

This disregard helps explain why *The Theatre of Insects*, completed circa 1589, was not finally published until 1634: the printers feared that a book on bugs would not turn a profit. Perhaps the most damning rebuttal to Moffett (whose name was also spelled Muffet) would come in the form of a famous nursery rhyme.[36] By bringing his puckish insects onto the stage, however, Shakespeare invites us to laugh at—rather than shriek with—the Little Miss Muffets of the world. Since the audience can see the shenanigans of the fairies while the characters in the play cannot, we can chuckle along with

8.4 Arthur Rackham, illustration from William Shakespeare, *A Midsummer-Night's Dream* (London: Heinemann, 1908). John Rylands Library, Manchester, R141968.

Puck as he "frights the maidens" (2.1.35). Robin Goodfellow, whom Reginald Scot, in a revealing etymological coincidence, lists among the "bugs" of English folklore, becomes a source of amusement, not an object of terror.[37] Onstage, the disproportion between the child and adult actors (representing the fairies and the Athenians) would serve to caricature the human dread of insects. If some of this aversion has a biological basis, much of it is learned behavior, transmitted via culture. In Japan, for instance, where children keep beetles as pets and crickets are admired like songbirds, insects are held in much higher esteem than in the West. It is also telling that entomophobia reached its peak during the Cold War, when insects became associated with the mindless drones of totalitarianism, an era that just happens to coincide with the mass-scale introduction of synthetic insecticides.[38]

Like the blacksmith Scaliot, Shakespeare harnesses insect performers to his artistic creations to showcase the power of the human mind to project itself into nonhuman dimensions. But in the early modern period, this collaboration tended to instill a sense of wonder, mirth, or humility rather than hubris. To read the fairies' spells and their physical assaults against insects as a yearning for the powers bestowed by DDT, then, might be projecting too far into the future. When Shakespeare wrote *A Midsummer Night's Dream*, the sixteenth-century delight in the miniature was helping to rehabilitate the lowly insect.[39] Naturalists like Moffett were "extending the reach of piety to insects, [and] developing an observational practice that . . . was leading to the investigation of matter and the processes of the natural world considered as ends in themselves."[40] On page after page, Moffett's text attests that the living theater of insects can evoke reactions besides revulsion. By associating them with the mysterious fairies, Shakespeare, too, emphasizes the beauty, exoticism, and subjectivity of insects, while purging them of their unpleasant flesh-crawling qualities. In attempting to replicate the microcosm of insects in the Elizabethan playhouse, Shakespeare seems to be testing Jaques's platitude that "all the world's a stage." At times, Shakespeare's fun-loving fairies even become invisible spectators of the "fond pageant" of the humans, as if inverting Moffett's theatrical metaphor. The ecocritical stakes of this experiment are, I think, significant. Imagining insects as actors and their ecosystems as quasi-theatrical spaces might make us more aware of the continuity between humans and nonhumans. In material terms, this might make us think twice about the nonchalance with which we poison them and, collaterally, the environment upon which our collective survival depends. Yet Shakespeare's comedy also preserves a salutary awareness of the irreducible differences between arthropods and humans. In representing the unrepresentable agency of insects, *A Midsummer Night's Dream* dramatizes the epistemological limitations of human sight, revealing that it is not coextensive with the environment. Insofar as insect theater makes plain these limitations, it helps imbue Shakespeare's *Dream* with some of its magical ambience. Plays like the *Dream* revel in theater's ability to derange our everyday perceptions of the natural world, making us believe that, say, insects can talk or that humans can become three inches tall. In our post-Enlightenment culture, that might be the closest we can come to enchantment.

NOTES

An early draft of this essay was presented at the European Shakespeare Research Association Conference in Montpellier in 2013. I am grateful to Amy Tigner, Jennifer Munroe, Rebecca Laroche, Stephen Guy-Bray, Joe Campana, Sharon O'Dair, Donovan Sherman, and Karen Raber for their helpful feedback.

1. See Fudge, *Perceiving Animals*; Boehrer, *Shakespeare Among the Animals* and *Animal Characters*; Höfele, *Stage, Stake, and Scaffold*; Raber, *Animal Bodies, Renaissance Culture*; Shannon, *Accommodated Animal*.

2. Notable exceptions include Eric C. Brown's outstanding collection *Insect Poetics* and Joseph Campana's recent article "The Bee and the Sovereign." This chapter echoes Campana's observation that a "certain neglect of insects . . . is oddly characteristic both of early modern and

posthuman approaches to the relation between human and non-human" (97). Karen Raber considers some microfauna in early modern London in "Vermin and Parasites."

3. This passage is indebted to Raffles, *Insectopedia*, 202–3. For more on entomophobia, see Lockwood, *Infested Mind*.

4. All Shakespearean citations are taken from *The Oxford Shakespeare* and are cited parenthetically in the text. For a critique of Schiller's *spieltrieb*, see Huizinga, *Homo Ludens*, 168.

5. Much of the commentary in Moffett's *Theatre of Insects* (hereafter cited parenthetically in the text) is indebted to Conrad Gessner and Edward Wotton, though extensively supplemented and illustrated by Thomas Penny, who spent two decades collecting specimens and information from dozens of naturalists. Upon Penny's death in

1588, his papers passed to his friend Moffett, who made his own additions and stylistic improvements. Though Moffett had the manuscript (BL 1404) ready the following March, publication was stalled by the high engraving costs. Forty-five more years would elapse before the work finally appeared in print. For more on the collaborations that produced this monumental text, see Neri, *Insect and the Image*, 45–60.

6. According to Eric C. Brown, this trope of insect behavior as a theater for naturalists dates back to Pliny: "we observe, detached, this other world unfolding before us, but we ourselves are kept somehow beyond." *Insect Poetics*, x.

7. It seems somehow appropriate that the major rival of the Royal Shakespeare Company in Stratford-upon-Avon is a butterfly zoo. Brown, "Performing Insects," 31.

8. Stow, *Annals*, 1195–96.

9. Holinshed, *Third Volume of Chronicles*, 1299.

10. Basse, *Helpe to Discourse*, 154.

11. Baker, *Microscope Made Easy*, 295. Tradescant the Younger records "flea chains of silver and gold with 300 links apiece and yet but an inch long" in his inventory of the family natural history collections. *Musaeum Tradescantianum*, 39. According to Ashmolean curators, however, the chains have been lost.

12. *OED Online*, accessed 17 January 2016, http://www.oed.com/, s.v. "atomy," n. 1, definition 2.

13. Woodhouse, *Flea Sic Parua*, C2r.

14. Watson, "Ecology of Self."

15. Huizinga, *Homo Ludens*, 1.

16. Latham, *Elizabethan Fairies*; Briggs, *Anatomy of Puck* and *Faeries in Tradition*; Purkiss, *Bottom of the Garden*; Woodcock, "Spirits of Another Sort." Recent articles have wrestled with the problem of "fairy belief" in Shakespeare's more skeptical Protestant milieu: see Hattaway, "Enter Caelia, the Fairy Queen"; Lander, "Thinking with Faeries."

17. Hendricks, "'Obscured by Dreams'"; Loomba, "Great Indian Vanishing Trick." On the possibility that the play's allusions to India refer to the New World, see Buchanan, "India and the Golden Age."

18. Evidence of the flower fairies of Midlands folklore is difficult to pin down. Historians must rely on written sources, and Briggs garners hers primarily from Shakespeare and the Warwickshire poet Michael Drayton, whose *Nimphidia, the Court of Fairy* postdates Shakespeare's *Dream* and was probably influenced by it. Contrary to Briggs, Diane Purkiss deems it "questionable whether Shakespeare knew *anything* about fairies from oral sources at all" (*Bottom of the Garden*, 158). If so, insect performers such as Scaliot's flea may have

been the decisive catalyst behind Shakespeare's shrinking of the fairies.

19. Day, *Parliament of Bees*, G2v–4r.

20. For more on insects in world culture, see Bernebaum, *Bugs in the System*, 315–21; and Raffles, *Insectopedia*.

21. Byatt, *Angels and Insects*, 120. Purkiss comes close to expressing this same insight: "perhaps fauna are our Victorian faeries—natural, unspoilt, sweet, always in danger of disappearing and being sickened by us, our modernity, our industry." *Bottom of the Garden*, 307.

22. Myrone, *Henry Fuseli*, 58.

23. See Brown, "Performing Insects."

24. Ibid., 36.

25. Purkiss, *Bottom of the Garden*, 182.

26. Reinhardt's legendary production of the *Dream*, which helped pioneer expressionist theater, drew huge audiences in the Čapeks' hometown of Prague in 1906.

27. Lyly, *Endymion*, 4.3.176.

28. See Scott, "Still Life?"

29. Brown, "Performing Insects," 36.

30. In "Gaia and the Great Chain," 61–62, Gabriel Egan considers how the Elizabethan worldview undergirds Titus's sympathetic plea for the fly. Simon Estok, however, offers a more critical appraisal of the Great Chain of Being in *Ecocriticism and Shakespeare*, 91–92. The seeming alterity of the insect world continues to pester philosophers; see the phenomenological debate incited by Uexküll's speculations on the *Umwelt* of the tick in Buchanan, *Onto-ethologies*, 24–25.

31. Margaret Farrand first proposed that Shakespeare parodied Moffett's poem in "Additional Source." Her arguments persuaded Kenneth Muir—who reiterates them at length in *Shakespeare's Sources*, 39–45—and Harold Brooks in his 1979 Arden edition. Moffett's most recent editor, Victor Houliston, is skeptical, since this scenario requires that Shakespeare have read the poem in a manuscript for which no evidence exists. Katherine Duncan-Jones is likewise unconvinced; see her "Shakespeare's Debt to Moffett Cancelled." The verbal and tonal parallels, however, strain coincidence: e.g., "O Lions . . . whose murdering mouth and not the sisters three, / Did Thisbe sweete, sweete Thisbe fowly quell." Moffett, *Silkewormes and Their Flies*, 14.

32. Čapek and Čapek, *R.U.R. and The Insect Play*, 110.

33. This reading differs slightly from Wolfe's. Her chapter emphasizes the early modern admiration for engineers whose miniature automata fostered a perception of actual insects as machinelike. While commentators do praise Scaliot for

his craftsmanship, none of the accounts I have uncovered suspects his flea of being mechanical.

34. Hall, *Virgidemiarum*, 24.

35. In "Politics of Fairylore," Marjorie Swann argues that Stuart fairy poetry aims to "satirize elite display as a grotesquely parasitic activity" (459).

36. Though some doubt the link (see Opie and Opie, *Oxford Dictionary of Nursery Rhymes*, 323–24), Moffett's evident obsession with spiders and his advocacy of curds and whey as a health food (as well as the alternative spelling of his name as Muffet) make the identification not only tempting but also highly plausible.

37. Scot, *Discoverie of Witchcraft*, 86. According to the *OED*, the first usage of "bug" to denote an insect dates from 1642. Fifty years earlier, however, Moffett had recorded it as a synonym for beetle (*Theatre of Insects*, 1005). Although there is no textual proof illustrating "how a word meaning 'an object of terror, bogle,' became a generic name for beetles, grubs, etc.," it seems a fair conjecture that it has to do with entomophobia. *OED Online*, accessed 20 January 2016, http://www.oed.com/, s.v. "bug," n. 2.

38. On Japanese fascination with insects, see Raffles, *Insectopedia*, 343–86. For more on entomophobia, see Lockwood, *Infested Mind*, 35–51, and Tsutsui, "Looking Straight at *Them!*"

39. Fumerton, *Cultural Aesthetics*, 67–110; Stewart, *On Longing*, 37–69.

40. Raffles, *Insectopedia*, 125.

9

MISS MAZEPPA AND THE
HORSE WITH NO NAME

KARI WEIL

Within theater history, the name Mazeppa might bring to mind the accomplished, if bawdy, stripper from the 1959 musical *Gypsy*, and the song "You Gotta Have a Gimmick," written by Stephen Sondheim. "Once I was a schlepper, now I'm Miss Mazeppa," the song goes, describing how one must have a particular gimmick in order to get ahead in show business. With her brash and belting alto, Mazeppa's "ballsy" stage presence in *Gypsy* was heightened by her particular gimmick: she will "bump it with a trumpet."

Almost a century before *Gypsy*, another feisty Mazeppa became the hit of the stage in Paris. An actress rather than a stripper, this Mazeppa also had a gimmick, which was to "bump," so to speak, with her horse, or at least that was how a central scene of the play was represented in the press of the time (fig. 9.1).

Performing in a new kind of hippodrama that was developed in the early nineteenth century and brought together elements of high and low, theater and circus, Mazeppa was played by Adah Menken, or "La Menken," as she was called, and she became the hit of Paris theater for her bold ride across the stage on horseback wearing only a revealing bodysuit. For the audience, this fleshy appearance highlighted a certain nakedness she shared with her mount. What exactly was revealed in this dance of "white" woman and black horse was a question many longed to answer.

In this chapter, I focus on this performance of woman and horse onstage and on its reception in the Parisian press. Such equestrian performances could be seen to merge or transgress boundaries of high and low art, much as *Gypsy* was advertised as burlesque's response to Shakespeare.[1] More remarkable, however, was the way that Adah and her horse performed and transgressed categories, not only of gender and race but also of species. The role of Mazeppa was a "breeches role," that is, a masculine role played by a woman; in the original legend, Mazeppa is a young Ukrainian page

9.1
La Lune, 10 February 1867. Getty
Research Institute, Los Angeles,
92-S402.

boy in the court of King John II Casimir who has an adulterous love affair with the wife of a count. His punishment consists of being strapped naked to the back of a horse and sent off at a gallop across the steppes of eastern Europe. For an all but naked woman to play Mazeppa on horseback was in many ways a seductive spectacle, and one that raised the specter of an interspecies love affair—thus the heart surrounding the dancers in figure 9.1. Moreover, by ditching her (riding) breeches for a transparent leotard, Menken opened herself to suspicions regarding the purity of her own whiteness, such that the interspecies performance of woman and horse was turned by the public into a provocative dance of permeable gender, race, and species identity. While the intricacies of how Menken wanted to be seen within this dance were not always clear, it was clear that horses were integral to her image (much as fighting buffalo had been to her childhood—or so she wrote), and on arriving in Paris, she took to the streets on a spirited horse to prove that she could handle her horses as well as her men. Indeed, as Daphne Brooks has observed, it was her ride across the stage that "transformed what could have been a scene of violent abjection and prurient delight for spectators into the pinnacle of her performance."[2] Unlike the schlepper's striptease in *Gypsy*, the success of Menken's performance depended on the equal participation of her equine mate and on the dance that the two performed together with utmost skill and precision.

Mazeppa: From Romantic Genius to Equestrian Circus

The Mazeppa tale and the image of a naked man on horseback inspired a generation of authors and painters, beginning with Byron's 1819 poem of the same name, and launched the notion of what Nigel Leask has called an "equestrian sublime": a new romantic celebration of the horse, not as the submissive "workaday engine of society" or servant of war popularized in the eighteenth century, but as an image of wild and animalistic, if poetic, fury.[3] The equestrian sublime draws upon Plato's dark horse from the *Phaedrus*, a symbol of uncontrolled appetites and bodily lust, to celebrate romanticism's resistance to aesthetic and political authority. Paintings of the Mazeppa legend by Géricault and Delacroix focused on a passive but eroticized male figure, with legs splayed across the back of a frenzied horse. Perhaps more cautious, Victor Hugo wrote his own version of the Mazeppa legend, published in *Les Orientales* in 1829, in which he insisted that the horse was only a symbol for the artist's "genius" and thus forestalled any hint of bestiality in the myth.

Thus when a mortal whom God protects,
Is bound alive to your fateful back,
     Genius ardent steed
In vain he struggles, alas! You leap you carry him off
Away from the real world, whose barriers you smash
     With your hooves of steel![4]

The sublimity of this equestrian image, however, became something less symbolic and more physical in the equestrian circus. And as the equestrian was revealed to be an "equestrienne," the sublime materialized into an alluring but potentially dangerous spectacle of interspecies corporeality—an image with which male riders were only beginning to be saddled.

Second Empire Paris could, by many accounts, be called the era of the horse. Whether hitched to a carriage or under saddle, in the streets or the Bois de Boulogne, horses were omnipresent in the city and became the focus of a dandified lifestyle that brought the world of the "grand monde" together with the world of entertainment and spectacle. Within this world, horses and their riders were objects of admiration and jealousy as well as of satire. According to the popular nineteenth-century writer and satirist Albert Cler, the words of the influential and widely admired eighteenth-century naturalist Georges-Louis Leclerc, comte de Buffon, had become "classic and proverbial"; Cler added that it was "impossible to pronounce the word *horse* without immediately inciting, orally and mentally, the inevitable tirade: 'the most beautiful conquest that man has ever made,' etc."[5] If Buffon's horse draws firmly and singularly upon the white horse of Plato's *Phaedrus*, the "lover of honor and modesty and temperance, and the follower of true glory,"[6] Cler's account of "the horsey world" in *La comédie à cheval, ou Manies et travers du monde équestre* (The comedy on horseback, or Fads and follies of the equestrian world) insists both on the unpredictable temperament of horses and on the growing numbers of bourgeois riders who know just as little about governing themselves as they do about controlling a horse.

For Cler, that is to say, if equestrianism ever merited Buffon's image of nobility, it had certainly lost it in this era of the horse, in which riding and racing had become popular sport and entertainment. The studied and serious training that once prepared horses and men together for war now turned them both into moneymaking spectacles for an increasingly crass consumer.

The penultimate chapter of Cler's book focuses on one of those forms of entertainment, and what was indeed a literal theater of the horse, known as the Cirque Olympique. Opened in 1807 by the Franconi brothers in the midst of the "hippo-mania" that had spread from London to Paris, but drawing upon France's unique equestrian traditions, the Olympic Circus was referred to as a "temple of equitation" where audiences could come to see the amazing and beautiful feats of haute-école dressage, and Laurent Franconi was considered the most accomplished horseman of any circus.[7] But if the classical and neoclassical image of horse and rider held sway in the early years, a rather different image of horse and rider eventually made its way to the circus. It was there that the increasingly popular acrobatic stunts were performed on "naked" horses, which was to say, without bridle or saddle.

It was in the Olympic Circus of 1825 that the Mazeppa legend made its first translation to the stage in a new "*mimo-drame*"—half play, half equestrian spectacle—starring Franconi in the title role. Franconi's performance brought the legend to a different, popular audience. As Patricia Mainardi explains, the historical background of the Mazeppa ride was muddled when the Franconi brothers turned the Cossack into a Tartar and the story of ethnic and sexual tension was supplanted by a more classic tale of prince and pauper. Far from focusing on the romantic symbolism of the horse, the *mimodrame* drew crowds thanks largely to the excitement generated by Franconi's famous equestrian tricks. In other words, the conflation of man and horse suggested by the title, *Mazeppa, or The Tartar Horse*, showcased the man and his skill, while the horse functioned as his tool of self-recognition.

Some forty years later, a different version of the Mazeppa story again found its way to the Paris stage, this time with Adah Menken in the equestrian role. The play was titled *Les pirates de la Savane*, and its most thrilling scene starred Menken, strapped to the back of a horse who "galloped" across the stage. Decried by one critic as a "Female Phenomenon," Menken became the hit of Paris as she indulged both the fantasies and the fears of the Parisian public and revealed the strength and power that a woman could discover in partnership with her horse. Taking advance publicity into her own hands, Menken worked to transform the image of shared vulnerability and victimization of man and horse that had been suggested by earlier literary and visual representations of Mazeppa into a performance of bodily agency and mastery uncommon for women onstage. At the same time, the potential dangers of the role for her and her horse were made apparent to the public in ways that had previously been taken for granted, even as they became part of the attraction. The poet Théophile

Gautier, who reviewed the play in *Le Moniteur Universel*, described the charm of this danger to a beautiful horse and a beautiful woman together: "If his foot slipped, if a plank broke, the audience would have the pleasure of seeing a superb beast and a charming woman of intelligence, level-headedness and bravery, break together in bits. What greater attraction could one imagine?"[8] At the same time, however, this partnership accentuated Menken's own ambiguous "breed" and the very ethnic attributes that had been washed out of Franconi's Mazeppa except in vague, Orientalizing ways. Menken was an American born in New Orleans of mixed, if ambiguous, racial ancestry and a converted Jew. Her "Creole" identity inspired commentaries and fantasies about the relationship between race and species and reports that translated the sublime "passion" of Mazeppa into the affections of kissing kin. Indeed, Menken's success turned to scandal as the "phenomenon" of this *écuyère* inspired stories regarding the perverse passions of women for horses, raising the specter of animalistic miscegenation. The partnership of woman and horse onstage was thus as striking as the manner in which the press perverted that partnership into a forbidden passion of interspecies intimacy.

Sex, Race, Species, and La Menken

Adah Menken arrived in Paris in the fall of 1866, visibly pregnant but without husband and eager to take on whichever lovers or horses were worthy of her. A poet, revered horsewoman, and celebrated female lover, she was, as one writer of *Le Mousquetaire* called her, the "example of a new species." In a letter to a male friend, she wrote that men should be married, but not women: "Somehow they all sink into nonentities after this epoch in their existence. That is the fault of the female education. They are taught from their cradles to look upon marriage as the one event in their lives. That accomplished, nothing else remains."[9] Menken was out to prove that there was more to life than marriage, and that "something more" most often involved a horse.

First starring as Miss Mazeppa in Albany, New York, in 1861, Menken was an instant star, and her exciting ride on the steed Tartar was seen on stages across the United States and in London before she made her debut in Paris. There, on 30 December 1866, she opened in *Les pirates de la Savane*, in the role of Léo, a part loosely based on the Mazeppa legend and written expressly for her. Léo is a young Mexican and a mute, the latter quality solving the problem presented by Menken's American accent and also strengthening the identification between woman and animal. The story takes place in Mexico, where the nephew of an old French colonist, with the help of local pirates, attempts to steal his uncle's property from the rightful hands of his cousin, Eva. A battle ensues in which the nephew is killed; with the help of Léo, Eva's inheritance is restored to her. Subsequently captured by the pirates, Léo is tied naked to the back of a wild horse and let loose across the plains. In the role of Léo, Menken's femininity was made all the more apparent by the sheerness of her costume. The play sold out for 150 performances, and almost overnight Menken's image hit the market, her picture decorating everything from shaving mugs to ladies' pins.[10]

Advance publicity had much to do with the attraction, as circulars featured a nearly nude woman, her shapely curves set off by the blackness of the galloping horse on which she lay strapped, back to back. In response to accusations of indecency by her English critics, Menken defended her apparent nudity onstage by comparing the aesthetic value of her bodily poses to those of the ballet or sculpture. "My costume, or rather want of costume, as might be inferred, is not in the least indelicate and in no way more open to invidious comment than the dress worn by Cerito [or] Rosatio. . . . I have long been a student of sculpture and my attitudes, selected from the works of Canova, present a classicality which has been invariably recognized by the foremost of American critics."[11] Thus Menken's pink body stocking transformed the limp, passive body of the legendary Mazeppa into the seductive and lithe body of an athlete. French reviewers were in awe of her sculptural qualities: "There are stars and stars," wrote one critic, and "this one has nothing to say, she appears and she seduces, she mimes and she carries you away. . . . She is surprising, this *amazone*, with her supple body, whose forms are worthy of the admiration of a sculptor."[12] Even as she compared her act to the art of ballerinas, however, Menken insisted on advertising her physical if not animal presence and power. Prior to her arrival, the theater published a fourteen-page biographical notice, approved by Menken, that told of her successes not only in translating Greek but in fighting buffalo in Texas, her being captured by Indians, and her marriages to a series of husbands. Upon her arrival in Paris, she reportedly donned her "amazon," or riding habit, leased the most spirited horse to be had, and rode through the streets to show the public that she could handle her horses as well as her men.

Adah Menken thus both fit and exploited the image of the woman rider, or *écuyère*, of the time. While initially male riders performed the difficult exercises at the hippodromes, in 1835 Caroline Loyo became the first of successive generations of *écuyères* to dominate the circus. The opening of riding to women was part of the larger process of democratization of horse culture that took place in Paris over the course of the century. Under Napoleon, horseback riding was largely reserved for the military and, secondarily, as a pastime for nobility. In the years of the Restoration, however, and especially under the July Monarchy of Louis-Philippe, France experienced an "Anglomania" that led to the establishment of its own Jockey Club in 1834, which quickly became a popular meeting place for the "golden youth" of Paris. Equestrianism thus became a bourgeois sport. Its popularity grew especially under Napoleon III, who—being an avid horseman, like his wife—purchased the Bois de Boulogne in 1852 as a kind of horse playground for the city of Paris. Depending on whom one wanted to see, or to whom one wanted to show off his or her mount, there were specific time slots for appearing in the Bois. According to Alfred Delvau's *Plaisirs de Paris*, published in 1867 and documenting the lifestyle of "le tout Paris," the ride through the Bois became "the privileged promenade of a good half of Paris, the richer half, of course."[13]

But this is not to say that only the richer half rode. Indeed, it was becoming increasingly difficult to distinguish class in the figure of the *amazone*, or woman rider, and the uncertainty over her class affiliation was linked to uncertainty over her sexuality: she "could be harlot or lady of fashion," as Patricia Mainardi quite rightly asserts.[14] By 1867, the professional *écuyère* was often the most sought after of courtesans, and Paris was rife with stories of *écuyères* who married their adoring counts. At the same time, it was not unheard of for girls of the upper classes to train for the haute école.[15] In this way, the woman rider became emblematic of the transitional epoch of Second Empire France, with its increasingly fluid social and sexual boundaries. For many, she was a disturbing emblem precisely because of the visibility of her enjoyment, which depended not on a man but on a horse. Perhaps this is why Albert Cler insisted that, despite their similarity of outfit, one could distinguish the "femme du monde" from the "lorette," or courtesan, by the way the former "doesn't appear to care about her horse, except to stroke him occasionally with her hand. The 'woman of leisure' likes riding, but the pleasure she takes from it is calm; she easily concentrates it and does not let it burst out in noisy or exaggerated expressions."[16] Displays of affection toward animals, in other words, were prescribed by protocols of class, and only a lower-class woman would deign to show passion for her horse, or so Cler suggests.

That there nevertheless existed a special, potentially passionate relationship between women and horses was hinted at in a variety of writings and cartoons, such as those of Cham, published in 1858 (fig. 9.2). Céleste Mogador, a prostitute-turned-*écuyère* who published her memoirs in 1858, wrote of how she found in her "true passion" for horses a way to give herself pleasure and help heal the wounds of an abusive childhood.[17] Comparing herself to Mogador, the anonymous author of *Les Amazones de Paris* (1866), a collection of stories said to be told in and about the city's stables, claimed in the preface to be a former *écuyère* at the hippodrome and a woman who "loves horses with passion." Having realized that she could make a far better living with a "position," however, she left the hippodrome to try her luck. "But I rode horses so ravishingly, that I resolved to exploit this new talent in my own way."[18] A very savvy woman, this *écuyère*-turned-courtesan feigns stupidity to attract the great names of Paris as her escorts and patrons, and they in turn must learn to ride if they wish to keep their position with her. In the stories that follow, love between woman and horse is portrayed as the most constant and true, even if it may defy bourgeois conventions. In only one instance is the *amazone* a victim of her mount: one Lady Seyton, who as an audacious child and adolescent was the only person able to ride a certain horse called Tom, is in the end killed by him. But this turning on his mistress is represented as an act of saving grace on the

9.2
Cham, cartoon from *Paris aux courses*, 1858. Getty Research Institute, Los Angeles, 92-b9510.

— Il monte un cheval de quinze mille francs, veux-tu que je le mène chez toi?
— Le cheval? je veux bien!

part of the horse, who in a heroic gesture sacrifices his mistress to rescue her from a melancholy future as wife and mother.

These stories of horse love and horse agency might be regarded as nineteenth-century precursors to the kinds of dog love written about by Donna Haraway, Marjorie Garber, and Alice Kuzniar. As Kuzniar writes, "trans-special love transcends the constrictions that gender and sexuality place upon the human body." This was especially true of the relations between women and horses, which were established essentially through the body, and through forms of physical, social, and sexual mobility that were understood to be the prerogative of men or the wrong kind of women. Kuzniar adds that "pet devotion has the potential to question the regulating strictures and categories by which we define sexuality, eroticism and love, though not in the banal sense that it offers different forms of genital stimulation."[19] Even before Freud, however, it was the fear of alternative eroticism and genital stimulation that made riding, or rather straddling a horse, a transgressive act for women. When the title character of George Sand's *Indiana* dons her riding habit and joins the hunt, she experiences a mixture of "terror" and "pleasure" and demonstrates a "masculine courage" unknown to her lover, Raymon: "Raymon was frightened to see her thus, giving herself fearlessly to the fury of this horse whom she barely knew."[20] Flaubert describes the "particular brutality" that comes from handling "thoroughbred horses and the society of fallen women," and the comparison sheds light on why Emma Bovary's adulterous affair begins with a gallop through the woods: "she abandoned herself to the cadence of the movement which rocked her in the saddle."[21] To ride sidesaddle or *en amazone*, however, was said to reduce one's contact with the horse's motions, and especially that "excitation of the genital organs and the propensity for pleasures of love" that Charles Londe's *Gymnastique médicale* (1821) confirmed was stimulated by riding.[22] Nevertheless, the *amazone*, which referred to either the woman rider, her sidesaddle position, or the masculine riding habit, signaled both a specificity and a blurring of gender. The riding habit, the top half of which was modeled on the male riding coat (redingote), did its job of tightly buttoning in the chest, while the skirt, made of an excessively heavy material, was at times tied around the woman's legs so as not to fly up with the wind and risk exposing her legs.[23] To compensate for the loss of the efficient use of her legs, however, the *amazone* always had to carry a whip. This ready phallic symbol completed the image of transgression.

If the whip and habit gave the suggestion of masculine mastery, it was as "mistress" of the horse, with all the sexual connotations of that term, that Menken was represented in the press. Shortly after she arrived in Paris, it was reported that her horse had turned angry and unmanageable after being left in London. When he finally joined his mistress in Paris, it was said that he "whinnied insanely with joy and began like a dog to lick Miss Menken's hands and face."[24] This scene was prominently featured on the cover of the newspaper *La Lune*, with which we began, where Menken is seen dancing arm in arm with her horse, he in white tie, she in a revealing tunic, as he eagerly licks her face (fig. 9.1). The picture's caption reads "Miss Dada Menken," playing on the nickname given to Menken by the French public, and alludes to a hobbyhorse or pet subject, identifying woman with equine and both with a form of "insane" obsession. The licking horse (an uncommon sight) might remind us of the well-known passage at the opening of *When Species Meet*, in which Donna Haraway describes the "darter-tongue kisses" of her Australian shepherd and wonders about the "becomings" produced by their mutual affection, about the way her cells may have been colonized by her dog, and about what record or "traces in the world" their touch might leave.[25] In 1860s France, the idea of symbiogenesis was, of course, far in the future, but fantasies of a different sort of coevolution and multispecies organism were figured in a cartoon image that appeared later that season on the cover of the satirical newspaper *Le Hanneton*. Whereas the "centaur ideal" was integral to constructions of masculinity in the eighteenth century, that ideal is feminized and racialized here, as Menken is depicted as a "centauress" with a black horse body, a small white torso dressed in African garb, and an enlarged head whose ethnic origins are marked by dark curls and large hoop earrings (figure 9.3).[26]

At the very time that "Oriental" horses were being imported to improve the stock of European breeds, Menken's Semitic and "Oriental" features turned her

9.3
Cartoon from *Le Hanneton*,
23 May 1867. Getty Research
Institute, Los Angeles, 92-S403.

into something other than, and for some less than, a woman. An article titled "Les femmes phénomènes" (Women phenomena), signed by Biloquet Fils, compared Adah Menken to Cora Pearl, a British actress, equestrian, and famous coquette performing at the Bouffes-Parisiens. According to the author, these women were interchange-able—"Pearl or Menken, Menken or Pearl, it's all the same"—and this because neither were "real women." He continued by delivering a eulogy on the real woman, the mother Eve with her "elegant limbs," Venus dressed in her blond hair. "She has to be white, our mother Eve, white with that whiteness beneath which life and blood cir-culate." But nineteenth-century women were neither white nor really women: "This is where the taste for phenomena like Cora Pearl and Miss Adah leads us. Today it is English women on horseback, tomorrow it will be Germans playing the clarinet, then Italians climbing a greased pole, which brings us to Lapps and hottentots, we will come to that . . . acrobats, tight-rope walkers, horse-women, . . . sword swallowers, women with two heads, seals, androgynes, monsters, this is what we need."[27] From Menken, in other words, it was a short step to the androgyne and Hottentot, unsexed or oversexed, racially other if not of another species.

The final racist scandal over Menken was initiated by the reproduction and wide-spread display of a number of photographs taken of her in the lap of her presumed lover, Alexandre Dumas.[28] In response, the well-known poet Verlaine published a jingle repeated throughout Paris, in which the rhetoric of horsemanship is used to contrast Adah's sexual vitality with the aging Dumas's questionable potency, while Dumas's own black ancestry is invoked with the name of "Uncle Tom."

L'oncle Tom avec Miss Ada

C'est un spectacle dont on rêve

Quel photograph fou soude,
L'oncle Tom avec Miss Ada?
Ada peut rester à Dada,
Mais Tom, chevauche-t-il sans trêve?
L'oncle Tom avec Miss Ada,
C'est un spectacle dont on rêve.[29]

Uncle Tom with Miss Ada,
It's a spectacle one dreams about
What crazy photographer soldered
Uncle Tom with Miss Ada?
Ada can stay on her hobbyhorse
But can Tom mount forever?
Uncle Tom with Miss Ada,
It's a spectacle one dreams about.

The dreamed-of equestrian "spectacle" of Menken and Dumas thus appears to invoke the more nightmarish specter of animalistic miscegenation, fed by female dominance and male impotence. While that fear is tempered by the suggestion of photographic soldering, as if the match were only of and for the camera and not made of flesh, it is nevertheless the female equestrian who remains on top.

Verlaine's mocking of Dumas's sexual escapades with Menken by reference to an aging Uncle Tom exposes the links between race and species within the French imaginary, even as the entertainment industry had come to capitalize on transgressions of the "proper" boundaries of race, gender, and species. Indeed, the stage at once fed into and fed off the very fears of degeneration and impotence of which such transgressions were regarded as symptomatic. Performances of transspecies passion thus threatened the presumed foundation of French culture and society and offered both a seductive backdrop and a rationale for efforts to promote proper breeding, especially proper horse breeding, as an industry of national importance. Since the beginning of the century, and especially since the foundation in 1833 of the "Society for the Encouragement of the Betterment of the Race of Horses in France," and of the Jockey Club in 1834 (itself a racially segregated club), France had been engaged in competition with England to produce the best "race" of horses, and to this end imported more and more "purebreds," mostly Thoroughbreds from England but also Arabians from northern Africa. The otherwise imprecise nineteenth-century definition of "race" was given "scientific" application to the equine population.[30] This was the rationale behind the "studbook," which was created in 1833 and first published in 1838, documenting both the paternal and maternal lineage of all purebreds, including workhorses or draft horses. Some fifty years after its conception, one equine specialist,

H. V. de Loncey, wrote that "the studbook shows better than any rationale, the importance that must be attached to the ancestry and confirmed race of the reproducers we
use . . . and we remain convinced of the mathematical truth of the old axiom: Good
blood cannot lie."[31]

This emphasis on good blood and race might shed a different light on Adah
Menken's suggestion that women refuse marriage. From stage to racetrack, women
and mares were valued above all for their performance in reproduction, and especially for upholding the purity of race. No amount of acting (or talent) could disguise
or compensate for the truth of breeding, so it was said, but as Menken's public kept
coming to see through her performance and pin down her truth, so did her intrepid
ride on horseback keep her secrets hidden, even in her nakedness.

Curtain Calls

It was perhaps prescient that Cler ended his book of horse "Follies" with a chapter on
Montfaucon, the Paris slaughter yards that closed in 1842. Cler described Montfaucon
as a "theater" of another sort, one where both working and noble horses met their
gruesome end and where every body part of the horse, including the blood, was
turned into steak, oil, or a particular paint known as "bleu de Prusse" (Prussian blue).
Distinctions among breeds or races mattered little in this final act, which had been
moved outside the city walls and beyond the view of the consumer because the spectacle was increasingly regarded as dangerous to see and might inure the audience to
violence or incite more of it. As coincidence would have it, horse meat was legalized
for human consumption the same year as Menken's debut on the Parisian stage, suggesting that the circus and stage did little to humanize the horse, however much the
horse animalized the woman.[32] Cler's flippant, satirical tone cannot conceal the horror
of this final chapter in the horse's life, and one can only wonder how the public came
to accept that a "dashing and brilliant steed, winner at the hippodrome and applauded
with the military solemnity, or that favorite mare, caressed by the hand of a lovely
amazon, could from one day to the next, be rushed from glory and honor into the mire
of the butcher."[33] Indeed, one wonders what "regimes" of emotion or affection allowed
a horse's companionship, talent, and affection to sink into oblivion, or onto the plate.[34]

Menken's death in 1868 after a brief illness was marked by a similar absence of
pomp or sorrow, despite her brilliant if brief stardom. According to reports, her
funeral procession included fifteen people in all, mostly her maids and grooms. Her
various friends and lovers had abandoned her, all but one. At the rear of the procession
was her horse, led by an attendant. His black color now took on new meaning for the
public as a symbol of mourning, but any idea of his own sense of loss or sadness was,

of course, unreported. For all the attention to his partnership in their performance, he mattered only as a reflection of her. His (or her?) name was never mentioned.

NOTES

1. Rich, "Gypsy Is Back."

2. Brooks, *Bodies in Dissent*, 182. Brooks's chapter is a brilliant reading of the racial politics involved in Menken's performances and their reception, especially within the American context. Beyond this one comment, however, she has little to say about the role of the horse or species identity.

3. On the notion of an "equestrian sublime," see Leask, "'To Canter with the Sagitarre.'"

4. Hugo, *Poésie*, 1.250–52. On the Mazeppa myth, see Mainardi's chapter "Many Ways to Ride a Horse: Mazeppa," in *Husbands, Wives, and Lovers*.

5. Cler, *Comédie à cheval*, 1.

6. Mainardi, *Husbands, Wives, and Lovers*, 189.

7. Thétard, *Merveilleuse histoire du cirque*, 2:167. On the "hippo-mania" that swept London, see Monica Mattfeld's chapter in this volume.

8. Théophile Gautier, "Miss Adah Menken dans *Les pirates de la Savane*," *Le Moniteur Universel*, 7 January 1867. All translations are my own unless otherwise noted.

9. Quoted in Falk, *Naked Lady*, 141.

10. Lesser, *Enchanting Rebel*, 194.

11. Quoted in Falk, *Naked Lady*, 78. A version of the letter is reprinted in French in *Le Mousquetaire*, 31 December 1866.

12. "Les pirates de la Savane," *Le Centaure*, 10 January 1867.

13. Delvau, *Plaisirs de Paris*, 31.

14. Mainardi, *Husbands, Wives, and Lovers*, 111.

15. See, for instance, the preface to de Vaux, *Écuyers et écuyères*, in which Henri Meilhac reprints a letter from a woman of some standing to the Countess Soperani, once an *écuyère* herself, asking her opinion on whether the woman's daughter should be allowed to pursue her wish to train as a rider of the haute école.

16. Cler, *Comédie à cheval*, 115–16.

17. *Mémoires de Céleste Mogador*, 139.

18. *Amazones de Paris*, 6.

19. Kuzniar, "'I Married My Dog,'" 208.

20. Sand, *Indiana*, 161–62.

21. Flaubert, *Madame Bovary*, 79, 234.

22. Londe, *Gymnastique médicale*, 208.

23. On the restrictive nature of the *amazone*, see Croqueville, *Paris en voiture à cheval*, chapter 30, and Pons d'Hostun, *Ecuyer des dames*, lettre X.

24. Jules Claretie, "Courrier de Paris," *L'Illustration*, 5 January 1867.

25. Haraway, *When Species Meet*, 15–16.

26. On the centaur ideal, see Kim Marra's chapter in this volume. Marra's chapter also demonstrates how horses acted to queer conventional boundaries of sex, race, and species on the American stage.

27. Biloquet Fils, "Les femmes phénomènes," *La Lune*, 10 February 1867.

28. A writer of poetry herself, Menken befriended a number of literary personalities in both France and Britain.

29. Quoted in Falk, *Naked Lady*, 182. *Uncle Tom's Cabin* was first published in France in 1853.

30. "The word *race* . . . has had many different accepted uses. Some have used it to encompass both race and species, others have made it a division of species. For us, who are polygeneticist, we consider the word race to be too abstract a term. In fact, where does a race begin and end?" Larousse, *Dictionnaire universel*, 13:596.

31. De Loncey, *Races de chevaux de trait*, 187.

32. On the legalization of horse meat in France, see Weil, "They Eat Horses, Don't They?"

33. Cler, *Comédie à cheval*, 153.

34. I borrow the idea of an "emotional regime," or prescribed displays (and speech acts) of emotion, from Reddy, *Navigation of Feeling*.

10

HORSES QUEER THE STAGE AND SOCIETY OF *SHENANDOAH*

KIM MARRA

The heart of the steed, and the heart of the master
Were beating like prisoners assaulting their walls,
Impatient to be where the battle-field calls
. . . .
The first that the general saw were the groups
Of stragglers, and then the retreating troops
. . . .
He dashed down the line 'mid a storm of huzzas,
And the wave of retreat checked its course there, because
The sight of the master compelled it to pause.
With foam and with dust the black charger was gray;
By the flash of his eye, and the red nostril's play,
He seemed to the whole great army to say,
"I have brought you Sheridan all the way
From Winchester, down to save the day."

Hurrah! hurrah for Sheridan!
Hurrah! hurrah for horse and man!
—THOMAS BUCHANAN READ, "SHERIDAN'S RIDE" (1864)

Verging into "horse drama," playwright Bronson Howard and producer Charles Frohman waited anxiously on opening night of the American Civil War play *Shenandoah* (9 September 1889) at Broadway's Star Theatre to see whether the appearance of a live horse in the climactic scene would elicit laughter or applause. They need not have worried. Already immortalized in verse and painting, General Philip Sheridan's fourteen-mile ride on his valiant steed Winchester (a.k.a. Rienzi) to rally Union troops for their pivotal victory in the 1864 Battle of Cedar Creek, reenacted in

Shenandoah as a fleeting gallop across the stage by an actor on horseback, launched one of the most profitable and popular plays of the late nineteenth century. The live horse effect proved so sensational that major Broadway revivals of the play in the 1890s boasted up to fifty horses to flesh out its numerous cavalry and other equestrian scenes. *Shenandoah* thrilled military and civilian audiences alike at a time when both equine and human Civil War veterans were dying off and receiving military honors, including Winchester himself, whose taxidermied body (later moved to the Smithsonian) was installed in the military museum on Governors Island in New York Harbor.[1]

Along with breaking the line separating serious drama from sensational spectacle, horses also crossed other conventional boundaries, queering cultural norms of gender and sexuality and interlocking categories of species, race, class, region, and, ultimately, life and death. Both on- and offstage in an era of military and civilian reliance on horsepower, this queering force operated in relation to the quintessential image of manliness: the mounted straight white male military officer in perfect command of his steed and his troops showcased in various *Shenandoah* scenes, most iconically in Sheridan's ride. Horses hugely magnified human corporeal presence and power, but in so doing they also greatly heightened human physical and social vulnerabilities. While achieving manliness on horseback, white men became highly subject to horsey unmanning, whether by the large, unpredictable animals themselves or by other riders, including women and free and enslaved African Americans, or by human enemies on the ground who targeted horses. Successive productions of *Shenandoah* highlighted such horsey queering vulnerabilities even as they reasserted northern white male equestrian supremacy and returned dead human and equine heroes to the living. In the process, horses also bent notions of performance itself, as equine actors blurred lines between real and make-believe in stage representation and operated in different registers of awareness from their human counterparts. To elucidate these ambivalent dynamics, this chapter draws on print archives of the 1889 Broadway premier production, Charles Frohman's revivals of 1894 and 1898, and Jacob Litt's even more massive 1898–99 remounting, as well as my own embodied knowledge of horses as a rider and former competitor in the cavalry-derived sport of three-day eventing, or equestrian triathlon. The analysis focuses on key moments in the staging of cross-species interactions, culminating in Sheridan's ride, and their meaning in relation to military and civilian equestrian cultures for spectators still struggling with the staggering losses and social upheavals of the Civil War.

The Horse as a Third Party

"Hurrah! hurrah for horse and man!" cheers Thomas Buchanan Read for both species together in his famous poem "Sheridan's Ride" (1864). An indispensable part of military and civilian life in and around the Civil War, horses massively constituted a third party in the interhuman relations of the conflict. According to best estimates, 750,000 human antagonists perished in this bloodiest of American wars; twice that number—1.5 million—horses and mules died serving along with them, vastly multiplying the carnage.[2] Equines carried soldiers into battles and countless other combat operations and hauled artillery and supplies, including provisions for themselves as well as for the more than three million men mobilized during the war. These huge animals gave their tremendous strength and power to the campaigns, but there were limits to what they could bear. Like humans, many more equines suffered and died from overexertion, horrible conditions, deprivation, disease, and other exigencies of war than from battle wounds. Combatants bore continuous witness to the horrific suffering and death of both species. Equine and human well-being determined strategy and outcomes; hence, General William Tecumseh Sherman's demand that "every opportunity at a halt during a march should be taken advantage of to cut grass, wheat, or oats, and extraordinary care be taken of the horses upon which everything depends."[3] Relying on their horses, and in many instances becoming quite attached to them, commanders and their troops also had to be prepared, when rations and forage ran out, to eat the flesh of their equine comrades to survive.[4] Yoked together in war, human and equine fates were inextricably intertwined. The corporeal needs, sensations, and character of one species viscerally entered and pulled on those of the other, altering bodies and identities.

When *Shenandoah* appeared on Broadway in 1889, twenty-four years after Appomattox, firsthand memories of Civil War experiences were still so palpable, and the more immediate circumstances of Reconstruction were so fraught, that the play, like other contemporary fictional representations, deliberately kept the bitter sectional politics and realities of slavery from view. Written from the northern perspective and never touring farther south than Baltimore, *Shenandoah* offered salving visions of reconciliation through North-South romance while triumphantly asserting Union victory through the famous battle reenactment. What distinguished it from similarly themed and skewed dramatic and literary fictions of the war were all the ways in which it cleverly interwove horses into the storytelling. This, among other aspects, prompted the retired General Sherman—an avid theatergoer who attended the opening and became a fixture, with his own box, for the duration of the initial New York run—to proclaim it "the most interesting war play I have ever seen."[5] Precisely in its human-equine interweaving, *Shenandoah* also proved uniquely revealing of the queering pull of cross-species intimacies.

Leading up to the brief, climactic appearance of Sheridan himself, the play introduces several officers of his cavalry, along with Major-General Francis Buckthorn and Sergeant Barket of the 19th U.S. Army Corps, all of whom figure in the North-South romance plots and derive manly authority from horses. The action opens in 1861, on the eve of Fort Sumter, at a residence on Charleston Harbor, where Colonel Kerchival West of Sheridan's cavalry, the play's leading hero, his sister Madeline, and his immediate commander, General John Haverill, have gathered with two Southerners, Colonel Robert Ellingham and his sister Gertrude, the play's leading heroine. After training together at West Point and fighting Indians together on the plains, Kerchival and Robert have grown as close as brothers, and now each is in love with the other's sister. General Haverill has served as guardian to Robert and Gertrude since their father died fighting alongside him in the Mexican War, an old allegiance that, like the filial and affectional bonds between these assembled characters, will be torn asunder in the impending War Between the States.

The officers of Sheridan's cavalry and the 19th U.S. Army Corps in *Shenandoah* arrive and depart on horseback when duty calls. Familiar with equestrian culture, audiences would have assumed this, and the dialogue makes reference to equestrian comings and goings even when the horses themselves do not appear. These men have to be mounted in order to have the mobility and visibility necessary to carry out missions and direct troops in the field. Moreover, they have to ride well to be effective; demonstrable command of their mounts literally undergirds their military command. This equestrian authority cannot be achieved simply by brute force, but rather requires years of training for the riders to meld with their horses' movements and gain their trust. Only then will these highly sensitive, thousand-pound prey animals with lightning-quick reflexes overcome their instinctual fears and, at their riders' behest, traverse strange terrain, jump imposing obstacles, and run into the manifest dangers of combat. Thus an exemplary officer of the Civil War era also had to be an accomplished horseman who commended his lower body to his horse, becoming, as was said of General Ulysses S. Grant, a centaur, no longer a discrete human but a mammalian hybrid, open to corporeal communion with another species.[6] Through that interspecies communion, the cavalry officer arrogated to himself the horse's potency and presence. For this reason, the best bred, most athletic, and most spirited mounts were designated officers' horses. In the play, by implication if not in flesh, the officers' steeds are always just offstage, waiting in the wings to complete their masters' manly military identities.

That equine proximity, which heightens the dramatic tension and the play's aura of realism, becomes immediately apparent in act 1, when the first horse to make a physical appearance, the male equine character called Jack, does so by sticking his head and neck through the set—a window panel in the back wall—while the assembled humans await the attack on Fort Sumter. This is the striking black steed whom Union forces later seize to bear General Sheridan, but who begins the play as southern belle Gertrude's pet and favorite mount. Bronson Howard invented this twist in the horse's story (Sheridan actually acquired the horse as a difficult three-year-old from an intimidated Michigan cavalry officer, named him Rienzi after his raid on Rienzi,

Mississippi, and then changed his name to Winchester, whence he valiantly galloped to Cedar Creek), but the playwright's dramatic license is not far-fetched. Invaluable resources, thousands of horses were captured by enemy forces and ended up fighting for both North and South. Some changed sides multiple times over the four years of the war. Because of Winchester's fame and his depiction in widely disseminated commercial illustrations (see, for example, fig. 10.1), the horse who played him had to convincingly embody his fine breeding and handsome bearing, relatively tall stature (sixteen hands, or sixty-four inches at the high point of the spine above the shoulder), jet black color, and distinctive markings—three white stockings and a star on his forehead, which could be effected with makeup.[7] The first equine to essay the role was a well-trained stage veteran named Black Bess after the steed who saved highwayman Dick Turpin by galloping until she dropped, a heroic act of equine self-sacrifice celebrated in romantic novels and hippodramas.[8] Although the horse's name indicates a mare, she looked the part of Winchester and earned rave reviews for her cross-gender star turn. Through repetition and reward, Black Bess learned her part exceptionally well; she performed for the duration of *Shenandoah*'s 250-performance run in New York, accompanied the show on tour, and starred again in Frohman's 1894 revival of the play.[9]

Black Bess as Jack makes only a partial appearance in the first act, but the stage business reveals much about the significance of horses and the gender politics of equestrian culture in the world of the play. Jack's mistress, Gertrude, enters in her riding habit with whip in hand, immediately marking herself as a bold equestrienne, and announces her intention to ride over to a neighbor's to solicit news about Confederate general Beauregard's maneuvers. Just as the officers call on orderlies to bring their horses, Gertrude tells the groom Old Pete to let Jack approach. That was the signal for the stagehand to move Black Bess into position from backstage. Holding up bonbons at an open window, Gertrude utters the words "I love you," which Kerchival hopes are for him, but the endearment is for Jack.[10] Black Bess obligingly stuck her head through the window on cue to take the treats with her lips from the palm of the actress's hand. This is but the first of several ways in which Gertrude's unabashed affection for Jack and her accomplished horsemanship pose challenges to her suitor Colonel Kerchival West's manhood and to wider masculine military authority.

Gertrude represents the rising mid-nineteenth-century generation of white middle- and upper-class women who began taking up the sport of riding en masse for recreation. Because equestrianism had for millennia been chiefly a male prerogative bound up in masculine power and identity, and because of how men experienced horsepower entering their bodies when astride, women's growing entrée into riding caused considerable social concern. Female equestrianism had to be carefully disciplined and kept within strict gender bounds, most notably through sidesaddle, which remained de rigueur for respectable women, at least in the eastern United States,

10.1   Chromolithograph of Thure de Thulstrop, *Sheridan's Ride*. Facsimile print by L. Prang & Co., 1886.
Library of Congress Prints and Photographs Division, Washington, D.C.

until 1915.[11] Supposedly to preserve modesty and chastity, the lady rider, fully skirted, corseted, and often veiled, did not straddle the horse with her crotch but rather kept both legs on the left side, with only the left foot in a stirrup and the right leg bent over the left knee. Brackets or "pommels" were attached to the sidesaddle for her to squeeze with her thighs so as to hold herself in place. Both the brackets and the long skirt made mounting and dismounting considerably more challenging and complicated for aside than astride riders. Although techniques were available to women for mounting sidesaddle on their own, these involved the indecorous practice, especially in the requisite skirts, of swinging the right leg over the horse and sitting briefly astride before moving the right leg back across the horse to place it in the bracket over the left leg.[12] Thus the most proper—and, by design, least autonomous—way for women to mount required the assistance of two men, a groom to hold the horse and a gentleman who, with acquired finesse and careful coordination, assisted her into the saddle. He had to cup her left foot in his hands while letting her push up with her left hand on his shoulder and then move with her as she sprang up on her right foot to lift her smoothly up to a side-sitting position in the saddle. He then helped her secure her left foot in the stirrup and adjust her skirts so that she could comfortably bracket her right leg. Reversing these steps for the dismount likewise required careful coordination with male assistance to maintain decorum. Helping a lady mount and dismount were skills akin to leading a ballroom dance, and a proper gentleman was expected to learn them. So that she would not travel unaccompanied, and lest she need to dismount and remount during the ride, two men—a groom and a gentleman—also customarily rode with her.[13]

In the space of her short first scene, Gertrude makes abundantly clear that she does not need all this male assistance and control over her riding. When Kerchival says that he'd be delighted to ride, presumably on his officer's mount, at her side in the gentleman's role, she scoffs, "At my side! There isn't a horse in America that can keep by the side of my Jack, when I give him his head, and I'm sure to do it. You may follow us." While caressing Jack's head and feeding him bonbons, Gertrude explains how she gets such winning performances from her steed: "Jack has been my boy ever since he was a little colt. I brought you up, didn't I, Jack? He is the truest, and kindest, and best of friends; I wouldn't be parted from him for the world, and I'm the only human he'll allow to be near him." As sparks of gunfire break out in the distance, opposing sectional loyalties quickly provoke tension in their conversation until Gertrude, secreting her underlying love for Kerchival, tersely asserts, "You need not ride over with me, Mr. West. . . . I choose to go alone! Old Pete will be with me; and Jack, himself is a charming companion." When Kerchival retorts by asking whether she prefers Jack's company to his, she replies over her shoulder as she exits the stage, "I do." "Damn Jack!" exclaims Kerchival. In a last-ditch effort to salvage his manly lover's pursuit, he exits after her, calling out, "But you will let me assist you to mount" (392–93). Spectators do not see whether she lets him do so or not, but the tenor of the scene suggests that she is more than capable of mounting—and doing almost anything else with a horse—on her own.

In a telling aside to the audience in this scene, Kerchival declares, "Jack embarrasses me. He's a third party" (390). The horse is a third party not only in stealing the lady's affections from her human suitor but also in providing the means for showing men up in what had historically been their preserve. If sidesaddle riding was designed to disadvantage women and keep them dependent on men, women quickly proved themselves to be highly effective in working with horses from the ground as well as on horseback. Generally smaller in stature than men and conditioned to be nurturers rather than aggressors, women tended to adopt more patient and gentle methods that were more conducive to horses' sensitive natures. Moreover, as asymmetrical and challenging a mode of equestrianism as sidesaddle is, it forces the rider to develop a strong seat, which is the key to good riding, whether aside or astride. At the time of *Shenandoah*'s production, women were publicly demonstrating that they could ride as well as or even better than men in respectable venues such as Central Park and the National Horse Show (begun in 1883) at Madison Square Garden.[14] These lady riders were from the same social demographic as the white middle- and upper-class women who increasingly dominated Broadway theater audiences, and they flocked to *Shenandoah* along with their male escorts and war veterans.[15]

Given the rise in women's equestrian pursuits and the use of live horses onstage, the actress who played Gertrude had to be credibly intimate with equines. The three female stars of the major Broadway productions of *Shenandoah* were all accomplished horsewomen whose fondness for and expertise with horses could radiate across the footlights. In a story about the star of the 1889 premiere production, a popular magazine reported, "Viola Allen's favorite exercise, naturally, is horse-back riding. Every morning at 11:30, accompanied by one of her brothers or an attendant from the riding school, she mounts her horse, whose name is Glory, and is off for a brisk canter along the bridle paths of the big, beautiful park."[16] The Georgia-born daughter of Confederate general William W. Kirkland, Odette Tyler, who starred in Frohman's 1894 revival at the Academy of Music, grew up riding horses. Likewise, Kentucky-born Mary Hampton, star of Jacob Litt's 1898–99 revival, was a southern belle who, in her own words, "was almost raised on a horse."[17] These Gertrudes were entirely comfortable letting Jack eat out of their hands, holding and caressing his head and neck, and kissing his velvet nose, because the actresses routinely had such interactions with horses in their daily lives. The sight of these cross-species intimacies onstage would have delighted female audience members who likewise knew a horse's touch. Crucially, such displays of woman-horse affection could remain chaste within the presumed proprieties of Anglo-American sidesaddle riding culture, in marked contrast to the still salient, bestiality-tinged specter of Adah Isaacs Menken's exotic, sexually provocative equestrianism in her Mazeppa role.[18] For the horse's part, Black Bess as Jack was only too happy to respond to the familiar offer of a treat and a rub. One backstage reporter followed Odette Tyler back to her dressing room and noted that she stopped to caress her equine scene partner along the way.[19] As horse lovers, Allen and Hampton probably did the same, because they too found horses irresistible and because the interaction fostered easy extension of the behavior from daily life to backstage and into onstage rehearsal and performance.

Although much is made of Gertrude's love for her horse, there are no indications in the script, or any mention in reviews of the play found to date, that male actors or their characters displayed affection for their equine comrades. In the face of so much equine death, disease, and suffering, soldiers had to adopt a utilitarian view of horses and see them as expendable. Yet many who fought in the war recorded their tender feelings for the horses in their charge, and they expressed sorrow when a valiant steed was shot out from under them or collapsed from exhaustion and had to be left behind. Some of the testimonials of the affectional bonds that formed between man and horse are quite poignant, such as the one left by Captain George Baylor of the 12th Virginia Cavalry:

> The cavalryman and his horse got very close to each other, not only physically, but also heart to heart. They ate together, slept together, marched, fought and often died together. While the rider slept, the horse cropped the grass around him and got as close up to his rider's body as he could get. The loyal steed pushed the trooper's head gently aside with his nose to get at the grass beneath it. By the thousands, men reposed in fields fast asleep from arduous campaigns with their horses quietly grazing beside them, and nary a cavalier was trod upon or injured by his steed.[20]

A picture in the Library of Congress print collection further illustrates the physical proximity of the two species (fig. 10.2). Lieutenant Williston from the U.S. Horse Artillery stands with the right side of his torso leaning comfortably against his horse's left side, ribs to ribs, while his right arm rests on the horse's back and the fingers of his right hand burrow into the horse's mane, scratching the skin just above the withers. This is a sweet spot that horses cannot reach themselves and thus love to have others scratch for them. In appreciation, the horse turns his head toward the lieutenant, who, while holding the rein in his left hand, reaches with his forefinger to rub the horse's lip. The two are standing so close to each other and are so relaxed that the man's bent left knee appears to touch the horse's left front knee, and the man's booted left foot rests on the ground practically up against the horse's hoof. The pose encapsulates the ease and familiarity that come from working intensively together, especially in the grave circumstances of military service.[21]

After soldiers returned from the war, however, the gender politics of displaying affection for horses shifted. As women's riding rose in popularity, it became institutionalized and commercialized in a burgeoning industry of riding academies, horse shows, suburban foxhunting clubs, and tack and clothing stores. Illustrated magazines such as *Harper's*, *Life*, *McClure's*, *Appleby's*, *Peterson's*, and the *Rider and Driver*, along with countless postcards and other ephemera, disseminated trends in female riding and equestrian couture nationwide. A prominent pictorial motif of women bussing and caressing horses fueled more female horse passion.[22] In this climate, a man who displayed tender affection for his horse risked being seen as womanly. Thus, despite the significant record of man-horse affection during the war, those male sentiments are almost entirely absent in the postwar print media record of civilian life. This helps explain the absence of those male sentiments in *Shenandoah*, a play of the fin de siècle, albeit set in the Civil War years, whose program ads for women's as well as men's equestrian attire, equipment, and services reflect its embeddedness in the now female-flooded equestrian sport. Of course, it is quite possible that men involved in

10.2   James Gardner, *Lt. Williston and Horse. U.S. Horse Artillery, Culpeper, Va. September 1863*. One negative: glass, wet collodion. Library of Congress Prints and Photographs Division, Washington, D.C.

Shenandoah's production gave the horses affectionate pats backstage; the two species waited together in close quarters in the wings. But such exchanges apparently were not publicized.

   Along with the pull of horses across gender boundaries, *Shenandoah*, while eliding the issue of slavery in the fraught postwar decades, perhaps unavoidably invoked equine disruptions of racial divisions. After Gertrude summons Old Pete to let Jack approach, and feeds her pet bonbons and caresses his head through the window, the stage direction reads, "An old Negro leads the horse away" (390). The word "slave" is not used, but in 1861 at a southern residence, the "old Negro" would have been an enslaved African American. An earlier version of the play called *Drum Taps* (1873), which did not evolve past three charity performances in Detroit, featured an "octoroon slave maid Nettie ('worth $2,000 in gold')" for Gertrude in addition to Old Pete.[23] Both characters, in keeping with the theatrical convention at the time, would have been played by white actors in blackface. A domestic worker, Nettie could be excised from subsequent versions without disrupting the war romance plot, but Old Pete remained necessary for the central horsey business in the expository first act because

10.3   W. S. L. Jewett, *Ladies' Riding-School*, *Harper's Bazaar*, 3 July 1869, 429.

the manual labor of horse care in the South fell to slaves. Working around horses for generations, enslaved African Americans acquired considerable knowledge of horsemanship. When Gertrude boasts to Kerchival that she is the "only human" Jack will allow near him, she implies that Old Pete, who obviously handles the horse, is not fully human, which is consistent with white attitudes toward enslaved African Americans in the South at the time. Nevertheless, love of horses and riding, and involvement in Jack's training, have kept this southern belle working closely with Old Pete, including taking instruction from him, in physical, tactile ways over many years.

For northern audiences, Old Pete corresponded to the free African Americans who found work as stable hands in the burgeoning urban riding industry. This trend was common enough to be portrayed in the July 1869 *Harper's Bazaar* illustration *Ladies' Riding-School* (fig. 10.3). Depicting riding instruction at several levels in the movement of pupils around the arena, the drawing captures the progression of the female rider, who begins instruction as a child riding astride with the African American stable worker's assistance and then grows up and graduates to full ladyship sidesaddle with a white male teacher. Viewed in a northern context, Gertrude's continuing closeness with Pete and her preference for riding with him alone as her companion does more than insult her suitor's manly white chivalry; it also suggests that she has not fully graduated to proper white female equestrianism and thus might be prone to backsliding, on and off the horse, a possibility that moves the plot in subsequent acts.

The immediate effect of her ride with Old Pete raises further concerns. Near the end of act 1, her voice is heard from offstage as she returns on horseback: "Whoa! Jack! Old boy! Steady, now—that's a good fellow. . . . O-h! Pete! You may take Jack to the stable. Ha-ha-ha!" After dismounting offstage (with or without Pete's help we don't know), she appears by thrusting her own head, Jack-like, through the window and informing Kerchival, "Old Pete, on the bay horse, has been doing his best to keep up with us, but Jack and I have led him such a race! Ha-ha-ha-ha!" (398). As with Gertrude's infamous theatrical prototype, Lady Gay Spanker in Dion Boucicault's *London Assurance* (1841), the gallop on horseback has infused Gertrude with the biblical "Ha-ha!" of horsiness—"He saith among the trumpets, Ha, ha" (Job 39:25, KJV); she fairly tosses her head and snorts in defiance of white female propriety. As hostilities escalate to cannon fire on Fort Sumter, and Kerchival, now in full Union cavalry attire, readies himself to assume his command on the field, he demands to know whether she loves him. Tapping her skirt with her riding whip, Gertrude withholds her feelings. Her suitor must ride into war and fight to regain his manhood.

Queering Battle Riding

Potentially emasculating challenges to military manliness increase over the next two acts on a set built for the rapid movement of live horses. After act 1, time jumps ahead three years to 1864, and the scene changes to the exterior of the Ellingham Homestead in the northern Virginia sector of the Shenandoah Valley. A low redbrick wall extends from the corner of a veranda across the stage, with a wide center opening flanked by two low, flat-topped pillars. Just behind the wall is a road that runs across the entire stage, and upstage of the road sits an elevation of rock and turf beyond which the valley and Three Top Mountain are visible. Gertrude and Madeline stand on the elevation on the other side of the road to watch the troops marching by. Gertrude remarks that a month ago it was the Confederate army; now Sheridan's Union cavalry is close at hand. In the premiere 1889 production, the troops were seen only in the distance, and the road was reserved for Sheridan's climactic ride at the end of act 3. But as equine actors were added in subsequent productions, the road in both acts 2 and 3 became a site for the actual comings and goings of horses and riders and for confrontations of women's versus men's equestrianism.

When a letter arrives with instructions for delivering a dispatch, Gertrude volunteers to take it herself. Lamenting that two years earlier enemy forces purloined her beloved Jack, she resolves to carry the dispatch on her remaining gray steed. News of the approach of regiment commander Colonel Kerchival West hastens the departure of this heroine, whom the press dubbed "the proud, high-spirited Southern girl," a moniker fit for a Kentucky racing filly.[24] In the 1894 and subsequent productions,

10.4
"The Greater Shenandoah, by Bronson Howard: 'A Fair Prisoner.'" Poster for the 1894 production of *Shenandoah*, featuring Odette Tyler as Gertrude Ellingham, sidesaddle on her horse fending off her captors, who are trying to help her dismount in act 2. Strobridge & Co. Lith.

Kerchival and then General Haverill and several attending officers ride up to the house "on steeds that are restive enough to make folks in the orchestra nervous" and dismount conspicuously unassisted in the manly way.[25] Shortly thereafter, Union cavalry capture Gertrude and bring her back to the house for questioning. One of the posters advertising the show, titled "A Fair Prisoner" (fig. 10.4), depicts her riding sidesaddle on her agitated white steed and swatting with her crop at the pair of captors who are trying to help her dismount. Although wearing the male military power regalia of uniform jackets, pants, tall boots, roweled spurs, and holstered sabre and rifle, the hapless soldiers cannot unseat the lady on horseback against her will. Odette Tyler then made a show of Gertrude's dismounting by herself before submitting to interrogation by Colonel West, her erstwhile suitor and, now that she is a prisoner of war, her commanding officer.[26]

Gertrude softens toward Kerchival briefly when an officer appears leading a large black horse (Black Bess), whom she instantly recognizes as Jack through the upstage center opening in the wall. She fervently hopes that Colonel West can restore him to

10.5 General Sheridan's horse Winchester. Taxidermied horse in the Division of Armed Forces History, National Museum of American History. Smithsonian Institution, Washington, D.C.

her. For the first time, the whole body of the famous horse becomes visible onstage. Preparing for the climactic dash to come, this appearance gives the audience as well as Gertrude a still moment to take "him" in. Riderless and fully caparisoned in military saddle and bridle, Black Bess posed as a living version of the real Winchester, who stood, taxidermied and wearing the same equipment, on public display less than five miles away from the theater (fig. 10.5). As relic, lore, and theatricality come together in this performance moment, Kerchival realizes that the horse is now Sheridan's; of course, he has no authority over him, which angers and disappoints Gertrude. Once again, her attachment to Jack, along with her southern rebelliousness, thwarts Kerchival's manly romantic desires. Only at the end of this act, when he is badly wounded and unconscious after defending his honor against the insults of the play's villain, the shifty Confederate secret service agent Robert Thornton, does Gertrude tell him that she loves him.

As Gertrude's desires bend excessively to her horse before "straightening" toward the play's romantic lead, the soubrette character, Jenny Buckthorn, offers a humorous portrayal of the queering effects of female absorption of mettlesome equine potency. She has ridden over to the Ellington mansion with Madeline, presumably sidesaddle; however, raised on the plains as the son her cavalry general father never had, she

10.6
"The Greater Shenandoah,
by Bronson Howard: 'Halt!'"
Poster for the 1894 production
of *Shenandoah* showing the
scene from act 2 where Jenny
Buckthorn imitates the movements of cavalry riders and their
horses as they pass by. Strobridge
& Co. Lith.

grew up riding with him, presumably astride. Yearning to join the ranks, she has
memorized all the snap-to military signals, which infuse the tone and rhythm of
their father-daughter conversations. Their surname, Buckthorn, connotes the thorn
in the horse's side that provokes bucking instead of straightforward motion. Both
characters zigzag through the norms of East Coast social propriety, but whereas her
military father comes across as affably crusty and rustic, Jenny's antics, though granted
a certain charm, verge on gender deviance played for laughs.

Jenny performs two comic dances of horse absorption in which she apes the
movements of both the cavalrymen and their mounts as they pass by the house to
the strains of martial band music. Vividly marking her entrance into the play, the
first dance was iconized in another poster for the Frohman revival (fig. 10.6). In
contrast to Gertrude's more ladylike dress, if not behavior, Jenny wears a military
hat, a form-fitting military-style jacket in white fabric over an A-line skirt with an
officer's sash at the waist, and riding gauntlets. She uses her folded parasol as a rifle
as she snaps to the trumpet signals, issues orders, and breaks out in her tellingly

horsey "Ha-ha-ha-ha!" (403). While General Haverill, a paragon of chivalric poise in the saddle, politely salutes her in passing, his trotting horse cocks its right ear and turns its head to eyeball her with its right eye—in a manner consistent with equine sightlines—to take in this strange human display. In a more sustained sequence, Jenny opens act 3, announcing:

> Boots and Saddles! Mount! I wish I was in command of the regiment. It was born in me. . . . Look at those horses' ears! Forward. (*A military band is heard without, playing "The Battle Cry of Freedom." JENNY takes attitude of holding a bridle and trotting.*) Rappity—plap—plap—plap, etc. (*Imitates motions of a soldier on horseback, stepping down to the rock at side of post; thence to the ground and about the stage, with the various curvettings of a spirited horse. . . .*) Ah! If I were only a man! (423–24)

Showcased onstage for intense public scrutiny and amusement, Jenny's quirky dances extravagantly display how the queering movements of horses can erupt through the female body in gender-bending performance.

Part of what makes Jenny's eruptions humorous, befitting a soubrette, and distinct from Gertrude's more thoroughbred leading lady antics, is that her horsiness cavorts with impurity. Nurtured on horseback and named for a female donkey—i.e., a "jenny"—she embodies the doubly queer world of equine genetic hybridity, an arcane phenomenon with which the more hippologically aware audiences of the time would have been generally conversant. Though charming, she consternates her male guardians. When ordered to travel with her, Sergeant Barket retorts, "I'd as soon move a train of army mules," implying that Jenny is odder and more problematic even than these reputedly difficult, if exceptionally strong and hardy, creatures (425). Over the long haul of horsepower, the vast majority of the many millions of mules who served civilian and military causes, with their hybrid vigor as beasts of burden, resulted from mating a male donkey with a mare. The crossing of a female donkey with a stallion, which Jenny's character suggests, was much rarer, and the result was usually not as big or strong, and less tractable. Because of the odd number of chromosomes, both mixes almost always yielded sterile—but still desirous—offspring. Hippo-gender-queer Jenny outrages her doting father with her romantic attraction to the ironically named military dandy Captain Heartsease, a "Fifth avenue exquisite."[27] The costume listings specify that whereas other officers' uniforms are "rough and war-torn," his "is as neat and precise as is consistent with active military service" (5). When Barket informs Buckthorn of Jenny's attraction, the general erupts, "Heartsease! That young jackanapes! A mere fop; he'll never make a soldier. My girl in love with—bah! I don't believe it; she's too good a soldier herself" (427). "Jackanapes," a combination of "jack" (as in "jackass") and "apes," constituted an equid-simian pejorative connoting the devolution ascribed to sexual inverts.[28] In spite of Buckthorn's protests, this jack and jenny fall irrepressibly in love. The play's deployment of the couple as comic relief highlights, even as it tries to diffuse through laughter, the potential threat that horsey queerness posed to the contemporary equine-reliant military and civilian orders.

By the time Sheridan's climactic ride comes at the end of act 3, both equestrian manliness and Union forces need resuscitation. Sergeant Barket runs up to the top of the elevation from the rear and yells downstage in his Irish brogue, "Colonel Wist! The devils have sprung out of the ground . . . and our own regiment is in full retrate [*sic*]!" (435). The original New York production, according to reviews, then showed "scattered and defeated troops moving slowly backward in droves across the stage, an occasional coward running at full speed, a wounded soldier falling unheeded by the way, a squad of men dragging a field piece," to which subsequent stagings added more supernumeraries, some carrying bodies on stretchers, and a mounted cavalryman with a bleeding soldier slung over the front of his saddle.[29] Now fully conscious, Kerchival calls for his horse and, though badly wounded, disappears into the fray to rally his regiment. Moved by his bravery to shift her regional allegiance, Gertrude cries out, "Men! Are you soldiers! Turn back! There is a leader for you! Turn back! Fight for your flag—and mine!" Soldiers start shouting, "Sheridan! Sheridan is coming! . . . The horse is down; he is worn out!" Seeing him in the distance, Gertrude yells, "No! He is up again! He is on my Jack! Now, for your life, Jack, and for me!" Sheridan "sweeps by" "at a good gallop," followed by "a whole troop of mounted cavalry" in the 1894 and 1898 productions, on the road across the full width of the stage. The famous general apotheosizes the pivotal action Kerchival has already started, as Gertrude channels her womanly hippophilia in service of manly military resuscitation, and the stream of retreat reverses *a vista* into attack. This theatrical synthesis worked brilliantly, except for one night early in the first run at New York's Star Theatre. The actor playing Sheridan missed his cue to mount, but Black Bess, still sharply attentive in the wings, with her neck all soaped into an artificial lather and dusted to look as though she had been running for miles, remained determined to charge ahead on the usual signal. She broke her handlers' hold on her bridle and galloped across the stage with an empty saddle.[30] A more spectacularly ill-timed deflation of military equestrian masculinity would be hard to imagine; certainly, this mishap encapsulates the fragility of chivalry's performative construction.

In spite of that disastrous symbolic rupture, Black Bess was nonetheless acting dutifully according to her training, running from one backstage mark and stopping at another on her appointed cue. Not all of the equine actors who performed in the burgeoning number of horse scenes in *Shenandoah*, however, proved as consistently obedient. One sweltering night in July 1898 on tour at Chicago's McVicker's Theatre, a mount was positioned backstage to gallop on with Sergeant Barket so he could deliver a dispatch, Rough Rider–like, to the waiting General Haverill. When Barket's impersonator, Augustus Cooke, a good actor but a timid and unaccomplished horse-man, tried to urge the hot and weary horse forward to no avail, a stage hand slapped the animal on the flank. Whereupon the horse, fed up with these oppressive human follies and seeing an exterior door open for some breeze, dashed across the stage for daylight and charged down the alley onto State Street with Cooke clinging on for dear life until mounted police came to the rescue. Some minutes later, a badly shaken Cooke reentered and delivered the dispatch on foot, never to ride again, onstage or off.[31] He received applause from a sympathetic audience, but the horse deserved some sympathy, too, for an understandably natural response to an unnatural situa-tion. Highlighting the poignancy of an animal trying to choose for him- or herself and the emasculating humiliation that can result for humans, the episode points to the gulf that exists between species no matter the degree of apparent connection and cooperation.

More subtly illustrative of chivalric masculinity's vulnerability are the rides that are not shown onstage but only alluded to in retrospective retelling in the final act. Set in General Buckthorn's residence in Washington a year later, in 1865, this denouement reassembles the war-scattered dramatis personae to bring the themes of romance and reconciliation to fruition. Robert and Madeline are reunited, as are Jenny and Heartsease; however, Gertrude and Kerchival are presumed lost. Sergeant Barket and General Buckthorn recount how the wounded Colonel West rode to rally his troops with Sheridan, was shot from his horse in the ensuing battle, always a hazard for necessarily conspicuous mounted commanders, but was not found among the dead. Like Evangeline and Clara Barton, Gertrude, Madeline, and Jenny wandered the bat-tlefield strewn with human and equine bodies looking for Kerchival in vain until dark. Whereupon Gertrude, using all the equestrian skill and independence she kept under her skirts, "suddenly seized the bridle of a stray horse, sprang upon its back and rode away to the South, into the woods" to continue on her own for months, in a peregri-nation left largely to the audience's imagination (442–43). Spectators could readily fill in vivid details, if not from their own and family members' firsthand memories then from the famous Matthew Brady war photographs and popular fictional and journalistic accounts of the hundreds of women on both sides who rode astride and cross-dressed, many in found uniforms, to serve the cause and look for loved ones.[32] Whom should the Amazonian Gertrude chance to encounter on her desperate quest but an unhorsed Heartsease, detained in a North Carolina prison accompanying "lots of jolly fellows" in a dramatic society and glee club on a one-string banjo. Such seem-ingly improbable horsey queer rendezvous could and did happen in what Buckthorn calls "the wilderness of this great war," the ravaged and shattering battle zone beyond the pale of normal civilization (445). The final plot resolution involves several gender realignments: Buckthorn acknowledges Heartsease's redeeming heroism in war; Jenny accedes to wifely duty in domestic society; and Gertrude and Kerchival appear reunited at the very end, in properly female and male civilian traveling clothes, to announce their marriage.

In subsequent productions, however, these straightenings proved insufficient to reaffirm ideals of American masculinity that still needed to be constructed on horseback, along with sectional reconciliation and national healing. Grandiose military tableaux were staged after the final scene of the play to tout federal triumph and white male equestrian power. The program for the 1894 revival on the huge stage of New York's Academy of Music concluded with a "Review of the victorious troops before President Andrew Johnson and his Cabinet—representing every branch of the service, led by Sherman, Sheridan, Logan, Custer, etc.," a scene that featured "more than a hundred actors, including the horses."[33] In Frohman's 1898 revival, produced during the Spanish-American War, the tableau was enlarged to thirty-one horses and 250 humans, "including a full military brass band, a full detachment of U.S. Marines, cavalry, and artillery, and a double fife and drum corps," with actors playing Grant and Sheridan reviewing the troops. The production so inflamed patriotism that the *New York Dramatic Mirror* advocated that "the Government should open a recruiting station at the Academy."[34] Capitalizing on the same flag-waving bravado, Jacob Litt's still more massive revival of 1898–1900 boasted, "CAVALRY! INFANTRY! ARTILLERY! 250 MEN. 50 HORSES," and employed actual human and equine veterans. According to a press release, Litt's agents purchased the fifty horses at a public auction of Rough Rider mounts "who fought so gallantly under the command of Col. Roosevelt" upon their return from Cuba. "It is astonishing how intelligent the animals are, for they have learned the business they have to do perfectly, and go through their part of the performance with an intelligence that is almost human."[35] Given the reality of the scenes of battle and military fanfare, cavalry training could indeed provide an effective foundation for equine stage performance. These warhorses provided the ultimate theatrical completion of cavalrymen's masculinity.

The grand tableau finale offered a lavish showcase for the actor playing the heroic Sheridan to return aboard the horse playing Jack to resounding cheers and applause during the review of troops. For hundreds of performances over several years, the valiant Black Bess, in revivifying Winchester, also played out the legacy of her popular theatrical namesake, who died galloping to save her master. Without the horses' giving their all at human behest, none of the wars waged on horseback could have been won. More ironically, Winchester's impersonator invokes another, less well known mare named Black Bess, who actually fought in the Civil War: she was the favorite mount of Confederate general John H. Morgan. When his memorial statue was created for installation in downtown Lexington, Kentucky, the sculptor insisted, "No hero should bestride a mare!" and added prominent "stallion attributes" to Bess's underside.[36] After so much horsey queerness during America's bloodiest war and its grandest stage reenactment, posterity demanded chivalric gender realignment and restoration cast in bronze.

NOTES

1. "General Sheridan's Horse, Winchester, Honored," *New York Times*, 5 June 1922, 8.

2. Hacker, "Census-Based Account"; Schofield, "Battlefield Dispatches."

3. Phillips, "Writing Horses"; Sherman, "Horse in the Civil War."

4. See *Memoirs of General William T. Sherman,* vol. 2, chapter 23, "Campaign of the Carolinas— February and March, 1865."

5. Quoted in Marcosson and Frohman, *Charles Frohman,* 122.

6. General James Longstreet, a West Point classmate of General Grant's, quoted in "Grant the Equestrian," Ulysses S. Grant homepage, accessed 13 March 2015, http://www.granthome page.com/grantequestrian.htm. See Mattfeld, "'Undaunted All He Views,'" 25, for analysis of the centaur ideal in the construction of influential eighteenth-century English masculinity.

7. Famous commercial depictions of Rienzi, a.k.a. Winchester, included the drawing by Thomas Nast on the cover of *Harper's Weekly* for 5 November 1864, two and a half weeks after the Battle of Cedar Creek, and the chromolithograph of the painting by Thure de Thulstrop distributed by L. Prang and Co. (fig. 10.1). In *The Memoirs of General P. H. Sheridan*, the general describes Rienzi as a Morgan horse of unusual height (sixteen hands) with a "thoroughbred appearance."

8. Various Turpin-inspired hippodramas featuring incarnations of Black Bess remained perennially popular on Anglo-American stages throughout the nineteenth century, e.g., William Barrymore's *Richard Turpin the Highwayman* (1819) and adaptations of Harrison Ainsworth's novel *Rookwood* (1834), including *Turpin's Ride to York, or Bonny Black Bess: An Equestrian Drama, in Two Acts* (1836) by H. M. Milner, and George Dibdin-Pitt's *Rookwood* (1840). These dramas endured in silent and color film versions into the twentieth century. For analysis of romantic constructions of this type of "ideal horseness," see Mattfeld's chapter in this volume.

9. Untitled newspaper clipping in *Shenandoah* clippings file, Billy Rose Theatre Collection, New York Public Library for the Performing Arts, Lincoln Center, New York (hereafter BRTC).

10. Howard, *Shenandoah* (1888), 390 (hereafter cited parenthetically in the text by page number).

11. Sprague, *National Horse Show*, 66.

12. See, for example, Houblon, *Side-Saddle*, 96–97.

13. Clarke, "Hints on Equestrianism."

14. See Marra, "Saddle Sensations."

15. See Butsch, *Making of American Audiences*, 66–80.

16. "Stars Seen by Day—Viola Allen at Home," *Ev'ry Month* (New York), 1 January 1899, 1–2, BRTC, vol. 12, 33.

17. Untitled magazine clipping in "Hampton, Mary," Robinson-Locke Collection of Dramatic Scrapbooks, BRTC, envelope 593.

18. See Kari Weil's chapter in this volume for more on Menken's Mazeppa, which circulated long after that actress's death (1868) through media lore and subsequent stage versions in England, France, and the United States, as the major cultural anti-type of the proper lady rider.

19. Untitled newspaper clipping, *Shenandoah* clippings file, BRTC.

20. Quoted in "The Faithful Steeds," accessed 5 March 2015, http://civilwarcavalry.com/?p=3521.

21. This image (fig. 10.2) can also be viewed at http://hdl.loc.gov/loc.pnp/cwpb.03759 (accessed 18 March 2015). Because of the human-equine bond the picture captures, Louis DiMarco used it on the cover of *War Horse*. It should be noted, however, that the handwritten number 344 on the photograph displayed on the LOC site is reversed; thus we have flipped the image to restore the orientation of the original exposure, whereas the DiMarco cover reproduces it as it appears on the LOC site.

22. See, for example, *The Comrades, Peterson's Magazine* (Philadelphia, 1888), accessed 5 April 2015, reproduced at http://www.oldpapershop .com/CG-014.jpg; Harrison Fisher, *Dumb Luck*, cover of the *Saturday Evening Post*, 28 November 1908.

23. Ryan, "Horse Drama," 44.

24. See, for example, Charles Henry Meltzer, "The Progress of Viola Allen—A Chat with the Future Heroine of The Christian," *Criterion*, 11 June 1898, BRTC, vol. 12, 21.

25. Untitled review of *Shenandoah* at the Academy of Music, New York, n.d., 1894, *Shenandoah* clippings file, BRTC.

26. "'Shenandoah' on a Large Scale," *New York Times*, 31 August 1894, 4.

27. This description appeared in the earlier version of *Shenandoah*, called *Drum Taps* (1873). Although the phrase was excised, the character traits remained. See Ryan, "Horse Drama," 44.

28. According to the *OED*, a *jackanapes* is "one who is like an ape in tricks, airs, or behaviour; a ridiculous upstart; a pert, impertinent fellow, who assumes ridiculous airs; a coxcomb." It is related to *jack-a-dandy*, "a little pert or conceited fellow; a contemptuous name for a beau, fop, dandy." *Oxford English Dictionary*, prepared by J. A. Simpson and E. S. C. Weiner, 2nd ed., reprinted with corrections (Oxford: Oxford University Press, 1989), 8:167–68. Beginning in the early nineteenth century, Robert and George Cruikshank frequently used ass and ape imagery in caricatures of Regency dandies that circulated widely in Anglo-American culture. Such imagery helped make these animals an integral part of the emerging visual lexicon of gender and sexual deviance that would, by the 1890s, be instantiated as sexual inversion.

29. "'Shenandoah' Splendidly Presented Last Evening," review of 1889 production in unnamed newspaper, and untitled review of 1894 revival, both in *Shenandoah* clippings file, BRTC.

30. The incident is described in an untitled newspaper clipping about the 1894 revival, *Shenandoah* clippings file, BRTC. The reporter hearkens back to the 1889 production, which opened at the Star Theatre and played for several weeks (9 September–12 October 1889) before moving to Proctor's 23rd Street Theatre. The incident is also reported in Marcosson and Frohman, *Charles Frohman*, 122.

31. Skinner, *Footlights and Spotlights*, 249.

32. See Blanton and Cook, *They Fought Like Demons*.

33. *Shenandoah* Programme, Academy of Music, MWEZ+ n.c. 12,442, BRTC; "'Shenandoah' on a Large Scale," *New York Times*, 31 August 1894, 4.

34. "Philadelphia War Plays Predominate—Shenandoah Revived," *New York Dramatic Mirror*, 30 April 1898, 10; "At the Theatres: Academy of Music—Shenandoah," ibid., 28 May 1898, 14; "Union Cheers and Rebel Yells," clipping from an untitled newspaper, *Shenandoah* clippings file, BRTC.

35. "Next Attraction," typed press release, n.d., *Shenandoah* clippings file, BRTC.

36. Loewen, *Lies Across America*, 164–65.

BIBLIOGRAPHY

Agamben, Giorgio. *The Open: Man and Animal.* Stanford: Stanford University Press, 2004.

Albala, Ken. *The Banquet: Dining in the Great Courts of Late Renaissance Europe.* Urbana: University of Illinois Press, 2007.

———. *Eating Right in the Renaissance.* Berkeley: University of California Press, 2002.

Alciato, Andrea. *Liber emblematum . . . Kunstbuch.* Frankfurt am Main: Sigmund Feyerabend, 1567.

Les Amazones de Paris. Paris: E. Dentu, 1866.

Anonymous. "May 1: Covent-Garden Theatre, Timour the Tartar Review." In *The Dramatic Censor, or Critical and Biographical Illustration of the British Stage*, edited by J. M. Williams, 241–46. London: G. Brimmer, 1811.

Aristotle. *The Works of Aristotle.* 12 vols. Translated by W. D. Ross. Oxford: Clarendon Press, 1931.

Astley, Philip. *Astley's System of Equestrian Education, Exhibiting the Beauties and Defects of the Horse; with Serious and Important Advice, on Its General Excellence, Preserving It in Health, Grooming, &c.* London: Sold by C. Creed, 1801.

Bacon, Francis. *The Advancement of Learning.* Vol. 4 of *The Oxford Francis Bacon*, edited by Michael Kiernan. Oxford: Clarendon Press, 2000.

———. *New Atlantis, with Sylva Sylvarum.* London, 1626.

———. *Novum Organum.* Vol. 4 of *The Works of Francis Bacon*, edited by James Spedding, Robert Leslie Ellis, and Douglas Denon Heath. Cambridge: Cambridge University Press, 2011.

Baker, Henry. *The Microscope Made Easy.* London, 1744.

Baker, Steve. *Picturing the Beast: Animals, Identity, and Representation.* Champaign: University of Illinois Press, 1993.

Baldwin, Elizabeth, Lawrence M. Clopper, and David Mills, eds. *Records of Early English Drama: Cheshire, Including Chester.* 2 vols. Toronto: British Library and University of Toronto Press, 2007.

Barad, Karen. "Posthumanist Performativity: Toward an Understanding of How Matter Comes to Matter." *Signs: Journal of Women in Culture and Society* 28, no. 3 (2003): 801–31.

Basse, William. *A Helpe to Discourse, or a Miscelany of Merriment.* London, 1619.

Bayreuther, Magdalena. *Pferde und Fürsten: Repräsentative Reitkunst und Pferdehaltung an fränkischen Höfen (1600–1800).* Würzburg: Ergon, 2014.

Beaumont, Francis. *The Knight of the Burning Pestle.* In *The Dramatic Works in the Beaumont and Fletcher Canon*, edited by Fredson Bowers, 2 vols., 1:1–110. Cambridge: Cambridge University Press, 1966.

Belknap, Maria Ann. *Horsewords: The Equine Dictionary.* London: J. A. Allen, 1997.

Bennett, Jane. *Vibrant Matter: A Political Ecology of Things.* Durham: Duke University Press, 2010.

Bentham, Jeremy. *Introduction to the Principles of Morals and Legislation.* Oxford: Clarendon Press, 1789.

Bepler, Jill. "Practical Perspectives on the Court and the Role of Princes: Georg Engelhard von Loehneyss' *Aulico*

Politico. . . ." *Daphnis* 32 (2003): 137–63.

Berger, John. *About Looking.* New York: Pantheon Books, 1980.

Berliner, Rudolf. "The Origins of the Crèche." *Gazette des Beaux-Arts* (October–December 1946): 249–78.

Bernebaum, May R. *Bugs in the System: Insects and Their Impact on Human Affairs.* New York: Basic Books, 1995.

Beschreibung der Verordnung / Wie es mit weilandt des Durchleuchtigen / Hochgebornen Fuersten und Herrn / Herrn Julii / Herzogen zu Braunschweig und Lueneburg etc. hochloeblicher und christmilter gedechtnus / Fuerstlichem Begrebnus / so den 11. Junii / Anno etc. 89 zu Juliusfriedenstedt bey der Heinrichstadt zum Gottslager geschehen / gehalten worden. Wolfenbüttel: Conrad Horan, 1589.

Beschreibung der Verordnung / Wie es mit Weilandt des Hoch=wuerdigen Durchleuchtigen Hochgebornen Fuersten und Herrn / Herrn Heinrich Julii / Postulirten Bischoffen des Stiffts Halberstadt / und Herzogen zu Braunschweigk und Lueneburgk / etc. Hochloeblicher und Christmilder Gedechtniss / Fuerstlichen Begrebniss / den 4. Octobris / Anno 1613 zu Wulffenbuettel gehalten worden. Wolfenbüttel: Elias Holwein, 1613.

Bewer, Francesca G. "'Kunststücke von gegossenem Metall': Adriaen de Vries's Bronze Technique." In *Adriaen de Vries, 1556–1626,* edited by Fritz Scholten, 64–77. Zwolle: Waanders, 1998. Exhibition catalogue.

Blanton, DeAnne, and Lauren M. Cook. *They Fought Like Demons: Women Soldiers in the American Civil War.* Baton Rouge: Louisiana State University Press, 2002.

Bliss, Matthew. "Property or Performers? Animals on the Elizabethan Stage." *Theatre Studies* 39 (1994): 45–58.

Boehrer, Bruce. *Animal Characters: Nonhuman Beings in Renaissance Literature.* Philadelphia: University of Pennsylvania Press, 2010.

———. *Shakespeare Among the Animals: Nature and Society in the Drama of Early Modern England.* New York: Palgrave, 2002.

Bogost, Ian. *Alien Phenomenology, or What It's Like to Be a Thing.* Minneapolis: University of Minnesota Press, 2012.

———. *What Is Object-Oriented Ontology?* http://bogost.com/writing/blog /what_is_objectoriented_ontolog/.

Boorde, Andrew. *A compendious regiment or a dyetary.* London, 1576.

Bredekamp, Horst. *The Lure of Antiquity and the Cult of the Machine.* Translated by Alison Brown. Princeton: Markus Wiener, 2005.

Briggs, Katharine M. *The Anatomy of Puck: An Examination of Fairy Beliefs Among Shakespeare's Contemporaries and Successors.* London: Routledge, 1959.

———. *The Fairies in Tradition and Literature.* London: Routledge, 1967.

Brooks, Daphne. *Bodies in Dissent: Spectacular Performances of Race and Freedom, 1850–1910.* Durham: Duke University Press, 2006.

Brooks, Peter. "The Melodramatic Imagination." *Partisan Review* 39, no. 2 (1972): 195–212.

Brown, Eric C. "Performing Insects in Shakespeare's *Coriolanus.*" In *Insect Poetics,* edited by Eric C. Brown, 29–57. Minneapolis: University of Minnesota Press, 2006.

Browne, Thomas. *Pseudodoxia Epidemica.* 2 vols. Edited by Robin Robbins. Oxford: Clarendon Press, 1981.

———. *Religio Medici.* In *Sir Thomas Browne's Works,* 2nd ed., edited by Simon Wilkin, 4 vols., 2:1–158. London, 1836.

Buchanan, Brett. *Onto-ethologies: The Animal Environments of Uexküll, Heidegger,*

Merleau-Ponty, and Deleuze. Albany: State University of New York Press, 2008.

Buchanan, Henry. "India and the Golden Age in *A Midsummer Night's Dream.*" *Shakespeare Survey* 65 (2012): 58–68.

Bullein, William. *The Government of Health.* London, 1595.

Burch, Preston. *Training Thoroughbred Horses.* Lexington, Ky.: Blood Horse, 1976.

Burke, Edmund. *A Philosophical Enquiry into the Origin of Our Ideas of the Sublime and Beautiful.* London: J. Dodsley, 1767.

Burt, Jonathan. *Animals in Film.* London: Reaktion Books, 2002.

Burton, Robert. *Versatile Ingenium.* Amsterdam, 1679.

Butler, Judith. *Gender Trouble: Gender and the Subversion of Identity.* New York: Routledge, 1990.

Butsch, Richard. *The Making of American Audiences: From Stage to Television, 1750–1990.* Cambridge: Cambridge University Press, 2000.

Butterworth, Philip. *Magic on the Early English Stage.* Cambridge: Cambridge University Press, 2005.

Byatt, A. S. *Angels and Insects.* New York: Random House, 1992.

Caius, John. *Of Englishe Dogges.* Translated by Abraham Fleming. London: Richard Johns, 1576.

Calarco, Matthew. *Zoographies.* New York: Columbia University Press, 2008.

Calendar of House of Lords Manuscripts, 1450–1678. Volume 7.1. Edited by Robert W. Monro and Merton A. Thoms. London: Historical Manuscripts Commission, 1879.

Campana, Joseph. "The Bee and the Sovereign: Political Entomology and the Problem of Scale." *Shakespeare Studies* 41 (2013): 94–113.

Čapek, Josef, and Karel Čapek. *R.U.R. and The Insect Play.* Translated by Paul Selver. Oxford: Oxford University Press, 1961.

Carlino, Andrea. *Books of the Body: Anatomical Ritual and Renaissance Learning.* Translated by John Tedeschi and Anne C. Tedeschi. Chicago: University of Chicago Press, 1999.

Cavendish, William. *A General System of Horsemanship.* Facsimile edition of the 1743 text. Vermont: J. A. Allen, 2000.

Chaudhuri, Una, and Holly Hughes, eds. *Animal Acts: Performing Species Today.* Ann Arbor: University of Michigan Press, 2014.

Chessa, Bernardo, Filipe Pereira, Frederick Arnaud, Antonio Amorim, Félix Goyache, Ingrid Mainland, Rowland R. Kao, et al. "Revealing the History of Sheep Domestication Using Retrovirus Integrations." *Science* 324 (April 2009): 532–36.

Clarke, Mrs. J. Stirling. "Hints on Equestrianism for the Fair." *Godey's Lady's Book* 37 (September 1848): 169–71.

Cler, Albert. *La comédie à cheval, ou Manies et travers du monde équestre.* Paris: Ernest Boudin, 1842.

Clopper, Lawrence M. "The History and Development of the Chester Cycle." *Modern Philology* 75, no. 3 (1978): 219–46.

Colombo, Realdo. *De re anatomica Libri X.* Venice: Bevilacqua, 1559.

Cox, Jeffrey N. *Romanticism in the Shadow of War: Literary Culture in the Napoleonic War Years.* Cambridge: Cambridge University Press, 2014.

Cox, Jeffrey N., and Michael Gamer. "Introduction to 'Timour the Tartar.'" In *The Broadview Anthology of Romantic Drama*, edited by Jeffrey N. Cox and Michael Gamer, vii–xxiv. Peterborough, Ont.: Broadview Press, 2003.

Croqueville. *Paris en voiture, à cheval, aux courses, à la chasse.* Paris: Librairie de la Nouvelle Revue, 1892.

Cuneo, Pia F. "Visual Aids: Equestrian Iconography and the Training of Horse, Rider, and Viewer." In *The Horse as Cultural Icon: The Real and the Symbolic Horse in the Early Modern World*, edited by Peter Edwards, Karl A. E. Enenkel, and Elspeth Graham, 71–97. Leiden: Brill, 2012.

Cunningham, Andrew. *The Anatomical Renaissance: The Resurrection of the Anatomical Projects of the Ancients*. Aldershot: Scolar Press, 1997.

Darvill, Richard. *Treatise on the Care, Treatment, and Training of the English Racehorse*. London: James Ridgway, 1840.

Day, John. *The Parliament of Bees*. London, 1641.

———. *The Travels of the Three English Brothers*. London, 1607.

de Loncey, H. V. *Les races de chevaux de trait: Études hippiques, documents et pratiques*. Paris: Bureaux de l'Acclimation, 1888.

Delvau, Alfred. *Les plaisirs de Paris*. Paris: A. Fauré, 1867.

Derrida, Jacques. *The Animal That Therefore I Am*. Edited by Marie-Louise Mallet. Translated by David Willis. New York: Fordham University Press, 2008.

Descartes, René. *Treatise on Man* and *Discourse on the Method*. In *The Philosophical Writings of Descartes*, translated by John Cottingham, Robert Stoothoff, and Dugald Murdoch, vol. 1, 99–108 and 111–51. Cambridge: Cambridge University Press, 1985.

de Vaux, Baron. *Écuyers et écuyères, histoire des cirques d'Europe, 1680–1891*. Paris: Rothschild, 1893.

Dibdin, Charles, the Younger. *The Manuscript Autobiography of Charles Dibdin the Younger, compiled by E. Rimbault Dibdin and now copied by L. G. Dibdin*. N.p., 1951.

Digby, Sir Kenelm. *Two Treatises in the one of which the nature of bodies, in the other, the nature of mans soule is looked into*. London, 1644.

DiMarco, Louis. *War Horse: A History of the Military Horse and Rider*. Yardley, Pa.: Westholme, 2008.

Dobson, Michael. "A Dog at All Things." *Performance Research: A Journal of the Performing Arts* 5, no. 2 (2000): 116–24.

Domingues, Clara. "Recherches sur les éditions grecques et latines à la Renaissance." PhD diss., Université Paris IV-Sorbonne, 2004.

Du Bartas, Guillaume Salluste. *His devine weekes and works*. Translated by Josuah Sylvester. London, 1611.

Duncan-Jones, Katherine. "Shakespeare's Debt to Moffett Cancelled." *Review of English Studies* 32 (1981): 296–301.

Durling, R. J. "Addenda et corrigenda to Diels' Galenica I-codices vaticani." *Traditio* 23 (1967): 461–76.

———. "Addenda et corrigenda to Diels' Galenica II-codices miscellanei." *Traditio* 37 (1981): 373–81.

———. "A Chronological Census of Renaissance Editions and Translations of Galen." *Journal of the Warburg and Courtauld Institutes* 24 (1961): 230–305.

Edwards, Peter. "Nature Bridled: The Treatment and Training of Horses in Early Modern England." In *Beastly Natures: Animals, Humans, and the Study of History*, edited by Dorothee Brantz, 155–75. Charlottesville: University of Virginia Press, 2010.

Egan, Gabriel. "Gaia and the Great Chain of Being." In *Ecocritical Shakespeare*, edited by Lynne Bruckner and Dan Brayton, 57–70. Aldershot: Ashgate, 2011.

Estok, Simon. *Ecocriticism and Shakespeare: Reading Ecophobia*. New York: Palgrave, 2011.

———. "Theory from the Fringes: Animals, Ecocriticism, Shakespeare." *Mosaic* 40, no. 1 (2007): 61–78.

Evelyn, John. *Numismata*. London, 1697.

Falk, Bernard. *The Naked Lady*. London: Hutchison, 1952.

Farrand, Margaret. "An Additional Source for *A Midsummer Night's Dream*." *Studies in Philology* 27 (1930): 233–43.

Fernel, Jean. *Universa Medicina*. Paris: Andreas Wechel, 1567.

Fettiplace, Elinor. *Elinor Fettiplace's Receipt Book*. Edited by Hilary Spurling. London: Faber and Faber, 1986.

Fisher, M. F. K. *How to Cook a Wolf*. New York: Farrar, Straus and Giroux, 1942.

Fitzpatrick, Joan. *Food in Shakespeare: Early Modern Dietaries and the Plays*. Burlington, Vt.: Ashgate, 2007.

Flandrin, Jean-Louis, and Massimo Montanari, eds. *Food: A Culinary History from Antiquity to the Present*. Translated by Albert Sonnenfeld. New York: Columbia University Press, 1999.

Flaubert, Gustave. *Madame Bovary*. Paris: Gallimard, 1972.

Fletcher, J. S. "A Stud Book of the Eighteenth Century." *Badminton Magazine of Sports and Pastimes* 16 (January–June 1903): 214–22.

Freeman, Margaret B. "Shepherds in the Fields." *Metropolitan Museum of Art Bulletin,* new ser., 11, no. 4 (1952): 108–15.

French, Roger. *Dissection and Vivisection in the European Renaissance*. Aldershot: Ashgate, 1999.

———. *William Harvey's Natural Philosophy*. Cambridge: Cambridge University Press, 2006.

Frisch, Karl von. *The Dancing Bees: An Account of the Life and Senses of the Honey Bee*. New York: Harvest Books, 1953.

Fudge, Erica. *Brutal Reasoning: Animals, Rationality, and Humanity in Early Modern England*. Ithaca: Cornell University Press, 2006.

———. "The Dog Is Himself: Humans, Animals, and Self-Control in *The Two Gentlemen of Verona*." In *How to Do Things with Shakespeare: New Approaches, New Essays*, edited by Laurie Maguire, 185–209. Malden, Mass.: John Wiley & Sons, 2008.

———. *Perceiving Animals: Humans and Beasts in Early Modern Culture*. London: Macmillan, 2000.

———. "Saying Nothing but Concerning the Same: On Dominion, Purity, and Meat in Early Modern England." In *Renaissance Beasts: Of Animals, Humans, and Other Wonderful Creatures*, edited by Erica Fudge, 70–86. Urbana: University of Illinois Press, 2004.

Fugger, Marx. *Von der Gestüterey*. Frankfurt am Main: Sigmund Feyerabend, 1584.

Fumerton, Patricia. *Cultural Aesthetics: Renaissance Literature and the Practice of Social Ornament*. Chicago: University of Chicago Press, 1991.

Fumerton, Patricia, and Simon Hunt, eds. *Renaissance Culture and the Everyday*. Philadelphia: University of Pennsylvania Press, 1998.

Galen. *On Anatomical Procedures*. Translated by Charles Singer. London: Oxford University Press, 1956.

———. *On the Natural Faculties*. Translated by A. J. Brock. Cambridge: Harvard University Press, 2006.

———. *On the Usefulness of the Parts of the Body*. Translated by Margaret Tallmadge May. Ithaca: Cornell University Press, 1968.

Gamer, Michael. "A Matter of Turf: Romanticism, Hippodrama, and Legitimate Satire." *Nineteenth-Century Contexts* 28, no. 4 (2006): 305–34.

Gifford-Gonzalez, Diane, and Olivier Hanotte. "Domesticating Animals in Africa: Implications of Genetic and Archaeological Findings." *Journal of World Prehistory* 24, no. 1 (2011): 1–23.

Grisone, Federico. *Federico Grisone's The Rules of Riding: An Edited Translation on Classical Horsemanship*. 1550. Translated by Elizabeth M. Tobey and Federica Deigan. Edited by Elizabeth M. Tobey. Tempe: Arizona Center for Medieval and Renaissance Studies, 2014.

Gross, Charles G. "Galen and the Squealing Pig." *Neuroscientist* 4, no. 3 (1998): 216–21.

Gross, Kenneth. *Dream of the Moving Statue*. Ithaca: Cornell University Press, 1992.

———. *Puppet: An Essay on Uncanny Life*. Chicago: University of Chicago Press, 2011.

Guerrini, Anita. *Experimenting with Humans and Animals: From Galen to Animal Rights*. Baltimore: Johns Hopkins University Press, 2003.

Hacker, J. D. "A Census-Based Account of the Civil War Dead." *Civil War History* 57, no. 4 (2011): 306–47.

Hale, Matthew. *The primitive origination of mankind*. London, 1677.

Halfpenny, John. *The Gentleman Jockey*. London, 1683.

Hall, Joseph. *Virgidemiarum*. London, 1598.

Haraway, Donna. *The Companion Species Manifesto: Dogs, People, and Significant Otherness*. Chicago: Prickly Paradigm Press, 2003.

———. *When Species Meet*. Minneapolis: University of Minnesota Press, 2008.

Harvey, William. *The Anatomical Exercises*. Translated by Zachariah Wood. London: Francis Leach, 1653.

———. *Anatomical exercitations concerning the generation of living creatures*. London: Pulleyn, 1653.

Haslewood, Joseph. "The Secret History of the Green-Room: Containing Authentic and Entertaining Memoirs of the Actors and Actresses in the Three Theatres Royal." In *Acting Theory and the English Stage, 1700–1830*, vol. 3, edited by Lisa Zunshine, 215–16. London: Pickering and Chatto, 2009.

Hattaway, Michael. "'Enter Caelia, the Fairy Queen in her Night Attire': Shakespeare and the Faeries." *Shakespeare Survey* 65 (2012): 26–41.

Hebb, David D. "Profiting from Misfortune: Corruption and the Admiralty Under the Early Stuarts." In *Politics, Religion, and Popularity in Early Stuart Britain: Essays in Honour of Conrad Russell*, edited by Thomas Cogswell, Richard Cust, and Peter Lake, 103–23. Cambridge: Cambridge University Press, 2002.

Hendricks, Margo. "'Obscured by Dreams': Race, Empire, and *A Midsummer Night's Dream*." *Shakespeare Quarterly* 47, no. 1 (1996): 37–60.

Heseler, Baldasar. *Andreas Vesalius' First Public Anatomy at Bologna, 1540*. Translated by Ruben Erikson. Uppsala: Almqvist and Wiksell, 1959.

Hocus Pocus Junior. *The Anatomy of Legerdemain*. London, 1638.

Höfele, Andreas. *Stage, Stake, and Scaffold: Humans and Animals in Shakespeare's Theatre*. Oxford: Oxford University Press, 2011.

Holcroft, Thomas, and William Hazlitt. *Memoirs of Thomas Holcroft, Written by Himself and Continued by William Hazlitt*. London: Oxford University Press, 1926.

Holder, Heidi J. "The Animal Actor and the Spectacle of Warfare: Lewis's *Timour the Tartar* at Covent Garden." In *War and Peace: Critical Issues in European Societies and Literature, 800–1800*, edited by Albrecht Classen and Nadia

Margolis, 599–618. Berlin: De Gruyter, 2011.

Holinshed, Raphael. *The Third Volume of Chronicles*. London, 1586.

Hooke, Robert. "An Account of an Experiment Made by Mr. Hook, of preserving Animals Alive by Blowing through Their Lungs with Bellows." *Philosophical Transactions of the Royal Society* 2 (1667): 539–40.

———. *Micrographia, or Some physiological descriptions of minute bodies made by magnifying glasses*. London, 1665.

Horst, Koert van der, ed. *Great Books on Horsemanship: Bibliotheca Hippologica Johan Dejager*. Leiden: Brill, 2014.

Houblon, Doreen Archer. *Side-Saddle*. New York: Scribner's, 1938.

Howard, Bronson. *Shenandoah*. 1888. In *Nineteenth Century American Plays: Seven Plays Including "The Black Crook,"* edited by Myron Matlaw, 375–452. New York: Applause, 2001.

———. *Shenandoah: A Military Comedy in Four Acts*. New York: Samuel French, 1897.

Hugo, Victor. *Poésie*. Edited by Bernard Leuillot. 3 vols. Paris: Seuil, 1972.

Huizinga, Johan. *Homo Ludens: A Study of the Play Element in Culture*. London: Routledge, 1971.

Hyman, Philip, and Mary Hyman. "Printing the Kitchen: French Cookbooks, 1480–1800." In *Food: A Culinary History from Antiquity to the Present*, edited by Jean-Louis Flandrin and Massimo Montanari, translated by Albert Sonnenfeld, 394–402. New York: Columbia University Press, 1999.

Ingold, Tim. *What Is an Animal?* London: Unwin Hyman, 1988.

Jha, Alok. "First Hamburger Made from Lab Grown Meat to be Served at Press Conference." *Guardian*, 5 August 2013. http://www.theguardian.com /science/2013/aug/05/first-hamburger-lab-grown-meat-press-conference.

Jones, Amelia. "Art History/Art Criticism: Performing Meaning." In *Performing the Body/Performing the Text*, edited by Amelia Jones and Andrew Stephenson, 39–55. London: Routledge, 1999.

Jonson, Ben. *The Alchemist*. Edited by Elizabeth Cook. London: Bloomsbury, 2010.

———. *The Workes*. London, 1616.

Kaplan, Edwin L., et al. "History of the Recurrent Laryngeal Nerve: From Galen to Lahey." *World Journal of Surgery* 33, no. 3 (2009): 386–93.

Kiser, Lisa J. "The Animals in Chester's *Noah's Flood*." *Early Theatre* 14, no. 1 (2011): 15–44.

———. "Animals in Medieval Sports, Entertainment, and Menageries." In *A Cultural History of Animals in the Medieval Age*, edited by Brigitte Resl, 103–26. Oxford: Berg, 2007.

Klestinec, Cynthia. "Medical Education in Padua: Students, Faculty, Facilities." In *Centres of Medical Excellence? Medical Travel and Education in Europe, 1500–1789*, edited by Ole Peter Grell, Andrew Cunningham, and Jon Arrizabelaga, 193–220. Burlington, Vt.: Ashgate, 2010.

———. *Theaters of Anatomy: Students, Teachers, and Traditions of Dissections in Renaissance Venice*. Baltimore: Johns Hopkins University Press, 2011.

Kuzniar, Alice A. "'I Married My Dog': On Queer Canine Literature." In *Queering the Non/Human*, edited by Noreen Giffney and Myra J. Hird, 205–26. Aldershot: Ashgate, 2008.

Lander, Jesse M. "Thinking with Faeries: *A Midsummer Night's Dream* and the Problem of Belief." *Shakespeare Survey* 65 (2012): 42–57.

Larousse, Pierre, ed. *Dictionnaire universel du XIXe siècle*. Vol. 13. Paris: Larousse, 1875.

Latham, Minor White. *The Elizabethan Fairies: The Fairies of Folklore and the Fairies of Shakespeare*. New York: Columbia University Press, 1930.

Latour, Bruno. *Reassembling the Social: An Introduction to Actor Network Theory*. Oxford: Oxford University Press, 2005.

Leask, Nigel. "'To Canter with the Sagitarre': Burns, Byron, and the Equestrian Sublime." *Byron Journal* 39, no. 2 (2011): 117–33.

Lesser, Allen. *Enchanting Rebel: The Secret of Adah Isaacs Menken*. New York: Beechhurst Press, 1947.

Lewis, Matthew. *Timour the Tartar: A Grand Romantic Melo Drama in Two Acts*. In *The Broadview Anthology of Romantic Drama*, edited by Jeffrey N. Cox and Michael Gamer, 97–116. Peterborough, Ont.: Broadview Press, 2003.

Liddell, Henry George, and Robert Scott. *Greek-English Lexicon*. Oxford: Clarendon Press, 1940.

Liedtke, Walter. *The Royal Horse and Rider: Painting, Sculpture, and Horsemanship, 1500–1800*. New York: Abaris Books, 1989.

Liedtke, Walter, and John F. Moffitt. "Velazquez, Olivares, and the Baroque Equestrian Portrait." *Burlington Magazine* 123, no. 942 (1981): 528–37.

Lietzmann, Hilda. *Herzog Heinrich Julius zu Braunschweig und Lüneburg (1564–1613): Persönlichkeit und Wirken für Kaiser und Reich*. Braunschweig: Selbstverlag der Braunschweigischen Geschichtsvereins, 1993.

Lippit, Akira. *Electric Animal: Toward a Rhetoric of Wildlife*. Minneapolis: University of Minnesota Press, 2000.

Lockwood, Jeffrey. *The Infested Mind: Why Humans Fear, Love, and Loathe Insects*. Oxford: Oxford University Press, 2013.

Loewen, James W. *Lies Across America: What Our Historic Sites Get Wrong*. New York: New Press, 1999.

Löhneysen, Georg Engelhard von. *Della cavalleria*. 2 vols. Remling, 1609–10.

———. *Vom Zeumen*. Gröningen, 1588.

Londe, Charles. *Gymnastique médicale ou l'exercise appliqué aux organes de l'homme*. Paris: Crouillebois, 1821.

Loomba, Ania. "The Great Indian Vanishing Trick: Colonialism, Property, and the Family in *A Midsummer Night's Dream*." In *A Feminist Companion to Shakespeare*, edited by Dympna Callaghan, 163–87. Oxford: Blackwell, 2000.

Lower, Richard. "An Account of making a Dog draw his Breath exactly like a Wind-broken Horse." In *Philosophical Transactions of the Royal Society* 2 (January 1666): 544–46.

Luckhardt, Jochen. "Herzöge als Sammler: Von den Anfängen bis zum Tod Herzog Augusts des Jüngeren (1666)." In *Das Herzog Anton Ulrich-Museum und sein Sammlungen, 1578–1754–2004*, edited by Jochen Luckhardt, 19–43. Munich: Hirmer, 2004.

———. "Kunst am Wolfenbütteler Hof um 1600." In *Hofkunst der Spätrenaissance: Braunschweig-Wolfenbüttel und das kaiserliche Prag um 1600*, edited by Jochen Luckhardt, 20–30. Braunschweig: Herzog Anton Ulrich-Museum, 1998.

———. "Die Rückkehr des Herzogs: Die Reiterstatuette des Herzogs Heinrich Julius von Adriaen de Vries." In *Neue Beiträge zu Adriaen de Vries*, edited by Schaumburger Landschaft, 156–67. Bielefeld: Verlag für Regionalgeschichte, 2008.

Lumiansky, R. M., and David Mills, eds. *The Chester Cycle*. 2 vols. Early English Text Society, supp. ser. 3 and 9.

London: Oxford University Press, 1974.

Lyly, John. *Endymion*. Edited by David Bevington. Manchester: Manchester University Press, 1996.

Maehle, Andreas-Holger, and Ulrich Tröhler. "Animal Experimentation from Antiquity to the End of the Eighteenth Century: Attitudes and Arguments." In *Vivisection in Historical Perspective*, edited by Nicolaas A. Rupke, 14–47. New York: Routledge, 1990.

Mainardi, Patricia. *Husbands, Wives, and Lovers: Marriage and Its Discontents in Nineteenth-Century France*. New Haven: Yale University Press, 2003.

Marcosson, Isaac F., and Daniel Frohman. *Charles Frohman: Manager and Man*. New York: Harper, 1916.

Markham, Gervase. *Cavelarice*. London, 1607.

———. *A Discourse of Horsemanship*. London, 1593.

Marra, Kim. "Saddle Sensations and Female Equestrian Prowess at the National Horse Show." In *Showing Off, Showing Up: Studies of Hype, Heightened Performance, and Cultural Power*, edited by Laurie Frederik, Kim Marra, and Catherine Schuler, 27–52. Ann Arbor: University of Michigan Press, 2017.

Massumi, Brian. *What Animals Teach Us About Politics*. Durham: Duke University Press, 2014.

Mattfeld, Monica. *Becoming Centaur: Eighteenth-Century Masculinity and English Horsemanship*. University Park: Pennsylvania State University Press, 2017.

———. "'Genus Porcus Sophisticus': The Learned Pig and the Theatrics of National Identity in Late Eighteenth-Century London." In *Performing Animality: Animals in Performance Practices*, edited by Lourdes Orozco and Jennifer Parker-Starbuck, 57–76. New York: Palgrave Macmillan, 2015.

———. "'Undaunted All He Views': The Gibraltar Charger, Astley's Amphitheatre, and Masculine Performance." *Journal of Eighteenth-Century Studies* 37, no. 1 (2014): 19–36.

Maurstad, Anita, Dona Davis, and Sarah Cowles. "Co-Being and Intra-Action in Horse-Human Relationships: A Multi-Species Ethnography of Be(com)ing Human and Be(com)ing Horse." *Social Anthropology* 21 (2013): 322–35.

Mayor, John. "King James I on the Reasoning Faculty in Dogs." *Classical Review* 12, no. 2 (1898): 93–96.

Meredith, Peter, and John E. Tailby, eds. *The Staging of Drama in Europe in the Late Middle Ages: Texts and Documents in English Translation*. Translated by Raffaella Ferrari, Peter Meredith, Lynette R. Muir, Margaret Sleeman, and John E. Tailby. Kalamazoo: Medieval Institute Publications, 1983.

The Mirror of Taste and Dramatic Censor. Vol. 3. Philadelphia: Thomas Barton Zantzinger and Co., 1811.

Moe, Aaron. "Zoopoetics: A Look at Cummings, Merwin, and the Expanding Field of Ecocriticism." *Humanimalia* 3, no. 2 (2012): 28–55.

———. *Zoopoetics: Animals and the Making of Poetry*. New York: Lexington Books, 2013.

Moffett [Moffet, Muffet, Moufet], Thomas. *Of the Silkewormes and Their Flies*. London, 1599. Facsimile edition, edited by Victor Houliston. Binghamton, N.Y.: Medieval and Renaissance Text Society, 1989.

———. *The Theatre of Insects, or Lesser living creatures*. Ca. 1589. Translated by J. Rowlands. London, 1658. Reprinted in Edward Topsell, *The History of*

Four-Footed Beasts and Serpents, 2nd ed., vol. 2. New York: Da Capo Press, 1967.

Mogador, Céleste. *Mémoires de Céleste Mogador*. Paris: Librairie Nouvelle, 1858.

Montaigne, Michel de. *An Apology of Raymond Sebond*. Translated by John Florio. London, 1603.

———. *Les Essais de Montaigne*. The Montaigne Project, University of Chicago, 1982–2015. http://www.lib .uchicago.edu/efts/ARTFL/projects /montaigne/.

Moody, Jane. *Illegitimate Theatre in London, 1770–1840*. Cambridge: Cambridge University Press, 2000.

Muir, Kenneth. *Shakespeare's Sources*. London: Methuen, 1957.

Myrone, Martin. *Henry Fuseli*. Princeton: Princeton University Press, 2001.

Nash, Richard. "Gentlemen's Recreation and Georgic Improvement: Lord Fairfax on Horse Breeding." In *England's Fortress: New Perspectives on Thomas, 3rd Lord Fairfax*, edited by Andrew Hopper and Philip Major, 235–58. Burlington, Vt.: Ashgate, 2014.

Neri, Janice. *The Insect and the Image: Visualizing Nature in Early Modern Europe, 1500–1700*. Minneapolis: University of Minnesota Press, 2011.

Nicolson, Marjorie. "The Early Stage of Cartesianism in England." *Studies in Philology* 26, no. 3 (1929): 356–74.

Nuss, Melynda. *Distance, Theatre, and the Public Voice, 1750–1850*. New York: Palgrave Macmillan, 2012.

Oldrey, David, Timothy Cox, and Richard Nash. *The Heath and the Horse: A History of Racing and Art on Newmarket Heath*. London: Philip Wilson, 2016.

Old Times, Oliver. "Equestrian Theatricals: To the Editor of the Morning Chronicle." In *The Spirit of the Public Journals: Being an Impartial Selection for 1811 . . .* , vol. 15, edited by Stephen Jones and Charles Molloy Vestmacott, 199–202. London: Printed for James Ridgway, 1812.

O'Malley, Charles. *Andreas Vesalius of Brussels: 1514–1564*. Berkeley: University of California Press, 1964.

Opie, Iona, and Peter Opie, eds. *The Oxford Dictionary of Nursery Rhymes*. 2nd ed. Oxford: Oxford University Press, 1997.

Orozco, Lourdes. *Theatre and Animals*. Houndmills: Palgrave Macmillan, 2013.

Orozco, Lourdes, and Jennifer Parker-Starbuck, eds. *Performing Animality: Animals in Performance Practices*. New York: Palgrave Macmillan, 2015.

Palmer, Barbara D. "Recycling the Wakefield Cycle." *Research Opportunities in Medieval and Renaissance Drama* 41 (2002): 88–130.

———. "'Towneley Plays' or 'Wakefield Cycle' Revisited." *Comparative Drama* 21 (1987–88): 318–48.

Palmer, Chris. "Lab-Grown Burger Taste Test." *Scientist*, 6 August 2013. http:// www.the-scientist.com/?articles.view /articleNo/36889/title/Lab-Grown -Burger-Taste-Test/.

Parikka, Jussi. *Insect Media: An Archaeology of Animals and Technology*. Minneapolis: University of Minnesota Press, 2010.

Park, Katharine. *Secrets of Women: Gender, Generation, and the Origins of Human Dissection*. New York: Zone Books, 2006.

Peterson, Michael. "The Animal Apparatus: From a Theory of Animal Acting to an Ethics of Animal Acts." *Drama Review* 51, no. 1 (2007): 33–48.

Phelan, Peggy. *Unmarked: The Politics of Performance*. New York: Routledge, 1993.

Phillips, Gervase. "Writing Horses into American Civil War History." *War in History* 20 (2013): 160–81.

Philostratus. *Vita Apollonii.* In *Flavi Philostrati Opera,* edited by Carl Ludwig Kayser, 2 vols., 1:1–344. Leipzig: B. G. Teubneri, 1870. http://www.perseus.tufts.edu /hopper/text?doc=Perseus%3Atex t%3A2008.01.0595.

Pick, Anat. *Creaturely Poetics: Animality and Vulnerability in Literature and Film.* New York: Columbia University Press, 2011.

Poliquin, Rachel. *The Breathless Zoo: Taxidermy and the Cultures of Longing.* University Park: Pennsylvania State University Press, 2012.

Pons d'Hostun, L. H. *L'écuyer des dames ou lettres sur l'équitation.* Paris: Librairie Mme. Huzard, 1817.

Powell, Thomas. *Humane Industry: A History of most manual arts.* London, 1661.

Power, Henry. *Experimental Philosophy.* London, 1664.

Prior, C. M. *Early Records of the Thoroughbred Horse.* London: Sportsman's Office, 1924.

Purchas, Samuel. *Purchas his Pilgrimes.* London, 1625.

Purkiss, Diane. *At the Bottom of the Garden: A Dark History of Faeries, Hobgoblins, and Other Troublesome Things.* New York: New York University Press, 2000.

Quiller-Couch, Arthur, ed. *The Oxford Book of Ballads.* Oxford: Clarendon Press, 1910.

Raber, Karen. *Animal Bodies, Renaissance Culture.* Philadelphia: University of Pennsylvania Press, 2013.

———. "Vermin and Parasites: Shakespeare's Animal Architectures." In *Ecocritical Shakespeare,* edited by Lynne Bruckner and Dan Brayton, 13–32. Aldershot: Ashgate, 2011.

Raffles, Hugh. *Insectopedia.* New York: Pantheon Books, 2010.

Rastall, Richard. "Music in the Cycle." In *The Chester Mystery Cycle: Essays and Documents,* edited by R. M. Lumiansky and David Mills, 114–30. Chapel Hill: University of North Carolina Press, 1983.

Read, Alan, ed. "On Animals." Special issue, *Performance Research* 5, no. 2 (2000).

Reddy, William. *The Navigation of Feeling: A Framework for the History of Emotions.* Cambridge: Cambridge University Press, 2001.

Remmert, Volker R. "'Docet parva pictura, quod multae scripturae non dicunt': Frontispieces, Their Functions, and Their Audiences in Seventeenth-Century Mathematical Sciences." In *Transmitting Knowledge: Words, Images, and Instruments in Early Modern Europe,* edited by Sachiko Kusukawa and Ian Maclean, 239–70. New York: Oxford University Press, 2006.

Resl, Brigitte. "Introduction: Animals in the Middle Ages." In *A Cultural History of Animals in the Medieval Age,* ed. Brigitte Resl, 1–26. Oxford: Berg, 2007.

Rich, Frank. "Gypsy Is Back on Broadway with a Vengeance." *New York Times,* 17 November 1989.

Rid, Samuel. *The art of jugling or legerdemaine.* London, 1612.

Ridout, Nicholas. *Stage Fright, Animals, and Other Theatrical Problems.* Cambridge: Cambridge University Press, 2006.

Roach, Joseph. *Cities of the Dead.* New York: Columbia University Press, 1996.

Robinson, J. W. *Studies in Fifteenth-Century Stagecraft.* Kalamazoo: Medieval Institute Publications, 1991.

Rosenthal, Erwin. "The Crib of Greccio and Franciscan Realism." *Art Bulletin* 36, no. 1 (1954): 57–60.

Rothfels, Nigel. *Savages and Beasts: The Birth of the Modern Zoo.* Baltimore: Johns Hopkins University Press, 2002.

Russell, Nicholas. *Like Engend'ring Like: Heredity and Animal Breeding in Early Modern England.* Cambridge: Cambridge University Press, 2007.

Ryan, Pat M. "The Horse Drama, with Supernumeraries: Bronson Howard's Semi-Historical *Shenandoah." Journal of American Drama and Theatre* 3, no. 2 (1991): 42–69.

Salisbury, Joyce E. *The Beast Within: Animals in the Middle Ages.* New York: Routledge, 1994.

Sand, George. *Indiana.* Paris: Gallimard, 1984.

Saxon, Arthur H. *Enter Foot and Horse: A History of Hippodrama in England and France.* New Haven: Yale University Press, 1968.

Schoenfeldt, Michael. "Fables of the Belly in Early Modern England." In *The Body in Parts: Fantasies of Corporeality in Early Modern Europe,* edited by Carla Mazzio and David Hillman, 242–61. New York: Routledge, 1997.

Schofield, A. W. "Battlefield Dispatches No. 208, 'War Horses.'" *Fort Scott (Kans.) Tribune,* 2 April 2010.

Scholten, Fritz, ed. *Adriaen de Vries, 1556–1626.* Zwolle: Waanders, 1998. Exhibition catalogue.

———. "Adriaen de Vries, Imperial Sculptor." In *Adriaen de Vries, 1556–1626,* edited by Fritz Scholten, 13–45. Zwolle: Waanders, 1998. Exhibition catalogue.

Scot, Reginald. *The Discoverie of Witchcraft.* New York: Dover, 1972.

Scott, Charlotte. "Still Life? Anthropocentrism and the Fly in *Titus Andronicus* and *Volpone." Shakespeare Survey* 61 (2008): 256–68.

Scully, Terence. *The Vivendier: A Fifteenth-Century French Cookery Manuscript.* Ca. 1450. London: Prospect Books, 1998.

Sebeok, Thomas. *Perspectives in Zoosemiotics.* Berlin: Mouton, 1972.

———. "Prefigurations of Art." *Semiotica* 27 (1979): 3–74.

Shakespeare, William. *The Complete Works.* Edited by David Bevington. 4th ed. New York: Harper Collins, 1992.

———. *The Complete Works of William Shakespeare.* Edited by David Bevington. 5th ed. New York: Pearson Longman, 2004.

———. *The Oxford Shakespeare.* Edited by Stanley Wells and Gary Taylor. 2nd ed. Oxford: Clarendon Press, 2005.

Shannon, Laurie. *The Accommodated Animal: Cosmopolity in Shakespearean Locales.* Chicago: University of Chicago Press, 2013.

———. "Invisible Parts: Animals and the Renaissance Anatomies of Human Exceptionalism." In *Animal Encounters,* edited by Tom Tyler and Manuela Rossini, 137–58. Leiden: Brill, 2009.

Sheridan, Philip Henry. *The Memoirs of General P. H. Sheridan.* 2 vols. New York: Charles L. Webster, 1888. Project Gutenberg EBook, 16 August 2006, http://www.gutenberg.org /files/4362/4362-h/4362-h.htm.

Sherman, Deborah Grace. "The Horse in the Civil War." Accessed 6 April 2015. http://www.reillysbattery.org/News letter/Jul00/deborah_grace.htm.

Sherman, William T. *Memoirs of General William T. Sherman.* 1889. Accessed 6 April 2015. http://www.gutenberg.org /files/4361/4361-h/4361-h.htm.

Shotwell, Allen. "The Revival of Vivisection in the Sixteenth Century." *Journal of the History of Biology* 46, no. 2 (2013): 171–97.

Sinanoglou, Leah. "The Christ Child as Sacrifice: A Medieval Tradition and the Corpus Christi Plays." *Speculum* 48, no. 3 (1973): 491–509.

Siraisi, Nancy G. *Medieval and Early Renaissance Medicine: An Introduction to Knowledge and Practice.* Chicago: University of Chicago Press, 1990.

Skinner, Otis. *Footlights and Spotlights: Recollections of My Life on the Stage.* Indianapolis: Bobbs-Merrill, 1924.

Smith, Helen, and Louise Wilson, eds. *Renaissance Paratexts.* New York: Cambridge University Press, 2014.

Smith, Pamela. *The Body of the Artisan.* Chicago: University of Chicago Press, 2004.

Sprague, Kurth. *The National Horse Show: A Centennial History, 1883–1983.* New York: National Horse Show Foundation, 1985.

Sprat, Thomas. *The History of the Royal Society of London for the Improving of Natural Knowledge.* London: J. Martyn, 1667.

States, Bert O. *Great Reckonings in Little Rooms: On the Phenomenology of Theater.* Berkeley: University of California Press, 1985.

Steel, Karl. *How to Make a Human: Animals and Violence in the Middle Ages.* Columbus: Ohio State University Press, 2011.

Stevens, Martin, and A. C. Cawley, eds. *The Towneley Plays.* 2 vols. Early English Text Society, supp. ser. 13 and 14. Oxford: Oxford University Press, 1994.

Stewart, Susan. *On Longing: Narratives of the Miniature, the Gigantic, the Souvenir, the Collection.* Durham: Duke University Press, 1993.

Stow, John. *The annales of England.* London, 1592.

———. *Annals.* London, 1580.

Strong, Roy. *Feast: A History of Grand Eating.* New York: Harcourt, 2002.

Stubbe, Henry. *Legends no histories.* London, 1670.

Swann, Marjorie. "The Politics of Fairylore in Early Modern English Literature." *Renaissance Quarterly* 53, no. 2 (2000): 449–73.

Tait, Peta. *Wild and Dangerous Performances: Animals, Emotions, Circus.* New York: Palgrave, 2011.

Thétard, Henri. *La merveilleuse histoire du cirque.* Vol. 2. Paris: Juilliard, 1947.

Thomas, Keith. *Man and the Natural World: A History of the Modern Sensibility.* New York: Pantheon Books, 1983.

Thomas of Celano. *The Lives of S. Francis of Assisi.* Translated by A. G. Ferrers Howell. London: Methuen, 1908.

Topsell, Edward. *The Historie of Foure-Footed Beastes.* London, 1607.

Tradescant, John, the Younger. *Musaeum Tradescantianum.* London, 1656.

Tsutsui, William. "Looking Straight at *Them!* Understanding the Big Bug Movies of the 1950s." *Environmental History* 12 (2007): 237–53.

Uexküll, Jakob von. *A Foray into the Worlds of Animals and Humans: With a Theory of Meaning.* Translated by Joseph D. O'Neil. Minneapolis: University of Minnesota Press, 2010.

Vesalius, Andreas. *De humani corporis fabrica. Epitome.* 1543. University of Cambridge Digital Library. Accessed 1 February 2017. https://cudl.lib.cam.ac .uk/view/PR-CCF-00046-00036/1.

———. *On the Fabric of the Human Body: Book I, Bones and Cartilages.* Translated by William Frank Richardson and John Burd Carman. San Francisco: Norman, 1998.

———. *On the Fabric of the Human Body: Book VI, The Heart and Associated Organs; Book VII, The Brain.* Translated by William Frank Richardson and John Burd Carman. Novato, Calif.: Norman, 2009.

Vialles, Noëllie. *Animal to Edible.* Translated by J. A. Underwood. Cambridge: Cambridge University Press, 1994.

Vitruvius, Marcus Pollio. *De Architectura libri decem.* Lyon, 1523.

Wade, Mara R. "Elisabeth von Dänemark (1573–1626) als Fürstin von Braunschweig-Wolfenbüttel: Dynastische Frauen und Kulturtransfer." In *Herzog Heinrich Julius zu Braunschweig und Lüneburg (1564–1613): Politiker und Gelehrter mit europäischen Profil*, edited by Werner Arnold, Brage bei der Wieden, and Ulrike Gleixner, 263–82. Wolfenbüttel: Braunschweigischer Geschichtsverein, 2016.

———. "Publication, Pageantry, Patronage: Georg Engelhard von Loehneyss' *Della Cavalleria*. . . ." *Daphnis* 32 (2003): 165–97.

Walchius, Joannes. *Decas fabularum humani generis sortem, mores, ingenium*. Strasbourg, 1609.

Walker-Meikle, Kathleen F. *Medieval Pets*. Suffolk, UK: Boydell and Brewer, 2012.

Wall, Wendy. *Staging Domesticity: Household Work and English Identity in Early Modern Drama*. Cambridge: Cambridge University Press, 2002.

Wanley, Nathaniel. *The wonders of the little world*. London, 1673.

Watson, Robert N. "The Ecology of Self in *Midsummer Night's Dream*." In *Ecocritical Shakespeare*, edited by Lynne Bruckner and Dan Brayton, 33–56. Aldershot: Ashgate, 2011.

Wear, Andrew, Roger K. French, and I. M. Lonie. *The Medical Renaissance of the Sixteenth Century*. New York: Cambridge University Press, 1985.

Weaver, John. *Essay Towards an History of Dancing*. London: Printed for Jacob Tonson, 1712.

Wecker, John. *Eighteen Books of the Secrets of Art and Nature, Being the Summe and Substance of Naturall Philosophy, Methodically Digested*. Translated by R. Read. London, 1660.

Weil, Kari. "They Eat Horses, Don't They? Hippophagy and Frenchness." *Gastronomica* 7, no. 2 (2007): 44–51.

———. *Thinking Animals: Why Animal Studies Now?* New York: Columbia University Press, 2012.

Weiss, Ulrike. "Die Königin hat (die) Hosen an: Caroline Mathilde von Dänemark zu Pferd." *Niedersächsiches Jahrbuch für Landesgeschichte* 85 (2013): 59–112.

Wilkins, John. *Mathematicall magick*. London, 1648.

Williams, David. "Inappropriate/d Others, or The Difficulty of Being a Dog." *Drama Review* 51, no. 1 (2007): 92–118.

Winstanley, William. *The new help to discourse, or Wit, mirth, and jollity*. London, 1680.

Wise, J. Macgregor. "Assemblage." In *Gilles Deleuze: Key Concepts*, edited by Charles J. Stivale, 91–102. Montreal: McGill-Queen's University Press, 2005.

Woodcock, Matthew. "'Spirits of Another Sort': Constructing Shakespeare's Fairies in *A Midsummer Night's Dream*." In *A Midsummer Night's Dream: A Critical Guide*, edited by Regina Buccola, 112–30. London: Continuum, 2010.

Woodhouse, Peter. *The Flea Sic Parua Componere Magnis*. London, 1605.

Worall, David. *Theatric Revolution: Drama, Censorship, and Romantic Period Subcultures, 1773–1832*. Oxford: Oxford University Press, 2006.

Wright, John P., and Paul Potter, eds. *Psyche and Soma: Physicians and Metaphysicians on the Mind-Body Problem from Antiquity to Enlightenment*. New York: Oxford University Press, 2000.

Wright, Louis B. "Animal Actors on the English Stage Before 1642." *PMLA* 42 (1927): 656–69.

Zunshine, Lisa, ed. *Acting Theory and the English Stage, 1700–1830*. Vol. 3. London: Pickering and Chatto, 2009.

CONTRIBUTORS

TODD ANDREW BORLIK is a senior lecturer in Renaissance drama at the University of Huddersfield. He is the author of *Ecocriticism and Early Modern English Literature* (2011) and more than a dozen scholarly articles on Shakespeare and his contemporaries. His work has appeared in such journals as *Shakespeare Survey*, *Shakespeare Quarterly*, *Shakespearean International Yearbook*, and *Shakespeare Bulletin*. He is currently at work on an anthology of early modern environmental writing and a comparative study on the staging of nature at the Rose and the Globe.

PIA F. CUNEO is a professor of art history at the University of Arizona. Since 1990, she has been researching and publishing on the nexus between visual culture, hippology, and identity in early modern Germany. In 2004, she was a research fellow at the Herzog August Bibliothek in Wolfenbüttel (Germany) and in 2009 a Daniels Fellow at the National Sporting Library and Museum (Middleburg, Virginia). She competes locally in dressage and enjoys jumping and trail riding. Both of her mares are rescue horses.

KIM MARRA is a professor of theater arts and American studies and an affiliate faculty member in gender, women's, and sexuality studies at the University of Iowa. Her publications include *Strange Duets: Impresarios and Actresses in American Theatre, 1865–1914* (2006), winner of the Callaway Prize; the co-edited volumes *Passing Performances: Queer Readings of Leading Players in American Theater History* (1998) and its sequel *Staging Desire: Queer Readings of American Theater History* (2002); *The Gay and Lesbian Theatrical Legacy: A Biographical Dictionary* *of Major Figures in American Stage History in the Pre-Stonewall Era* (2005); *Showing Off, Showing Up: Studies of Hype, Heightened Performance, and Cultural Power* (2017); and numerous essays on gender, horses, historiography, and performance. She is currently an associate editor of the Animal Lives series of the University of Chicago Press.

MONICA MATTFELD is an associate professor of history and English literature at the University of Northern British Columbia. She is the author of *Becoming Centaur: Eighteenth-Century Masculinity and English Horsemanship* (Penn State University Press, 2017), along with multiple publications on equestrian culture, animals, and illegitimate theater in the eighteenth century. She is currently working on a history of eighteenth- and nineteenth-century hippodrama and the sporting poetics of William Somerville.

RICHARD NASH is a professor of English at Indiana University, specializing in eighteenth-century British literature and culture and animal studies. Among his publications are numerous essays on the history of thoroughbred horse racing and, most recently (with David Oldrey and Timothy Cox), *The Heath and the Horse: A History of Racing and Art on Newmarket Heath* (2016).

SARAH E. PARKER is an assistant professor of English at Jacksonville University in Florida. Her current research focuses on the early modern medical genre of popular errors treatises by Laurent Joubert, Girolamo Mercurio, Thomas Browne, and others. She has published in *Renaissance and Reformation/ Renaissance et Réforme*, the *Disability*

Studies Journal, and *Tulsa Studies in Women's Literature*. Most recently, she co-edited, with Sara Miglietti, "Reading Publics in Renaissance Europe, 1450–1650," a special issue of *History of European Ideas*.

KAREN RABER is a professor of English at the University of Mississippi. She is the author of *Animal Bodies, Renaissance Culture* (2013) and the editor or co-editor of several volumes, including *The Culture of the Horse: Status, Discipline, and Identity in the Early Modern World* (2005), with Treva J. Tucker, and *Early Modern Ecostudies: From the Florentine Codex to Shakespeare* (2008), with Ivo Kamps and Thomas Hallock. She has written numerous essays on early modern women, gender, animals, ecostudies, and related topics; her current and forthcoming projects include *Shakespeare and Posthumanist Theory* for the Arden Shakespeare and Theory series, and *Shakespeare's Animals: A Dictionary*. She is currently also working on a monograph on meat called *Animals at the Table: Making Meat in the Early Modern World*, and editing the series Perspectives on the Non-Human in Literature and Culture for Routledge.

ROB WAKEMAN is a postdoctoral fellow in English at the University of South Florida. His research centers on medieval and early modern drama, animal studies, and food studies. He is currently working on a book titled *Eating Animals in Tudor and Stuart Theaters*. He has written articles on medievalism in the Reconstruction-era South in *Arthuriana*, on grease as a medium for transformation in *The Merry Wives of Windsor* in *Object Oriented Environs* (2016), and on the resacralization of sheep-corn husbandry in *Ground-Work: English Renaissance Literature and Soil Science* (2017).

KARI WEIL is a University Professor and director of the College of Letters at Wesleyan University. She is the author of *Androgyny and the Denial of Difference* (1992) and *Thinking Animals: Why Animal Studies Now?* (2012) and has published numerous essays on literary representations of gender, feminist theory, and, more recently, theories and representations of animal otherness and human-animal relations. Her chapter in this volume is part of a longer monograph (tentatively titled *Meat, Motion, Magnetism: Horses and Their Humans in Nineteenth-Century France*) on the riding, breeding, beating, and eating of horses in nineteenth-century France, and their prominent role in literature, art, performance, and theories of education.

JESSICA WOLFE is a professor of English and comparative literature at the University of North Carolina, Chapel Hill, and director of UNC's Medieval and Early Modern Studies program. She is the author of *Humanism, Machinery, and Renaissance Literature* (2004), *Homer and the Question of Strife from Erasmus to Hobbes* (2015), and various articles and essays on English and European Renaissance literature. She is currently co-editing Thomas Browne's *Pseudodoxia Epidemica* for a new Oxford University Press edition of Browne's complete works.

INDEX

Typeset by

REGINA STARACE

Printed and bound by

SHERIDAN BOOKS

Composed in

MINION PRO AND BODONI

Printed on

NATURES NATURAL

Bound in

ARRESTOX